Situation and Human Existence

PROBLEMS OF MODERN EUROPEAN THOUGHT

Series editors
Alan Montefiore
Jonathan Rée
Jean-Jacques Lecercle

Already published
Consciousness and the Unconscious
David Archard

Humanism and Anti-Humanism
Kate Soper

Philosophy Through the Looking-Glass
Language, nonsense, desire
Jean-Jacques Lecercle

Reflexivity
The post-modern predicament
Hilary Lawson

Situation and Human Existence
Freedom, subjectivity and society
Sonia Kruks

Situation and Human Existence
Freedom, subjectivity and society

SONIA KRUKS

London
UNWIN HYMAN
Boston   Sydney   Wellington

© S. Kruks 1990
This book is copyright under the Berne Convention. No reproduction without permission. All rights reserved.

Published by the Academic Division of
Unwin Hyman Ltd
15/17 Broadwick Street, London W1V 1FP, UK

Unwin Hyman Inc.,
8 Winchester Place, Winchester, Mass. 01890, USA

Allen & Unwin (Australia) Ltd,
8 Napier Street, North Sydney, NSW 2060, Australia

Allen & Unwin (New Zealand) Ltd in association with the Port Nicholson Press Ltd,
Compusales Building, 75 Ghuznee Street, Wellington 1, New Zealand

First Published in 1990

British Library Cataloguing in Publication Data

Kruks, Sonia
 Situation and human existence : freedom, subjectivity and society. – (Problems of modern European thought).
 I. Title II. Series
 301
 ISBN 0-04-445456-2

Library of Congress Cataloging in Publication Data

Kruks, Sonia.
 Situation and human existance : freedom, subjectivity, and society / Sonia Kruks.
  p. cm. — (Problems of modern European thought)
 Includes bibliographical references.
 ISBN 0-04-445456-2. — ISBN 0-04-445457-0 (pbk.)
 1. Situation (Philosophy) 2. Existentialism. I. Title
 II. Series.
 BD340.K78 1990   89–16650
 128'.4—dc20   CIP

Typeset in 10/12 Garamond by Gecko Ltd, Bicester, Oxon.
Printed by Billings and Son, London and Worcester

Contents

Editors' foreword	ix
Acknowledgements	xi
List of abbreviations	xiii
Introduction	1
Part One: Individual Situations	21
1 Marcel: embodiment and situation	23
2 Sartre: individual constitution of situation	51
Part Two: Social Situations	81
3 Beauvoir: the weight of situation	83
4 Merleau-Ponty: situation and social world	113
5 Sartre: praxis in situation	146
Conclusion	181
Notes	190
Index	210

Editors' foreword

During most of the twentieth century, philosophers in the English-speaking world have had only partial and fleeting glimpses of the work of their counterparts in continental Europe. In the main, English-language philosophy has been dominated by the exacting ideals of conceptual analysis and even of formal logic, while 'continental philosophy' has ventured into extensive substantive discussions of literary, historical, psycho-analytic and political themes. With relatively few exceptions, the relations between the two traditions have been largely uncomprehending and hostile.

In recent years, however, continental writers such as Heidegger, Adorno, Sartre, de Beauvoir, Habermas, Foucault, Althusser, Lacan and Derrida have been widely read in English translation, setting the terms of theoretical debate in such fields as literature, social theory, cultural studies, marxism, and feminism. The suspicions of the analytical philosophers have not, however, been pacified; and the import of such continental philosophy has mostly been isolated from original philosophical work in English.

PROBLEMS OF MODERN EUROPEAN THOUGHT series is intended to help break down this isolation. The books in the series will be original philosophical essays in their own right, from authors familiar with the procedures of analytical philosophy. Each book will present a well-defined range of themes from continental philosophy, and will presuppose little, if any formal philosophical training of its readers.

Alan Montefiore
Jonathan Rée
Jean-Jacques Lecercle

Acknowledgements

This book owes much to the generosity and patience of Alan Montefiore and Jonathan Rée, my series editors. Their willingness to engage in prolonged discussions of both substance and form has gone far beyond the normal bounds of editorial duty. Many others have also contributed to the writing of this volume, either by commenting on the manuscript itself or through conversations which have helped to shape my ideas. I would like, in particular, to mention Perry Anderson, David Archard, Ronald Aronson, Elizabeth Bowman, Joseph Catalano, William Connolly, Fred Dallmayr, Thomas Flynn, Christina Howells, William McBride, Anthony Manser, Phyllis Morris, Robert Stone and Joseph Walsh.

Thanks go also to Osborne Wiggins, previously my colleague at the New School, and to all the students there who participated in our seminars on Sartre's *Critique*. From them, and also from the students in my seminar on French Political Philosophy, I have learnt much.

Thanks of a different kind must go to my daughter, Gabi, for her good humour and tolerance in the face of my preoccupation with this work. Thanks also to Leo and Sima Kruks for their assistance. Finally, my deepest gratitude goes to Ben Wisner, who has lived with this project and supported it not only intellectually but in many other ways.

List of abbreviations

I have placed references to frequently cited works in the text, using the following abbreviations to refer to them.

BH   Marcel, Gabriel, *Being and Having*, translated by Katherine Farrer (New York: Harper and Row, 1965); French original: *Etre et avoir* (Paris: Aubier, 1935).

BN   Sartre, Jean-Paul, *Being and Nothingness, An Essay in Phenomenological Ontology*, translated by Hazel E. Barnes (New York: Philosophical Library, 1956 and London: Methuen, 1957); French original: *L'Etre et le néant, Essai d'ontologie phénoménologique* (Paris: Gallimard, 1943). NOTE: where page references diverge, I have given first the British edition and then the American edition reference.

CDR   Sartre, Jean-Paul, *Critique of Dialectical Reason*, Vol. I, 'Theory of Practical Ensembles', translated by Alan Sheridan-Smith, edited by Jonathan Rée (London: New Left Books, 1976); French original: *Critique de la raison dialectique*, Tome I, 'Théorie des ensembles pratiques' (Paris: Gallimard, 1960; revised edition, edited by Arlette Elkaïm-Sartre. Paris: Gallimard, 1985).

DP   Foucault, Michel, *Discipline and Punish. The Birth of the Prison*, translated by Alan Sheridan (London and Harmondsworth: Penguin, 1977); French original: *Surveiller et punir: Naissance de la prison* (Paris: Gallimard, 1975).

EA   Beauvoir, Simone de, *The Ethics of Ambiguity*, translated by Bernard Frechtman (New York: Citadel Press, 1967); French original: *Pour une morale de l'ambiguïté* (Paris: Gallimard, 1947).

EPC	Marcel, Gabriel, *Essai de philosophie concrète* (Paris: Gallimard, 1967); originally published as *Du Refus à l'invocation* (Paris: Gallimard, 1940).
HT	Merleau-Ponty, Maurice, *Humanism and Terror*, translated by John O'Neill (Boston: Beacon Press, 1969); French original: *Humanisme et terreur* (Paris: Gallimard, 1947).
HV	Marcel, Gabriel, *Homo Viator*, translated by Emma Crauford (Chicago: Regnery, 1951); French original: *Homo Viator* (Paris: Aubier, 1944).
MAMS	Marcel, Gabriel, *Man Against Mass Society*, translated by G.S. Fraser (South Bend, Ind.: Gateway, 1978); French original: *Les Hommes contre l'humain* (Paris: La Colombe, 1951).
MB	Marcel, Gabriel, *The Mystery of Being*, 2 Vols, translated by G.S. Fraser (South Bend, Ind.: Gateway, 1978); French original: *Le mystère de l'être* (Paris: Aubier, 1951).
MJ	Marcel, Gabriel, *Metaphysical Journal*, translated by Bernard Wall (Chicago: Regnery, 1952); French original: *Journal métaphysique* (Paris: Gallimard, 1927).
PC	Beauvoir, Simone de, *Pyrrhus et Cinéas* (Paris: Gallimard, 1944).
PM	Sartre, Jean-Paul, *Problem of Method* (US edition: *Search for a Method*), translated by Hazel E. Barnes (London: Methuen, 1964 and New York: Vintage Books, 1968); French original: 'Questions de méthode', prefatory essay in *Critique de la raison dialectique*, tome I (Paris: Gallimard, 1960).
PP	Merleau-Ponty, Maurice, *Phenomenology of Perception*, translated by Colin Smith (London: Routledge and Kegan Paul, 1962); French original: *Phénoménologie de la perception* (Paris: Gallimard, 1945).
S	Merleau-Ponty, Maurice, *Signs*, translated by Richard C. McCleary (Evanston, IL.: Northwestern University Press, 1964); French original: *Signes* (Paris: Gallimard, 1960).
SNS	Merleau-Ponty, Maurice, *Sense and Non-Sense*, translated by Hubert Dreyfus and Patricia Dreyfus (Evanston, IL.: Northwestern

LIST OF ABBREVIATIONS

University Press, 1964); French original: *Sens et non-sens* (Paris: Nagel, 1948).

TSS   Beauvoir, Simone de, *The Second Sex*, translated by H.M.Parshley (New York: Knopf, 1953 and Harmondsworth: Penguin, 1972); French original: *Le deuxième sexe*, 2 Vols (Paris: Gallimard, 1949). NOTE: since page references are different, I have given first the British edition and then the American edition reference.

TW   Marcel, Gabriel, *Tragic Wisdom and Beyond*, translated by Stephen Jolin and Peter McCormick (Evanston, IL.: Northwestern University Press, 1973); French original: *Pour une sagesse tragique* (Paris: Plon, 1968).

Situation and Human Existence

Introduction

I

'Existentialism? But surely no one takes that seriously any more!' Such comment is typical of reactions to the kind of philosophy this book examines. Indeed, today the very name 'existentialism' has a quaint and old-fashioned ring. It evokes images of Parisian café life and jazz cellars in the late 1940s, of earnest but faded novels about anguish and the absurdity of life. And if we need firmer evidence that existentialism is but a relic of a bygone era, we need only look at the opening pages of a recent biography of Jean-Paul Sartre.[1] There we find a description of Sartre's papers being sold off for a song at an auction of literary manuscripts in Paris: the market is surely a true indicator of a thinker's current worth. Or is it?

We live in a century of fast-moving intellectual fashions. Indeed existentialism was itself an intensely fashionable movement in its day. But it dropped abruptly from the French intellectual scene in the early 1960s, as the star of 'structuralism' rose, a star in turn to be eclipsed by 'post-structuralism' during the early 1970s. Although by the 1980s post-structuralism too had lost its dominant position in French intellectual life, both structuralism and post-structuralism have, with time-lags and changes of emphasis *en route*, crossed the English Channel and the North Atlantic. At a time when many French thinkers are returning to more classical, even Enlightenment, themes and thinkers, particularly to Kant, and to foundational questions in ethics and politics,[2] both structuralism and post-structuralism remain alive and well in the English speaking world.

However their reception has been more enthusiastic in the social sciences and cultural studies than into philosophy proper.[3] Indeed, Anglo-American philosophy has, with some exceptions, remained militantly impervious to foreign importations. Prognostications as dire as those Gilbert Ryle made about phenomenology in 1929 – that it would all end 'either in a ruinous subjectivism or a windy mysticism' [4] – have been repeated about each and every foreign vogue. With regard to social and political philosophy – my main area of concern in this book – hegemony in the 1970s and 1980s has been located in the USA, in the work of Rawls and his adherents. Today discussion is above all focused on issues of justice and rights within the framework of the liberal state.[5] But it is striking that these debates within political philosophy have continued as if the arguments of structuralism and post-structuralism had done nothing to put into question the very status of the agents, persons, or 'subjects', whose capacity for rational analysis and action political philosophers continue to take for granted. Thus Rawls, to take the most influential example, simply tells us, at the beginning of *A Theory of Justice*, that when we formulate principles of justice they must be acceptable to 'free and rational persons concerned to further their own interests',[6] as if the notion of 'free and rational persons' were wholly unproblematic.

In the social sciences and social theory it has been otherwise. While American behaviourism and its methodological-individualist assumptions were successfully imported into some areas of both British and French sociology and political science in the late 1950s and early 1960s, there has since been a reverse geographical movement, particularly from France. Structuralism, with its frequently proclaimed mission of eliminating 'man', or 'the human subject' – such as Rawls's 'free and rational person' – from the framework of all social analysis, has established itself since the late 1970s as a counter-orthodoxy to behaviourism within several of the Anglo-American social sciences. With, for example, the adoption by many anthropologists of Lévi-Strauss's use of structural linguistics as a model for explaining diverse forms of social organization, or with the use of Althusser's concept of structural 'conjuncture' in political science to explain such phenomena as 'class formation', 'state formation' and revolutions, neither individual behaviour nor the human subject as an effective agent retains a place in the methodological agenda of the new orthodoxy. This is true, it is interesting to note, as much for Marxist work as for non-Marxist. Marxist theory ceases, with structuralism, to be methodologically distinctive: the difference lies only in the choice of structures to be studied. Moreover, hard on the heels of the structuralist revolution in the Anglo-American social sciences, post-structuralism has arrived. It is now particularly fashionable among some anthropologists and historians, and in some areas of political and social theory, including feminist theory.

Neither structuralism itself nor post-structuralism has been a unified or highly coherent movement, even in France. Nor has it been wholly clear to what extent post-structuralism entails a rupture with or an internal development from structuralism. Foucault, whose influence in certain fields of Anglophone history, anthropology and political and social theory is now extensive, certainly appears to have bridged both movements. But others, such as Derrida, have tried more emphatically to distance themselves from structuralism.[7] However, from the point of view of their absorption into Anglo-American social science and theory, what is significant about both, and what allows us to treat them as variations on one single theme, is their common hostility to those central assumptions of the Western philosophic tradition which are tacitly presupposed by Rawls's notion of 'free and rational persons' between whom relations of justice may be established. Both structuralists and post-structuralists attack what they (pejoratively) call 'humanism': the set of assumptions which have their *locus classicus* in Descartes but which are also present (albeit in diverse formulations) in the tradition of Western political and social philosophy from Hobbes to Rawls. These assumptions concern the attribution of rationality and of subjectivity to all human beings who, by virtue of these attributes, can be assumed to have epistemological (and moral) autonomy and a capacity to act as free and responsible agents. From Lévi-Strauss's insistence that the aim of the human sciences is 'to dissolve man' and the claims of Lacan and Althusser that 'the subject' is a mere 'effect', through to Derrida's attacks on the metaphysics of 'presence' and Foucault's argument that subjects are 'constituted' in discourse, what has been under attack are those notions of human autonomy and agency which still remain central to normative theory.[8]

Of course, ever since Hume there has been an acknowledged problem concerning the relation between normative judgements and factual descriptions. The problem has been a pervasive one since the birth of the modern social 'sciences'. It is evidenced, for example, in Weber's now classic wrestling with the 'fact-value' dichotomy. But although earlier social science, including that of Marx and Durkheim, has offered explanations of social phenomena which rest on claims as to the objective existence of supra-individual social entities of one kind or another, prior to French anti-humanism these claims have rarely been linked with an attempt explicitly to deny any degree of effective autonomy to individual consciousness and volition. There is, then, at present a particularly wide gulf between the basic assumptions about agency and subjectivity in the discourse of Anglo-American liberal philosophy and those of the theoretically informed social sciences, non-Marxist and Marxist alike. The main discourse of normative philosophy is still concerned with the actions of agents who are assumed above all to be thinking subjects (indeed, Rawls claims, Kantian subjects) and responsible agents. However, for the new discourses of the social sciences 'the subject' is a piece of obfuscating ideology (or at best a construct), and there exist only supra-individual logics, structures, or plays of significations. And if we are still to talk of 'the subject' at all, it 'must be stripped of its creative role' and analysed as an effect only.[9] Between a Foucauldian (or an Althusserian) and a Rawlsian, there would appear to be little basis for dialogue.

Yet if the anti-humanists' claims are valid, then Rawls's 'basic structure' of society can have nothing to do with the 'interests' of 'free and rational persons', and the whole project of normative theory is arguably put into question. For if the self is uniquely constituted by supra-individual structures, etc., then the basic assumptions about human agency which support such concepts as responsibility for our actions or equal respect for persons are untenable. Equally, Marxism as an appeal to action, guided by 'a morality of emancipation',[10] ceases to be possible, and Marxism can be nothing more than a descriptive science. However, the gulf is not quite as wide as it appears at first sight. For, on the one hand, anti-humanism has arguably failed, after all, wholly to expunge the autonomous subject from its analyses, while, on the other, some post-Rawlsian liberal theory has begun to challenge Rawls's unproblematized notion of the subject.

With regard to the difficulties which anti-humanism has encountered in its efforts to expunge the autonomous or 'constituting' subject, Foucault's work is instructive. For although he was one of the most emphatic critics of the notion of the constituting subject, he was the one who ended by most clearly resurrecting a version of it in his attempt to distinguish truth from polemic and to justify his own political judgements. His trajectory suggests that it may not be possible for social theory ever consistently to eliminate from itself all notions of active subjectivity. For many years Foucault held that 'truth' is simply a function of a 'discursive regime' which organizes a field of knowledge (such as the study of madness or criminality). He developed essentially a historical sociology of knowledge, which described how truths come to be created and altered, and which attempted to demonstrate their inseparability from relations of power. This project, with its suspension of normative judgement, was consistent with the claim that subjectivity is only a construct. 'One has', he wrote, 'to dispense with the constituent subject, to get rid of the subject itself, that's to say, to arrive at an analysis which can account for the constitution of the subject within a historical framework'.[11] Both truth and subjectivity are constructs, emerging from discursive practices which function in ways which nobody controls.

Foucault's method seems to imply a stance of ethical indifference. However, he became increasingly involved in the later years of his life with groups in France defending the rights of prisoners and homosexuals. With this, criteria for evaluating truth claims, rather than simply describing their emergence or function, became important to him. We thus find Foucault returning, somewhat abruptly, to a rather different notion of subjectivity, one linked to the claim that there can, after all, be a real autonomy of thought. Thought, he stated near the end of his life, can be distinguished from those representations and attitudes present in routine conduct by its ability freely to step back from action and to 'problemize' it. In a strikingly Cartesian formulation, he observed:

> Thought is not what inhabits a certain conduct and gives it meaning; rather, it is what allows one to step back from this way of acting or reacting, to present it to oneself as an object of thought and question it as to its meaning, its condition, and its goals. Thought is freedom in relation to what one does, the motion by which one detaches oneself from it, establishes it as an object, and reflects on it as a problem.[12]

Along with this account of thought, Foucault also now insisted that a valid distinction can be made between the search for truth and the use of polemic.[13] For the former can, after all, be distinguished by its refusal of the power dimensions which he had previously attributed to all knowledge claims. The possibility of such a refusal again implies an autonomy of the subject which his earlier work had militantly precluded.

To turn now to the alternative position, the unquestioning assumption of the autonomy of the subject, this too is undergoing modification. Within normative liberal theory itself a questioning of such a notion of the subject has begun to emerge with what is often called the 'communitarian' critique of liberalism. Michael Sandel, for one, has argued that Rawls's theory implicitly assumes a 'constitutive conception' of the community – that is, a conception in which 'community would not just describe a feeling but a mode of self-understanding partly constitutive of the agent's identity'.[14] However, to sustain such a notion of the community one must – as Sandel realizes – begin to rethink the nature of the agent or subject in more social and less individualistic terms. Thus Sandel critically observes that:

> Rawls conceives the self as a subject of possession, bounded in advance, and given prior to its ends, and he assumes furthermore that the bounds of the subject unproblematically correspond to the bodily bounds between individual human beings.[15]

Sandel is not, of course, here calling for the 'deconstruction' of the subject or the 'end of man'. Nor is he implying that the notion of citizens as rational agents acting within a political community is a total fiction. All he wants to point out against Rawls is that 'we cannot be wholly unencumbered subjects of possession, individuated in advance and given prior to our ends'.[16] But his critique raises a set of issues about the nature of the subject, about the relations of agents or persons to the societies in which they live and about the relations that may (or may not) exist between social structures and the ability of individuals to act as free agents, which shift the ground toward the questions with which structuralism and post-structuralism have also been concerned. Indeed, the autonomous, or 'unencumbered', subject has now been sufficiently put in question within liberal thought itself that my own concern in this work is less to contribute further to its critique than to defend at least a revised notion of subjectivity against anti-humanism.[17]

As already indicated, debates about the relations of subjectivity, agency and social structure are not new. They have in recent times been played out in the social sciences between defenders of positivism and its critics and between methodological-individualists and holists.[18] In Marxism, the same issues have arisen in debates over the respective roles of concrete agents and determining historical laws in bringing about epochal change. 'Men make their own history', Marx had said, 'but they do not make it just as they please; they do not make it under circumstances chosen by themselves, but under circumstances directly encountered, given and transmitted from the past.'[19] But what are 'circumstances'? How do they come into being, and how far do they shape action? And what are these 'men' who 'make history', yet who cannot do so 'as they please'? Are these 'men', as structuralist Marxism (and other structuralisms) would have it, simply the passive vehicles, or 'supports' of those grand historical forces which are the 'real subjects' of history,[20] or are they the mere constructs of discursive practices, as Foucault tells us? Or are 'men', as conscious actors and as the responsible possessors of their own lives, the primary agents of history?

To reply affirmatively to either alternative is to open oneself to persuasive criticism from the other. A consistent anti-humanism not only leaves us bereft of criteria for making ethical or political judgements, it also runs up against the problem of the status of the theorist him- or herself. Is Foucault, for example, really only performing (as he insists) an 'author function' in which he plays no 'creative role' as a subject?[21] And is he writing to address an audience of persons who lack any autonomous judgement as to how they will respond to his work? The very project of scholarship, as Foucault admitted shortly before his death, belies such claims. But there is no reason to privilege authors and readers above other human beings: if the project of scholarly or other written communication implies a relation of freely thinking subjects, then we must grant that human subjectivity in general is more than a mere 'effect'. Yet, this having been said, both anti-humanist works and much other macro-analytic social science (of various complexions) do offer considerable evidence in support of the critique of the autonomous subject. We are to some degree the products of external circumstance, not only in the sense that, for example, economies or state systems develop functions that are beyond individual control, but in the stronger sense that there is ample evidence to support the claim that what we experience as personal values, beliefs, tastes, etc., are culturally specific. The 'unencumbered', or self-constituting, notion of the subject is as open to criticism as its anti-humanist obverse.

There is, however, a third alternative open to us: the task of exploring the ground between these two positions. That is, the task of investigating (sociologically and philosophically) the hypothesis that subjectivity is at once constituting and constituted, that structures (discursive practices, systems of signifiers, or what you will) and subjects act and re-act upon each other, so that we must talk of an 'encumbered' subjectivity and of 'human' structures. This book is intended as a contribution to such a project. It aims, through a reconsideration of the social philosophy of the French existentialists, to complement, along the philosophical axis, the work of those few Anglo-American scholars who have, in recent years, begun to undertake such an exploration.

Among social scientists in this group one would have to name above all Anthony Giddens. While acknowledging that structuralism has effectively criticized naïve notions of the agent and forms of methodological-individualist explanation in the social sciences, Giddens insists that

> the pressing task facing social theory today is not to further the conceptual elimination of the subject, but on the contrary to promote a recovery of the subject without lapsing into subjectivism.[22]

To undertake this task, he suggests, the social sciences must focus neither at the level of individual experience and action alone, nor only at the level of structures and totalities. Rather they must develop a 'theory of the acting subject', in which the embeddedness of individual action in 'social practices ordered across time and space' should be the main locus of analysis. What Giddens calls 'structuration theory' is different from structuralism. The latter deals with rules and institutions as universals, independent of the particularities of time and place, and as causally dominant; but for structuration theory the role of specific individuals who actively maintain structures through their own 'recursive practices' is all-important.[23]

In more philosophic vein than Giddens, one could point to a few thinkers who are attempting, in somewhat different modalities, also to 'recover the subject' rather than to abandon the notion in the light of structuralist and post-structuralist attacks. Fred Dallmayr's contributions to what he has called 'a post-individualist theory of politics' are a good example. Dallmayr attempts, as he puts it, to steer a course 'between the recent reaffirmations of individualism (on both empiricist and transcendental humanist premises) and the radical counter-currents proclaiming the "end of the individual" or "end of man"'.[24] In steering this course, Dallmayr explores what he calls a non-'egological' or a non 'possessive individualist' notion of the subject. In such a notion, subjectivity is seen always to imply intersubjectivity and community.

Similarly, starting from the standpoint of epistemology, Richard Bernstein's book, *Beyond Objectivism and Relativism*, also exemplifies the call to rethink subjectivity. The movement 'beyond objectivism and relativism' in both the natural and the human sciences requires,

Bernstein argues, an understanding of the 'dialogical' nature of scientific rationality. It requires a notion which stresses its 'practical, communal character'[25] and thus its intersubjective nature. Moreover, in a world in which the possibility of such dialogue is threatened, to recognize the intersubjective nature of rationality is to issue a call for action, a call to foster and protect what Bernstein calls 'dialogical communities'. '[W]hat has become manifest', he concludes, 'is that the movement beyond objectivism and relativism is not just a theoretical problem but a practical task'.[26]

But what, one might well ask, has 'existentialism' to do with all of this? After all, was not existentialism *par excellence* an unreformed 'philosophy of the subject', an inveterate Cartesianism? Indeed, was it not French existentialism which furnished that very naïve model of 'man' as pure subjectivity, as pure freedom, against which French structuralism and post-structuralism so properly rebelled? Was it not the 'humanism' of the existentialists which was the justified target of the 'anti-humanists'? Well, as we shall see, 'yes' and 'no'.

II

If one takes 'existentialism' to be synonymous with Sartre's early work, especially *Being and Nothingness* (1943), then it deserves at least some of the anti-humanist opprobrium that it has received since the 1960s. For Sartre's early work can indeed be read as developing a notion of the subject as the irreducible possessor of pure consciousness and pure freedom. But the reduction of existentialism to early Sartreanism, effected by its anti-humanist critics, is a gross distortion. For there are major shifts in Sartre's own philosophy over time and the notion of the subject elaborated in *Being and Nothingness* was significantly put into question by Sartre himself by the time he wrote the *Critique of Dialectical Reason* (1960). In addition, although Sartre was undoubtedly the central figure in the public eye when existentialism was at its peak of popularity, it remains a mistake to identify it – even in France – uniquely with him.

The term, 'existentialism', has been used to cover the work of a wide array of nineteenth- and twentieth-century thinkers, ranging from Kierkegaard to Jaspers, Heidegger, Sartre and many others. Some of them – Sartre at times included – have objected to the term, or denied that it applied to them. Even so, there are grounds for at least loosely grouping together those thinkers to whom the name has most frequently been applied. For they do share certain general starting points: a rejection of philosophic 'system building' which finds its classic formulation in Kierkegaard's work, and a commitment instead to the elucidation of individual lived experience as the aim of philosophic (or in some instances, literary) activity. Taking the movement as a whole, this commitment has indeed led to a tendency to conceive subjectivity as an intrinsically individual phenomenon. 'Men' have been conceived as the autonomous possessors of their own subjectivity, the creators of their own values, shapers of their own destinies. But such a blanket characterization of existentialism misses the many nuances and divergences within the movement. In particular, it obscures the fact that in one strand there has emerged a far more sustained and significant consideration of the *social* aspects of subjectivity than the general characterization acknowledges. This strand is that of French existentialism, particularly after the Second World War.

My aim in what follows is not, therefore, to give a faithful or a full historical account of the entire intellectual movement known as 'existentialism'. Nor, although I am sympathetic to such an undertaking, is it to write the kind of intellectual history which examines in detail the emergence of ideas in relation to the complex interplay of political, cultural and intellectual contexts.[27] My aim is rather to construct a selective history of that strand of existentialism which has most pervasively concerned itself with the relation of subjectivity to society and history. With this in mind I have chosen (for reasons discussed more fully below) to focus on the work of four thinkers: Gabriel Marcel, Jean-Paul Sartre, Simone de Beauvoir and Maurice Merleau-Ponty.

One way of proceeding would have been to try to produce a unified, conceptual account, drawn from the common elements in the notion of the subject developed by these four thinkers. This composite model could then have been neatly compared and contrasted with, say, a Foucauldian notion of the subject on the one hand, or perhaps a Rawlsian one on the other. But rather than creating set-piece debates between ostensibly monolithic positions, I have chosen to proceed thinker by thinker, elucidating continuities and filiations, divergences and disagreements between them, by examining their explicit and implicit quarrels as much as their common ground. Such a method transgresses the boundary, generally accepted in Anglo-American philosophy, between history of ideas and philosophy 'proper'. But I have chosen to use this mixed genre (more common in continental philosophy) for several reasons.

INTRODUCTION

Firstly, there has been a tendency within social philosophy and theory to regard the French existentialists as simply irrelevant. This tendency, always present in Anglo-American scholarship, has been reinforced in recent years by an overly uncritical acceptance of the reading the French anti-humanists have offered of their existentialist forebears. This reading, as hostile as it is inaccurate, portrays them as naïve proponents of a romantic, individualistic subjectivism. Against such exclusion and misreading, my aim is a setting straight (albeit an interested setting straight) of the present historical record: to set out what, as a group of thinkers, they had to say about the problem of social subjectivity and to suggest that much of it is still of relevance today. However, for all their insights, none of them offered a 'definitive' theorization of the relations of subjectivity to social being – indeed there could not be one. Thus it is preferable to avoid conceptual over-simplification and to lay out their quarrels and divergences as much as their areas of agreement. In addition, such a way of proceeding is more consonant with the methodological strength of the thinkers under discussion. For it is one of their merits that they repeatedly warn us that diversity and singularity should not be eradicated in the name of theoretical parsimony.

In undertaking the task of tracing this history, I have selected the notion of *situation* as a guiding thread. For in this notion, central to the work of all four thinkers, the presence of an internal bond, a relation of mutual permeability between subjectivity and its surrounding world, is always asserted. Exactly how this permeability should be theorized, and just how great or small is the degree of autonomy that subjectivity has from its surroundings, are not, however, matters on which there is unanimity. In tracing the notion of situation through the work of Marcel, Sartre, Beauvoir and Merleau-Ponty, what is explored is, as it were, a set of somewhat dissonant variations on a theme. Before immersing ourselves in these variations it may be helpful to sketch out, rather baldly, what I take to be the initial or unifying theme. For although at times this theme will be temporarily obscured, submerged beneath others, or developed in tangential ways, it will always re-emerge as the continual point of reference present within the variations.

The concept of *situation* most immediately engages us with the perennial problems of epistemology. Indeed, most of the thinkers I examine explicitly develop their own positions through a critique of epistemology. Traditionally, epistemology concerns itself with the question of whether or not we can establish a realm of certain, or even objective, knowledge – that is, a knowledge which does not depend on the subjective particularities of the knower and which is thus the same for anybody. For such a knowledge to be possible, a knower has to be presupposed who can come to have real knowledge of objects that are independent of his or her own existence. It is against such a view of the possibility of knowledge that the notion of situation is powerfully deployed by the French existentialists.

In insisting that the relation of knower to known, of subject to object, always takes place *in situation*, the existentialists challenge the assumption that there can be an autonomous subject, a detached contemplator and knower of objects. In so doing they risk, however, asserting the impossibility of any trans-individual knowledge. Relativism and even solipsism seem to beckon – as they have done since the Skeptics – as the only viable alternative to a theory of objective knowledge. But neither relativism nor solipsism has necessarily to be the terminus of an epistemology of the situated subject. For if there can be shown to be a commonality to human situations, then situated knowledge is not uniquely private. It can be a shared and thus, at least in a minimal sense, an objective knowledge, even while it remains also a particular knowledge.

However, to defend such an epistemological position, one which argues that situated knowledge is both particularistic and common, it is necessary to go beyond the confines of the traditional epistemological domain and to ask what it is *to be* a situated human being. Thus the autonomy of epistemology as a field of inquiry is challenged, and the notion of situated knowing leads us to ontology: to the exploration of the notion of situated human being, or 'being-in-situation'.

Situated human being is necessarily embodied being. 'I am my body', as both Marcel and Merleau-Ponty put it. This apparently unexceptionable little statement, has profound implications. Firstly, it implies that the notion of subjectivity must itself be broadened to acknowledge that the 'self' is irreducibly sentient: it is not to be conceived as an exclusively, or perhaps even a primarily, thinking, knowing, or self-conscious subject. Secondly, it implies that, through the contingencies of physical birth, subjectivity comes to discover itself as *being* of a particular physique, race, gender, etc., and as born into a human situation – a particular spatial and temporal location, a general and a personal history, a cultural and economic context, etc.

The claim that subjectivity is irreducibly sentient is explored along diverse axes. For Marcel, it is examined through a phenomenology of feelings and moods; for Merleau-Ponty through the elucidation of perception; for Beauvoir and (late) Sartre respectively, through the phenomenology of oppression and the logic of need. But what each of them arrives at by a separate route is the recognition that being 'in situation', being as embodied subjectivity, cannot but be *intersubjective*. Far from solipsism or relativism resulting from the challenge to traditional epistemologies, situated subjectivity can be shown to inhere, because embodied, in more general modes of human being. There is thus an opening of individual subjects into one and the same world, which ensures that experience and knowledge are not closed in on themselves.

On the contrary, in so far as embodied subjects discover themselves to be situated in a specific human context, the notion of situated subjectivity implies also the social and cultural permeability of subjectivity and its historicity. Subjectivity can no longer be synonymous, as for Descartes, with freedom or autonomy. It emerges in the way we live our body, our gender, our family and our wider social and economic relations, and our relation to their past. Moreover, as such, subjectivity must no longer be conceived as pure contemplation or reflection, whether of objects or ourselves. Situated subjectivity is not only sentient but *practical*, inseparably bound up with action and with the multiplicity of social bonds that emerge in human action.

Yet, for all its permeability by physical, inter-human and sociohistorical being, situated subjectivity remains something other than a mere effect of social practices. It is hard to find a language to describe this 'something'. It is not the free consciousness, the rationality, of a Descartes, a Kant, or a Rawls. But nor is it a product, reducible to the sum of exterior conditionings. It involves a freedom which admits of degree, a self that is both a responsible agent and a victim of circumstance. Merleau-Ponty's notion of an 'impure subject' perhaps best indicates what is involved in the notion of situation: a subjectivity that is neither the 'constituting consciousness' of normative philosophy, nor the 'constituted consciousness' of anti-humanism; a subjectivity that, as situated, is embodied, intersubjective and practical, and yet which is not reducible to any of these dimensions.

III

In writing this history, I have chosen to begin my account with the work of Gabriel Marcel (1889-1973). For his work, beginning in the 1920s and drawing extensively on Bergson (1859-1941), is the point of origin of this distinctive, French strand of existentialism. What initially makes this strand distinctive is the presence there to a greater degree than elsewhere of Cartesianism as a point of reference and area of contestation. There is no one figure in English-language philosophy whose influence has been as enduring and far-reaching as that of Descartes has been for French philosophy. However, Cartesianism is not identical with the work of Descartes himself. For, in the long history of Descartes interpretation in France, he has come to be read in differing ways. In the nineteenth and early twentieth centuries Descartes has been read predominantly through neo-Kantian lenses: the *res cogitans* has been interpreted as a uniquely knowing or epistemological subject, rather than as an acting or a more broadly experiencing subject. Thus Cartesianism, as Marcel confronts it, is synonymous with the assertion that consciousness is the individual possession of an autonomous knowing subject. Cartesianism also stands for a dualistic ontology in which that autonomous subject, the *res cogitans*, is taken to be a self-subsistent entity, ontologically distinct from the *res extensa*, which it confronts as its object of knowledge.

Although Sartre, Beauvoir and Merleau-Ponty – the postwar generation of French existentialists – were to immerse themselves in German phenomenology and existentialism, frequently (if inaccurately) drawing on the work of Husserl and Heidegger, their work also should be read as a series of more direct arguments with the ghost of Descartes. While their debt to German thought cannot be discounted, it should not be overlooked that there is also an extended tradition of specifically French philosophical debate behind their arguments. French existentialism, as Jean Wahl put it, 'picked up the baton from Bergsonism'[28] and, before that, from a tradition that goes back to Maine de Biran, or even to Pascal. But it is to Marcel, writing in the 1920s, that we must look for the first major attempt to elaborate a notion of existence as the central element in the attempt to refute Cartesianism.

Seminal though it is, Marcel's work stands in many ways apart from the work of the postwar generation. This is not merely a question of his temporal priority or his lack of familiarity with German phenomenology. It is also to do with the religious and political tenor of his work. Although he challenges the Cartesian notion of the subject by developing one of the richest notions of situated subjectivity as embodied, his philosophy finally has recourse to theological premises to account for the possibility of human communication and community. It thus fails to engage adequately with the question of the relations of subject and social structure and remains, in spite of itself, still a highly individualistic philosophy of the subject.

Moreover, Marcel's religious commitments made him deeply hostile to Marxism, whereas it was the additional factor of their profound encounter with Marxism which makes the work of the postwar existentialists unique. At no other time and place has a group of thinkers felt obliged simultaneously to confront such a philosophically hegemonic Cartesianism and such a politically hegemonic objectivist Marxism as that of the French Communist Party. It is the location of their work at this intersection which makes the reflections of the French existentialists on subjectivity and its relations to social life so distinctive. It is for this reason that they, rather than say Heidegger or Jaspers, are the focus of my investigation. This is not to say that the latter have no bearing on my topic, but that the French thinkers are of greater interest because of their encounter with Marxism.

Sartre was born in 1905, Beauvoir and Merleau-Ponty in 1908. All three studied philosophy at the Ecole Normale Supérieure in the late 1920s. All three, rebelling against the complacent and scholastic idealism of their teachers, turned to German philosophy (Heidegger and Husserl) to search for a way of philosophizing about 'lived experience'. Yet they also continued to draw on their French heritage, Sartre observing late in life that it was his encounter with Bergson's work which first engaged him in philosophy, while Merleau-Ponty was to hail Marcel as a major influence.[29]

Sartre's *Being and Nothingness*, begun in a German prisoner of war camp during the Second World War and published in occupied Paris, is the culmination of that interwar student rebellion. Remarkably untouched by the political context in which it was written, it (like Marcel's work) must be read as a partly failed engagement with the ghost of Descartes. For although Sartre criticizes the Cartesian notion of the thinking subject, attempting to develop an account of situated subjectivity, he still ends by reconfirming the Cartesian identity of consciousness and freedom, and by asserting the absolute autonomy of individual subjectivity. Marcel's work and Sartre's early philosophy may, for all their manifest divergences, both be read as unsuccessful attempts to escape from Cartesianism. They remain, in the last analysis, philosophies of the subject which are unable adequately to address the relation of subject to social structure. Yet, their difficulties not withstanding, they raise key issues about the relation of subjectivity to intersubjectivity, to embodiment and to the social world, which later work addresses more fully. Part One of this book, 'Individual Situations', develops such a reading of their work as both seminal and yet flawed.

In Part Two, 'Social Situations', I set out to reconstruct the social turn which existentialism took by the end of the War. I demonstrate how this turn called for a modification (though not an abolition) of the notion of the subject and an exploration, through the notion of situation, of the grounds of intersubjectivity in order to account for the experience of social existence. This social turn, according to all three thinkers I focus upon, took place initially as a response to the experience of the German Occupation. They learned, as Merleau-Ponty put it, 'that their former freedom had been sustained by the freedom of others and that one is not free alone'.[30] The twin experiences, German oppression on the one hand and the solidarity of the Resistance on the other, served, said Merleau-Ponty, to shatter what he called the 'Cartesian' view of society – a view which they had all previously shared of society as an aggregate of self-contained, autonomous, individual consciousnesses. It put into question both the previous social and political order and their own prewar philosophical concerns. Moreover, thinking through new alternatives involved, for each of them, a fundamental encounter with the Marxism of the time.

In France the Communist Party had become, long before the War, both a major political and an intellectual force. It also exercised an almost total hegemony over what properly constituted 'Marxism' or, more precisely, 'Marxism-Leninism'. With the role of the Soviet Union in the defeat of Nazi Germany and the key role of communists in the Resistance, the reputation of communism ran high in the immediate postwar period. Indeed, communism appeared to many people to represent the only viable alternative to a return to the *status quo ante*. It was thus impossible for the postwar existentialists to work out their own alternatives to the old order without confronting the party and its claims to a monopoly of theoretical and political legitimacy. Given the contradiction between the intense anti-subjectivism of orthodox Marxism and the strength of the existentialist's residual Cartesianism, it is this confrontation which gives a unique character to their work. It is, moreover, this confrontation that makes their work of current as well as historical interest. For, in addressing the anti-subjectivism of orthodox Marxism, arguments were developed that remain pertinent as responses to later 'anti-humanism'.

In tracing the social turn of existentialism, as I do in the second part of this book, I have chosen to begin with the work of Simone de Beauvoir. This is because, exploring the issue of oppression (in a series of works which culminated in *The Second Sex*, 1949), Beauvoir pushed the early Sartrean notion of the subject as absolute freedom to its limits and beyond. Her work implied that the notion of subjectivity must be rethought in terms of the significance of the body and the weight of social institutions for human situation. Beauvoir herself never explicitly developed the reformulations that her analysis implied. But Merleau-Ponty, whose work I next examine, did. In Merleau-Ponty's writings of the 1940s we find a radical reformulation of the notion of the subject. The subject is no longer the possessor of private, individual consciousness, but is an 'impure' subject. The situated subject is an opening, through the body and perceptual experience, on to a common being and is always an intersubjectivity.

In the 1940s it was Beauvoir and Merleau-Ponty who undertook the most significant attempts to rework the notion of the subject. But by the late 1950s, Merleau-Ponty having turned away from any extended explicitly social and political inquiry, it was Sartre whose work became most pertinent. Thus, rather than examining Merleau-Ponty's posthumous 'late' work, I end Part Two by returning to Sartre and examining the first volume of his monumental *Critique of Dialectical Reason*. Although for reasons of space I do not trace Sartre's entire intellectual trajectory, I argue, contrary to most other commentators, that in this work Sartre significantly modified his earlier notion of the subject. Moreover, in attempting to synthesize that revised notion with Marxism, he developed a highly original account of practical subjectivity, in which the inseparability in human situations of materiality and consciousness, of social structure and self, of historical necessity and freedom, is demonstrated. This account, I end by arguing, provides the basis for a continuing project of the 'recovery of the subject', provided that it is broadened to include other aspects of embodiment, subjectivity and intersubjectivity to which Marcel, Beauvoir and Merleau-Ponty had pointed.

As I have indicated, my primary purpose in writing this book is to present, through the guiding thread of the notion of situation, the history of a strand of important theory which has been unjustifiably neglected by social philosophers and theorists alike. Thus, although I allude to the implications of this kind of theory for other positions, particularly 'anti-humanist' ones, in the course of my exposition, I do not enter into direct or extended confrontation with them. However, in the Conclusion, through a brief treatment of Foucault, I focus more directly on what I take to be at issue between anti-humanists and those who would take up the project of recovering the subject, not as a Cartesian or autonomous subject, but as a subject 'in situation'.

IV

This book aims primarily to elucidate the accounts of *social* existence offered by the French existentialists. But, in order to grasp the full import of their social philosophies, we need to approach them informed about their epistemologies and ontologies. These are not generally well known to English-speaking audiences. Moreover, they employ a vocabulary that is largely alien to the Anglo-Saxon philosophic tradition, let alone to the social sciences. For these reasons, I have in general adopted the method of beginning each chapter with an account of the epistemology and ontology of the thinker under discussion, focusing on the notion of 'being-in-situation'. I have tried in general to keep my own critical interventions to a minimum during this exegesis. I have also tried to write in such a way as to render the ideas comprehensible to those unfamiliar with the philosophic style of the existentialists. It is only when I have set out each thinker's account of human existence as being-in-situation that I then proceed to show what notions of intersubjectivity and interpersonal human relations emerge from it, what account of social being it implies, and that I try critically to assess what it contributes to the development of a conception of a socially situated, or 'impure', subjectivity. For those who are already familiar with the material under discussion some parts of the book will inevitably seem self-evident or redundant. I hope they will bear with me, however. For, given current neglect of the work of the existentialists, they will surely be the minority of my readers.

Finally, a word on the problem of gendered language. All of the existentialists, Beauvoir included, are guilty of what today is often called phallocentrism. They collapse humankind into 'man'; persons into 'men'. The examples they use (apart from Beauvoir's in *The Second Sex*) are invariably ones drawn from masculine experience. My own objections to such gendering have, however, been difficult to reconcile with the task of accurate presentation. To substitute *person* for *man* is to conflate terms that have distinct meanings for my authors; to recast their examples in the female voice is to distort the style of their texts. I have thus decided to leave their masculinist tone and vocabulary intact where I am giving an account of their ideas. Where I stand at a greater distance and give my own comments, I have tried to avoid phallocentric language.

Part One
Individual Situations

1

Marcel: embodiment and situation

Today, not many people read the works of Gabriel Marcel (1889–1973). Yet, as a few perceptive commentators have observed, Marcel's thought, initially elaborated in the interwar period, is seminal in the development of existentialism and phenomenology in France. For example, writing in a now classic volume, which did much to introduce recent French philosophy to English-speaking audiences in the early 1950s, Jean Hering insisted that: 'even if German phenomenology (to suppose the impossible) had remained unknown in France, nevertheless a phenomenology would have been constituted there; and this, to a large extent would have been due to the influence of Gabriel Marcel'.[1] More recently Paul Ricoeur has observed that it was Marcel who 'laid the foundation of what Merleau-Ponty and others later called the phenomenology of perception'.[2]

The reason for the general neglect of Marcel's work is its primarily religious character. There is a long tradition of Christian philosophizing in France, much of it Catholic, within which we might attempt to locate him. But this tradition is alien both to the concerns of recent non-Catholic philosophy in France and to the mainstreams of twentieth-century Anglo-American philosophy. For those, myself included, who do not share it, the theological framework within which Marcel thinks must to some extent limit the significance of his work. This is particularly the case with his discussion of social and political life, which he tends to reduce to issues of 'evil' and 'love'. But in other dimensions, the import of what Marcel has to say most definitely transcends his theological framework.

Moreover, Hering and Ricoeur are surely correct in pointing to Marcel's influence over the atheistic postwar existentialists. For in his pursuit of ways of grasping religious experience Marcel developed a powerful critique of Cartesianism which they were to echo. He also proclaimed the need for a philosophy that would grasp 'lived experience' from within. He was the one who first demanded a situated or a concrete philosophy, as opposed to the kind of detached speculation which Merleau-Ponty was later to designate 'high altitude thinking' (*pensée de survol*). Both in his critique and in his call for a situated philosophy of lived experience, Marcel anticipated and influenced the work of the later generation of existentialists. If Sartre was to insist so emphatically that 'there are two kinds of existentialists', the Christians and the atheists,[3] this point had to be made because they were two subspecies of one and the same philosophical orientation.

French existentialism is often described as a variant of German phenomenology. But in the light of Marcel's contribution to the birth of a specifically French tradition, such a designation is clearly inadequate. For Marcel had already elaborated the broad lines of an existential phenomenology well before the 1930s. And he had done so in splendid ignorance of the work of Husserl and Heidegger (not to mention Kierkegaard and Jaspers), and with only indirect reference to Hegel.[4] If, as Hering argued, Marcel had been able to initiate a distinctly French phenomenological tradition, without reference to the German schools, he did so, however, by building above all on an indigenous French tradition of philosophizing. This came to him through Henri Bergson, who was professor of philosophy at the Collège de France from 1900 to 1921.[5]

Bergson's popularity before the First World War appears to have been comparable to that of Sartre after the Second World War. However, as has been pointed out, there were arguably two Bergsons – Bergson the 'cosmologist', originator of a spiritualist theory of evolution, and Bergson the Cartesian or 'semi-Cartesian' philosopher of consciousness.[6] While Bergson's contemporary fame was won by the former, it was the latter whose work bore fruit in the work of the existentialists. Arguing against positivists such as Taine and Renan, Bergson distinguished an external realm, where causality and mechanism operate, from a distinct but equally real realm of inner experience. The external realm could be comprehended through the analytical methods of mathematics, natural science and practical or instrumental reason which, together, Bergson called 'intellect'. However, the inner realm – where causality is inoperative and where human freedom resides – was to be grasped only through 'intuition', a non-conceptual and immediate kind of knowledge. Knowledge of our own selves is, according to Bergson, of this intuitive kind. For we experience ourselves only through our immersion in the non-objective flow of time which he calls *durée*, or 'real time', which mathematical or physical models of time can never capture. Bergson also developed a social theory based on these distinctions. He called 'closed' those societies which mechanically and statically perpetuate themselves by imposing religious and moral norms on their members as external, quasi-natural, forces. These he contrasted to 'open' societies, in which individual moral and religious creativity freely shine forth, and in which society is engaged in a process of spiritual evolution which transcends mere survival.[7]

While the postwar existentialists also acknowledged a direct debt to Bergson, it was largely through Marcel that they came to him. Of the postwar existentialists, it was Merleau-Ponty who most explicitly acknowledged the influence of Marcel on his own work. In a talk given in 1959, he cited Marcel as one of the figures who had most influenced his generation in their efforts to develop, in opposition to the dominant idealism of Brunschvicg, a 'philosophy of existence'.[8] It was, Merleau-Ponty suggested, especially in Marcel's treatment of the theme of 'incarnation' – the notion that 'I am my body' – that they found the central premise for their attack on the current orthodoxy. For, Merleau-Ponty argued, the idea of incarnation, of the centrality of my body in my existence, implied a particular manner of philosophizing, a 'new way of thinking'. In particular, it implied that the philosopher could no longer conceive of himself as a detached 'spectator' of reality. Sartre too was familiar with Marcel's work. Indeed, before he achieved notoriety as the symbol of 'Left Bank' existentialism, he even attended philosophical *soirées* which Marcel used to hold in his own home. Marcel claims that it was at his suggestion that Sartre developed his phenomenology of *le visqueux* (variously translated as 'the slimy' and 'the viscous') in *Being and Nothingness* and *Nausea*.[9]

Marcel was born in 1889 and began to study and to write philosophy in Paris in the era before the First World War, when Bergson's influence was at its height. Marcel described his childhood as sorrowful, overshadowed by the death of his mother when he was very young. It was also, he has said, 'a desert universe', imbued with the 'arid' positivist rationalism and the 'invincible agnosticism' of his father and the aunt who brought him up. This in turn was compounded by the scholasticism and competitiveness of a *lycée* education which, he said, he endured in misery.[10] It was to a philosophy of 'inner experience', to a somewhat mystical religiosity and also to music and the writing of drama that he turned in repudiation of this ultra rationalistic childhood experience. Thus, it would seem, his conversion to Catholicism in 1929 was a fulfilment of his earlier tendencies and presented no rupture with his prior thought or life. It was his hostility to rationalism that also prepared him to fall under the spell of Bergson, whose classes at the Sorbonne he began to attend in 1906. Of all his professors, he later wrote, Bergson was the one 'whose thought and words took a sure and lasting hold of me'.[11] It was not Bergson the evolutionist, but the philosopher of *durée* and opponent of abstract system, whose work Marcel absorbed and creatively reworked.

Marcel's first major work of philosophy, the *Metaphysical Journal*, was written over the period 1914–1923 in an intimate diary form. It was published (with his major 1925 essay, 'Existence and Objectivity', as an appendix) in 1927. Marcel dedicated the volume to Bergson. Years later, in the preface he wrote to the 1950 English translation, he continued to emphasize his debt to Bergson. '[M]y thought', he observed,

> should appear as the prolongation of a fundamentally anti-dogmatic tradition; and if it is linked up with Bergson that is in the measure in which Bergson himself gave us the means for proceeding beyond him when in his last work he made use of the category 'open'... Though I did not realise this in the beginning, my researches have a bearing on the conditions that permit us to maintain thought in a state of 'openness' in contradistinction to a systematised dogmatics closed in on itself.[12]

Although Bergson's influence was great at the turn of the century, it lessened considerably after the First World War. By the 1920s and 1930s what Marcel regarded as a 'systematised dogmatics' was all too prevalent in French academic philosophy. There predominated a rather scholastic idealism, epitomized in the work of Brunschvicg, against which Sartre, Beauvoir and Merleau-Ponty were also to rebel. In calling for a non-systematic philosophy which attempted to 'evoke' what Marcel called *existence* – that is, our immediate experience of life, prior to the abstracting and objectifying interventions of thought – Marcel anticipated the next generation of existential philosophers, creatively transforming and handing on to them Bergson's insistence on the reality of lived time and the priority of 'intuition' over 'intellect'.

Central to Marcel's work is the distinction summed up in the title of his 1925 essay, 'Existence and Objectivity'. There is, he asserts, an 'absolute priority of existence ... of the existential', which leads us 'to the affirmation of a *pure* immediate, that is to say to an immediate which by its very essence is incapable of mediation' (MJ 329). Existential philosophy must undertake the delicate and paradoxical task of trying to 'evoke' those unthought and unspoken experiences – of self, of love, of fear, etc. – in which we are directly immersed, yet do so without in the process destroying them by turning them into objects of contemplation. The task of philosophy is thus similar to that of poetry or drama: to express that which is unexpressed and can be only indirectly expressed. Talking of his own work, Marcel was emphatic that the unity between philosophical and dramatic work 'describes without doubt what is most original as well as most essential in my contributions'.[13] Like Marcel, Sartre and Beauvoir also moved back and forth between literary and philosophical genres and wrote (as did Merleau-Ponty) a rather literary style of philosophy. This style of existential philosophy has been the butt of criticism from 'hard-boiled' logical positivists and analytical philosophers. The kind of strictures Bertrand Russell passed on Bergson early in this century have been frequently echoed in criticism of his successors. 'Of course', Russell complained,

> a large part of Bergson's philosophy, probably the part to which most of its popularity is due, does not depend upon argument, and cannot be upset by argument. His imaginative picture of the world, regarded as poetic effort, is in the main not capable of either proof or disproof. Shakespeare says life's but a walking shadow, Shelley says it is like a dome of many coloured glass, Bergson says it is a shell which bursts into parts that are shells again. If you like Bergson's image better, it is just as legitimate.[14]

But this and other such criticisms miss the point of what Bergson, Marcel and their successors are arguing. What they seek to establish is that there are certain kinds of experience – even we might say certain kinds of truth – that are not subject to 'proof' of either a strictly logical or an empirically verifiable kind. The dramatic, the poetic, the metaphorical are appropriate forms of philosophic discourse because they alone enable us to approach dimensions of experience which are destroyed if we try to evaluate them by objective criteria. Although Marcel overstates his case, his work remains a useful corrective to the kind of philosophy which defines its task as no more than linguistic and logical clarification.

Both positivism and those forms of Cartesian and neo-Kantian idealism prevalent in France were, according to Marcel, guilty of objectivism. Instead of evoking our immediate inherence in existence, they rupture that immediacy by positing a world of objects distinct from the consciousness that knows and judges them: they de-situate, establishing a distance between a thinking subject and the objects thought about. They thus chop up and destroy that seamless reality which Bergson had called *durée* and which Marcel calls existence. The aim of a philosophy of existence, by contrast, must be to reveal 'the indissoluble *unity of existence and of the existent*' (MJ 322) by demonstrating that subject-object distinctions collapse when we attempt to analyse such fundamental human experiences as embodiment, love, human communication, or the communion with God.

But what is at issue for Marcel in his unceasing effort 'to dissociate existence and objectivity' (MJ 314) is not merely a matter of philosophical error. Objectivist approaches to reality – what in later works he will call the 'spirit of abstraction' – are not only philosophically mistaken. They involve an attitude to life, a way of being, that is destructive of the distinctly human qualities of our existence. Scientists treat natural phenomena as constituting an objective order: they regard them as objects of inquiry laid out for scrutiny before the detached scientific mind. Marcel doubts whether this assumption of distance is justified even in the domain of natural science. But what is certain for him is that if we treat our own inner experiences in this way, or take this attitude when we think about other people – as do many social scientists – we destroy what is distinctively human about our existence. The detached attitude of objectivism invites not only to indifference but also to callousness towards our fellows. It is, in Marcel's view, the ultimate source of violence and oppression in human affairs, the point of origin of political conflict. However, before examining Marcel's views on collective human affairs and politics in more detail, it is necessary to sketch the general aspects of his thought.

Beyond the 'cogito'

Marcel developed his philosophy of existence initially through a critique of what he called Idealism. Empiricism, which he regarded as the traditional alternative to Idealism, he found so unacceptable that he rarely engaged in an extended or serious critique of it. Indeed, the *Metaphysical Journal* began by virtually dismissing empiricism out of hand, and it is hard even to know which thinkers he had in mind. Empiricism, Marcel asserted, cuts us off from all possibility of grasping the plenitude of human experience, or of approaching the non-objective truths of human existence, because it conceives sense data as the only possible source of truth.

According to Marcel, it is reflection, or what he calls the 'self-activity of mind', that at least begins to take us beyond the standpoint of the empiricist's 'immediate existence' to 'successive planes on which things become intelligible'(MJ 1). But these higher planes of intelligibility cannot be grounded in the immediacy of sense perception. It is not, as empiricism claims, a question of starting from objectively given sense data and building up, from knowledge acquired through the senses, to higher kinds of knowledge through the additional operations of reflection. The starting-point for proceeding towards higher planes of intelligibility is wholly other than pure sense data, and the kind of knowledge aimed at is not the 'objective' knowledge empiricism seeks. It is thus to the examination of idealism that the *Journal* rapidly turns, although only to show that (while to be taken more seriously than empiricism) it too is seriously flawed.

Marcel's style of philosophizing is deliberately non-systematic, since he regards systemization as the imposition of false (because external) ordering principles on experience.[15] The task of philosophy for Marcel is one of 'evocation', not of ordering or analysis. However, this refusal of systemization gives rise to a lack of terminological precision even in Marcel's critique of other philosophical positions. In the *Metaphysical Journal*, the journal form itself, with its breaks in continuity and rambling interior monologue, compounds the lack of clarity. Thus, in the *Journal*, 'idealism', 'rationalism', 'intellectualism' are all discussed, without it ever being clear why Marcel sees these all as roughly synonymous and yet as sufficiently distinctive to merit separate designations. Nor does Marcel attribute any one of these positions consistently to a specific philosopher. However, there are two philosophers – Kant and, above all, Descartes – who are explicitly discussed at length as illustrating both the achievements and the limitations of what Marcel most frequently calls Idealism.

From some philosophical perspectives Marcel's own thought, with its emphasis on spiritual experience and its religious foundations, could reasonably be described as 'idealist'. However, Marcel describes his own philosophy as 'concrete' (*une philosophie concrète*). This suggests the source of his uneasiness with the tradition that links Descartes to Kant and to their successors. 'Idealism', according to Marcel, suffers from *abstractness*. It commits the error of granting such a degree of autonomy to reason that reason and what Marcel calls 'experience' are sundered. The 'self-activity of mind' might well, as idealists claim, be the source of 'intelligibility' but, Marcel points out, 'self-activity' belongs to the minds of human beings each of whom is a bodily and situated existent. To comprehend the 'self-activity of mind' we have to know whose mind in particular we are discussing: we cannot talk of Mind in general. In a discussion of Kant, Marcel makes this point as follows:

> We need to admit that thought (reason) does not constitute itself as thought for itself save in the measure in which it is realised in experience . . . In other words, the idea of a pure thought anterior – even in a rational sense – to all experience is certainly a pseudo-idea; it is the product of a schematic and illusory reflection. (MJ 75)

Both Kant's deduction of the categories of the understanding and Descartes' attempt, in the *Meditations*, to found indubitable knowledge solely in mind fail, according to Marcel's perhaps eccentric reading, to examine the relation of thought to the existence of particular thinking subjects; that is, they fail to recognize the 'incarnate', or embodied, and situated nature of consciousness. As a result, Marcel claims, thought is radically separated from sensation and feeling. Mind is posited as independent of, or at any rate prior to, body and concrete situation. A fundamental dualism is established which leaves us with two realms of being, each closed in on itself, yet whose self–evident interpenetration remains an inexplicable paradox. For idealism, as much as for empiricism, this dualism involves the designation of a realm of things wholly distinct from consciousness, an 'order' of objectivity divorced from the 'order' of human existence.

When Descartes writes in the third of his *Meditations*, 'I am a thing which thinks', he is stating the very paradox which Marcel wishes most centrally to address: how can 'I' be both a 'thing' and yet be also a thinking 'I' if, as Descartes asserts, my thinking being is independent of my bodily form? What is it that links these two 'I's together, assuming their conjunction in my 'self' is something more than mere chance? In the *Metaphysical Journal*, Marcel approaches this problem –

which he sums up as the problem of the *cogito* – from the standpoint of *faith*.[16] The difficulties of this *cogito* are, as he sees it, twofold. Firstly, the 'I think' is, he asserts, radically different from the 'I believe'. Faith has to be a wholly personal experience, involving its own particular mode of immediate 'knowing', which Marcel calls *mystery*. But the *cogito* implies the universality – and thus the impersonality – of the 'thinking subject'. Thus:

> Inasmuch as I think, I am universal, and, if knowledge is dependent on the cogito, that is precisely in virtue of the universality inherent in the thinking ego. In faith there is nothing of the kind. (MJ 40)

The experience of faith thus implies a different kind of 'knowing self' than the *cogito*, and it also implies – as Sartre and Merleau-Ponty were to insist – that there can be a qualitatively different kind of knowledge than that attained by the thinking subject; a knowledge which is neither universal nor abstract but which is none the less valid. To achieve such knowledge, Marcel suggests, we must embark on an act of faith in which we choose to surpass the experience of the self as a *cogito*, as distanced from the world.

> Through faith I affirm a transcendental foundation for the union of the world and of my thought, I refuse to think of myself as purely abstract, as an intelligible form hovering over a world which is what it may be. (MJ 45)

It is thus also through faith that what Marcel regards as the second major difficulty of the *cogito* – namely its dualism – can be resolved. Descartes' 'I think' posits an object of thought distinct from the contemplative thinking subject, such that 'no relation is thinkable' between the two. His *cogito* thus ends up, according to Marcel, in a 'radical dualism which places an intelligible nature and an empirical (irrational) nature in absolute opposition to one another' (MJ 43).

Marcel demands an initial act of faith as the basis for 'surpassing' this dualism and he conceives it in explicitly religious terms – a faith in an 'Absolute Being', who is also an 'Absolute Thou' with whom I can communicate. However, as he explores this surpassing, his notion of faith takes on different connotations and becomes amenable to less theological interpretations. In opposition to the *cogito* he elaborates an account of our relation to the world which posits an 'existential' faith, grounded in the indubitability of our bodily, or 'incarnate' existence. It is such a notion of existential, rather than theological, faith which is taken up but transformed by later thinkers, particularly by Merleau-Ponty, who also insisted on the 'indubitable' quality of our experience of our own existence.

If, says Marcel, there is an indubitable such as Descartes sought to establish, it is an 'existential indubitable' (MB 88) – my own existence. For if I were to deny my own existence, I would not be able to assert that there is any other kind of existence. To say that 'I exist' means, says Marcel, that I am more than a consciousness, that 'I am manifest... I have something to make myself known and recognized both by others and by myself' (MB 90–1). That 'something' is not my self as *cogito*, but my self as body. As a bodily existent I feel, I sense, my existence. It is as body that I 'participate' directly in the being of the world. 'I exist', says Marcel, 'means not I *think*, not even I *live*, but I *experience*'.[17] Such a notion of 'experience' might arguably bring us very close to empiricism after all.[18] But Marcel insists that his notion of immediate experience implies a creative relation to the world, rather than the passive reception of sense data. Thus, experience must be discovered 'at a level beyond that of traditional empiricism' (TW 229). But Marcel also sometimes suggested there is, perhaps, what he called a 'higher empiricism' to be attained. For, 'after all, the error of empiricism consists only in ignoring the part of invention and even of creative initiative involved in any genuine experience'.[19]

'Participation' – a central concept in Marcel's philosophy – implies above all a non-objective relation to Being. Reflective consciousness involves relations that are mediated, distanced; it conceives of the world of objects (including the body as object) as detached from the thinking subject. By contrast, in participation there is no distance, only a co-presence, a 'being with' the world which 'can no longer be translated into the language of outer objects' (MB 116). It follows also that participation must be beyond judgements of the kind we pass on the objective world. For sensations and feelings are our direct experience of the world, our mode of co-presence with it, while judgement requires always the mediation of objectifying reflection. It is only at the level of 'ideas of feelings' (MJ 131) that we can evaluate our experience or ever begin to doubt it.

It is a striking coincidence that in the same year in which Marcel published the *Metaphysical Journal*, 1927, Heidegger published *Being and Time*.[20] Marcel had no familiarity with Heidegger's work until much later. Indeed, Heidegger's work appears to have become known in France only after 1929, when he attended a major meeting of French and German philosophers held in Switzerland, and the earliest reference to Heidegger I have found in Marcel's work is a journal entry dated 31 March 1931 (BH 73).[21] However, the parallels between the two thinkers deserve comment. Drawing from Bergson, Marcel developed, through the notion of participation, an account of our lived experience of being which in many ways overlaps with Heidegger's account of 'being-in-the-world'. The Heideggerian notions that human beings *inhabit* the world and that it is revealed to them through *care*, express very similar insights to those which Marcel developed in discussing embodiment and mystery. However, for Marcel, unlike Heidegger, the possibility of participation was finally assured by the existence of the Absolute Being, or God. As Marcel put it, although they both shared a sense of the 'sacred' quality of being, he was a Christian while Heidegger was 'a Greek' (TW 242–3). The postwar generation of existentialists, Sartre in particular, claimed to draw on Heidegger as one of their main sources of inspiration. But in many instances, their reading of Heidegger served only to supplement or to justify notions they had already received through Marcel.

Embodied and situated existence

It is most fundamentally as 'my body' that I participate in Being. But we need further to clarify what the phrase 'my body' means for Marcel. Can I conceive of myself apart from my body, Marcel asks. Or, conversely, am I no more than my body? Marcel answers 'no' to both questions. If one were to conceive of a self apart from the body, this would imply that the body is no more than an object, a tool or 'instrument' in the service of a 'self' which is a disembodied thinking subject – and we would return to the problems of Cartesianism. But on the other hand, it would not do to say that I am identical with, or no more than, my body. For if all that were in the world were bodies, what would distinguish 'mine' from another? (EPC 32–4)[22] While it is possible to say what the phrase 'my body' or the related statement 'I am my body' do *not* mean, Marcel finally concludes that it is not possible to give them a positive meaning:

> To say 'I am my body' is in reality to utter a negative judgement: 'it is not true to say, there is no sense in saying that I am other than my body'. (EPC 34)

This is not because we still lack the right words, or because the analysis has yet to be worked out. It is because my relationship to my body, because immediate, is intrinsically opaque. If I were to conceive my body as a 'body-object' (*corps-objet*), it would be comprehensible to me, but merely as an instrument whose function was to transmit sensations to me. If, however, I conceive my body – as indeed I must – as a 'body-subject' (*corps-sujet*), then all I can say is that it is immediately revealed to me through 'sensation', but that I cannot identify myself with it through any 'logic' (EPC 44). My body is, to use Marcel's terminology, a *mystery* to me.

The term *mystery*, counter-posed to the term *problem*, used initially in the *Metaphysical Journal*, remains central to Marcel's entire body of work. But it takes on new dimensions after his conversion to Catholicism in 1929. Problems, according to Marcel, are posed when we inquire into the world of things, or when we consider people as things, fully distinct from the inquirer. When addressing a problem, the inquirer assumes him- or herself to be a detached spectator:

> Whenever a problem is found, I am working upon data placed before me; but at the same time the general state of affairs authorises me to carry on as if I had no need to trouble myself with this Me who is at work: he is here simply presupposed. (BH 171)

Scientific inquiry proceeds in such a detached manner. It 'only speaks of the real in the third person' (MJ 137) – that is, as 'it'. A problem-oriented approach invites us to search for 'solutions' and to manipulate the world: technology is thus the product of problem-oriented investigation. In some of Marcel's later works he is highly critical of the encroachment of technological approaches in human affairs. For example, by treating people as mere data, as the objects of impersonal manipulation, bureaucracy reduces human beings to what Marcel calls *abstractions*; it dehumanizes them.

By contrast, in exploring a mystery I do not assume myself to be distinct from the data placed before me. When he uses the term 'mystery' Marcel does not mean an encounter with the wholly impenetrable or indecipherable. Rather, mysteries are inaccessible only to an objectifying reflection, because no clear distinction can be maintained between what is experienced and the experiencer. There is a relationship of 'encroachment' which precludes the distance necessary for objective thought. Marcel put the idea thus in an autobiographical essay of 1947:

> Perhaps I can best explain my continual and central metaphysical preoccupation by saying that my aim was to discover how a subject, in his actual capacity as subject, is related to a reality which cannot in this context be regarded as objective, yet which is persistently required and recognised as real.[23]

A mystery, then, is not amenable to rational analysis, nor to any process of formal reflection, yet we can still apprehend it as meaningful. However, Marcel is careful not to call the experience of mystery subjective. For we are not dealing here with a realm of subjective reality opposed to that of objective reality, but with an order of experience which denies such a distinction. My relation to my body is perhaps the most pervasively encountered example of mystery, but it is for Marcel but one manifestation of the mystery of Being in general – of what Marcel called in an essay of 1933, 'the ontological mystery'.[24] Even before he became a Catholic, Marcel conceived this central mystery in religious terms, as an immediate relation to God. For example, an entry from 1918 in his *Metaphysical Journal*, states:

> I would be prepared to say dogmatically that every relation of being to being is personal and that the relation between God and me is nothing if it is not a relation of being with being, or, strictly, of being with itself. (MJ 137)

Mysteries, as immediate experiences, imply our situatedness in Being. The mystery of embodiment involves my *situation* in space and time, but not as objective dimensions. Space and time, in so far as 'I' am situated as a substantial but finite body within them, are not independent 'givens' or externalities which define me. That 'I am my body' means rather that 'I *am* also my habitual surroundings' and that '*I am my past*' (MJ 259). The space and time in which I am situated are, then, specifically *mine*, invoked by my own participation in Being. Or, we could say, space and time and my situation within them, pertain to the order of existence and not to that of objectivity.

From the fact that my situation is existential rather than objective, various conclusions follow. For one, the spatial dichotomies of 'interiority' and 'exteriority' are reduced or even obliterated: 'if one deeply investigates being-in-situation, one will find there perhaps not the synthesis but at least the junction of exteriority and interiority'. Thus to talk of being in situation is not only to talk about a position in space. For 'determinations which appear purely spatial are able to be qualified in an increasingly internal manner' (EPC 130). For example, if I say that I am 'at home' (*chez moi*) somewhere, I do not mean that I am in a place which formally or legally belongs to me. What I mean is that I experience a certain 'harmony' between myself and the place, that I 'find' myself or have a 'recognition' of myself there (EPC 138–9).

In situated existence we do not only pass beyond the antinomies of inside and outside, we also pass beyond that objective order in which necessity and contingency operate. My 'being-in-situation' cannot be necessary in the sense of being subject to an external constraint (MJ 100). 'Things', for Marcel, are regulated in a domain where necessity is present in the form of causal relationships. But if I were to posit myself (or other people) as the product of anterior causes, then I would fail to grasp what is distinctive about my own relation to Being. I am not situated as a rock, for example, is situated in a landscape because, unlike the rock, I participate actively in my situation. I call it forth; I *exist* it. Agreeing with Sartre in this one instance, Marcel writes:

> We shall be tempted, of course, and we must resist the temptation, to think of a man's given circumstances, or of the self's situation, as having a real, embodied, independent existence *outside* the self ... But, in fact, as Sartre has very lucidly demonstrated, what we call our given circumstances come into our lives only in connection with a free activity of ours to which they constitute either an encouragement or an obstacle. (MB 134)

If for Marcel it is impossible to talk of a human situation in terms of a necessary relation between the self and what surrounds it, it is equally impossible to conceive that relation in terms of contingency, for the concept of contingency is meaningless except in relation to that of necessity. Moreover, were I to regard my situation as contingent I would be treating it as radically separated from my self. If I were to say that it is a matter of contingency that I have been born in a particular place, or with particular physical characteristics, or that I earn my living in a particular way, it would be implied that I have a self which is distinct from such attributes. It would be, as Marcel puts it, to posit an 'empirical self' as a dispensable husk which surrounds a 'transcendental kernel' and which can be stripped away. However:

> I can only carry out this stripping in so far as I arrogate to myself the right to abstract myself from a given circumstance and, as it were, to stand outside it. Let us ask ourselves whether the assumption that we can step outside of our skins in this spry and simple fashion is not merely an illusion or even a lie. In abstracting myself from given circumstance, from the empirical self, from the situation in which I find myself, I run the risk of escaping into a real never-never or no-man's land – into what strictly must be called a *nowhere*. (MB 133)

And to be nowhere is to be disembodied and unsituated; it is to cease to exist any more. To conceive of oneself as such a disembodied *cogito*, or perhaps spirit, is as erroneous as to conceive of oneself as a purely material 'thing'.

What runs through Marcel's account of 'being-in-situation', as through his account of embodiment, is the primacy of communication and the possibility of harmony. The realm of the truly human is the realm of mystery, where we encounter Being in all its plenitude. There is 'creative development', says Marcel, 'as soon as there is *being in a situation*' (MB 139). Love, religious vocation, artistic creation are, for Marcel, the fullest resonances of 'being-in-situation'. What, however, is striking about Marcel's account of 'being-in-situation', as of embodiment and our relation to the Absolute Thou, is the rigid nature of the distinction he draws between our immediate, existential 'knowledge' of such mysteries and the order of 'objective' knowledge. There can be *no* passage from one order of knowing to the other. It is for this reason that he writes in the *Metaphysical Journal* that, 'no demonstration of the existence of God is possible. There is no logical transition by which we can mount up to God from a starting point which is not God' (MJ 262). Similarly, there could be no proof of the existence of 'my body' that was not already given with my body.

Thus, Marcel's world ultimately seems as dualistic as that of a Cartesian. Between the orders of objectivity and existence, between the detached knowledge of problems (including scientific knowledge) and the immersed knowledge of mysteries, no passage is possible. Yet although the order of objectivity can, for Marcel, have no place in what he conceives as the properly human order of existence and mystery, it is real. Indeed, he sees it as continually threatening existence. Moreover, there is an overwhelming temptation for us to treat our own lives and those of our fellows as problems rather than as mysteries. Paradoxically, there is for Marcel a fundamental bifurcation both of Being itself and of our knowledge of Being. These bifurcations are as total – and one might add as problematic – as those which Marcel had set out to overcome in Cartesian thought.

Human relations: communication and objectification

These bifurcations have profound consequences for Marcel's treatment of the question of relations between human beings. A real meeting of two human beings is, for Marcel, a mystery; it is not the encounter of two distinct consciousnesses, nor does it involve the perception by each of the other as an object. Rather, other people are, like 'my body' and like God, already present with me. I meet another person – a 'Thou' – within my own field of incarnate being, and thus in no way as a threat to myself or as a potential negation of myself. On the contrary, the other person is integral to my self-fulfilment. Marcel goes so far as to claim at one point: 'I cannot communicate effectively with myself except insofar as I communicate with the other, that is to say that the latter becomes thou for me' (EPC 56). In the most intense I-Thou relations the boundary between myself and the other person becomes blurred. There is 'a sort of fertile indistinction where beings communicate, where they *are* in and through the very act of communication' (EPC 59).

It is striking that the kinds of relations between people that Marcel discusses – especially prior to the 1930s – are predominantly positive ones: love, friendship, faith in others, loyalty, etc. But what is also striking is that Marcel very rarely discusses what we might call social relations, those involving more than a self and one other person. The fundamental human relationship (replicating our relationship with God) involves for him only two people: the dyad of I and Thou. This dyad is mutually supporting and the possibility of its existence appears to be independent of the presence of any kind of wider collectivity. Its foundation is what Marcel calls Love, a transcendental relation which takes us beyond the experience of self and other, and beyond mere 'desire'.[25]

It is, of course, possible to conceive of a community of persons involved in multiple I-Thou relationships, but only a very small, face-to-face one, in which intense personal communication between all the members was possible. Indeed, Marcel observes, 'it is only within groups that are fairly restricted in size and animated by a spirit of love that the universal can really embody itself' (MAMS 267). Wider collectivities – political parties, for example, or nations – preclude such personal ties and are thus regarded by Marcel as always dehumanizing. Marcel's insistent focus on the I-Thou relation as the only fully human relation leads to some interesting critical insights into modern mass society. But it also leads to considerable inadequacies in his treatment of social and political life. For while it allows him to develop a critical description of such 'depersonalizing' and 'evil' phenomena as bureaucracy and mass conformity, it does not permit Marcel to develop any explanation of them.

As we will see, Simone de Beauvoir, Merleau-Ponty and (somewhat belatedly) Sartre, also all try to elucidate personal or individual experience. But they do so in ways which also illuminate the relation of individual experience and action to social institutions and processes of change. Indeed, one of the central problems they address is the complex, and often unintended, consequences which arise on the social plane from the interplay of individual actions. But from Marcel's perspective all institutions pertain equally to the order of objectivity rather than that of existence. They are thus inherently dehumanizing, forces of evil; 'history is an abstraction' (MAMS 241), and events and processes that take place at the macro-social or macro-historical level are always a threat to truly human existence. But since the fully human person must not play the enemy's game by, for example, joining a political party to organize against dehumanizing forces, major historical events, however catastrophic, must always be lived through at the personal level only. They become above all a 'trial of faith' for the individual.

There is, in the final analysis, a paradoxical reductionism in Marcel's perspective: since he expels all mundane transpersonal phenomena to the order of objectivity, he can admit no significance to macro-historical events except at the level of individual experience, where they become 'trials'. And there can be no call therefore to engagement in actions or movements that might require us to act beyond the sphere where 'I-Thou' communication is possible. Accordingly, Marcel's reaction to the horrors of the Second World War and the German Occupation was above all to appeal for a yet stronger spiritual life; in the face of such evil, greater hope, fidelity, faith in immortality were needed. It was a response that called for individual strength, but not for political engagement of the kind which might require that we do violence to another.[26] Emphasizing the possibility of maintaining an 'inner' spiritual purity in the face of extreme dehumanization, Marcel's views amounted to the claim, against Sartre and Merleau-Ponty, that it is possible after all to have 'clean hands' in any situation.[27]

Marcel insisted that his position was not one of indifference. On the contrary, the philosopher in particular has a duty to fight inhumanity in any form. But this requires only an 'inner attitude', expressed in our own personal sphere of activity (MAMS 244). Marcel warns against the role of 'philosopher king'. For 'it is not the business of the philosopher or the sage to take charge of a technocratic world; he could only do so by making himself a slave' (MAMS 271). Even in the age of nuclear war and the possibility of the destruction of humanity, the task of the philosopher is never to enter the world of politics *per se* (for example, to address mass meetings, to write to newspapers, to join demonstrations). For this world is part of 'the order of things', while the domain in which the philosopher has responsibility is 'what can be very generally called the spiritual domain' (TW 31). Discussing Bertrand Russell's activity in nuclear disarmament campaigns in the 1960s, he criticizes him for engaging in 'showy demonstration' in which the philosopher does not have the duty, 'or perhaps even the right' to participate (TW 28). To the end, Marcel remained emphatic that the order of existence is distinct from that of objectivity, and that it alone is the source of all that is significant in human life.

However, this is not to say that the realm of objectivity does not exist. In the *Metaphysical Journal* Marcel had dwelt at length on our participation in Being, and on our experience of communion with God and our fellows. But from the early 1930s he became increasingly preoccupied with what he called (in the title of a play) 'The Broken World'. In such essays as 'On the Ontological Mystery' and 'Outline of a Phenomenology of Having',[28] pessimism and despair become, in an age dominated by technocracy and depersonalization, the 'trials' against which we must struggle in faith and hope. Thus, already in 1933 he wrote:

> The characteristic feature of our age seems to me to be what might be called the misplacement of the idea of function . . . The individual tends to appear both to himself and to others as an agglomeration of

functions ... Life in a world centered on function is liable to despair because in reality this world is *empty*, it rings hollow.[29]

While Marcel's conversion to Catholicism no doubt offered him a range of traditional theological concepts with which to express his growing misgivings about the human condition – sin, evil, despair – it was above all the changing political climate of Europe in the early 1930s which was reflected in the changing tone of his work.[30] With the War and the German Occupation and, subsequently, with what he regarded as the Soviet threat and the threat of nuclear war, Marcel's feeling of menace continued to grow. In such volumes as his wartime essays, *Homo Viator*, his postwar critique of mass dehumanization, *Man Against Mass Society*, or the collection *Tragic Wisdom and Beyond*, there is less a celebration of the communication and love in human existence than a struggle to affirm such values in the face of overwhelming threat.

But to return for now to the early 1930s, it is in the material published as *Being and Having*, particularly the essay 'Outlines of a Phenomenology of Having', that Marcel began to explore what he saw as the source of such threat – a source that lies in individual moral failure. It is when we seek to *have*, or to possess, rather than to *be*, that forms of self-objectification (which lead us also to objectify other people) arise. It is in our relation to our bodies that such an objectifying self-relation most easily appears. We can, in the terminology Marcel now develops, conceive of our bodies as something which we *have* instead of what we *are*; we can conceive of them as things 'possessed', and thus as external to us. But when things are external to us, it is inherent in the kind of relation we have with them that they can become separated from us. For the individual whose attitude to him- or herself and to the world is primarily one of having, or proprietorship, life becomes dominated by the fear of loss. This fear is destructive:

> Having as such seems to have a tendency to destroy and to lose itself in the very thing it began by possessing, but which now absorbs the master who thought he controlled it. It seems that it is of the very nature of my body, or of my instruments in so far as I treat them as possessions, that they should blot me out, although it is I who possess them. (BH 164–5)

Thus, says Marcel, a tendency can develop for the order of objectivity increasingly to destroy that of existence. This is a not uncommon state of affairs in the world and is the source for most social ills. However, it is not an inevitable or an irreversible state of affairs. For, far from such a tendency being central to the human condition, it arises from what Marcel calls 'an act of desertion' (BH 165) – from the choice to become thing-like and to relinquish our affirmation of the mystery of Being. The person who wishes to *have* operates at the level of mere 'desire', rather than love or creation. But there is no ontological necessity that we operate at this level, and it is always possible to transcend it in 'love'.

Marcel concedes that there are some kinds of suffering which do not come to us through such 'acts of desertion': sickness, for example, or the death of a loved one. But such afflictions may be accepted as mysteries and taken up as 'my trial' or 'my test'. A serious illness, Marcel says, may appear 'as a pathway and not merely an obstacle' (MAMS 126). Indeed, he insists, 'faith' could not exist unless it were tested: 'Faith is in essence something which ought to be tried and wants to be tried' (MJ 201). [31] Suffering and misery have their place as a ground for the faith in which I affirm my being and the being of the Absolute Thou. But the evils and suffering which pervade whole epochs and societies – wars, totalitarian regimes, the threat of nuclear annihilation – do not have this providential quality, although the individual may still live them as a trial. For, with dogged single-mindedness, Marcel insists that the origin of such societal evils lies in the increasing predominance of relations of having over those of being, of objectivity over existence.

The 'mass-man': abstraction and depersonalization

Writing shortly after the Second World War, Marcel laments that, in the modern world, technological approaches to life and the 'spirit of abstraction' have come to predominate, along with the predominance of the 'masses'. Most men – the 'masses' – are incapable of experiencing mystery. We are witnessing a profound crisis, in which 'man is in his death throes'. By this Marcel does not mean that the 'idea of man' is dying, but that the latent possibilities for total self-destruction, always inherent in human existence, have now come to predominate. There is, he argues, 'a secret bond' between 'the physical destruction wrought by the atomic bomb and the spiritual destruction wrought by techniques of human degradation' (MAMS 14). This bond, which links together phenomena as apparently diverse as Nazi concentration camps and Soviet 'totalitarianism', the dominance of a debased public opinion in France, increased urbanization and the ubiquity of bureaucracy and technocracy, lies, he believes, in the pervasiveness of the 'spirit of abstraction'. The crisis is at root 'metaphysical', a crisis of values, and it is to be overcome not by political or other problem-oriented action but only through 'grace' and God's 'light'. Indeed, Marcel firmly warns us:

> There is probably no more dangerous an illusion than that of imagining that some readjustments of social or institutional conditions could suffice in itself to appease a contemporary sense of disquiet which arises, in fact, from the very depth of man's being. (MAMS 37)

However, we should not give way to the sin of despair. Rather, those of us who wish to resist the evils of the modern world must, in small communities of like-minded people, hold ourselves 'available' (*disponible*) for God's grace, allowing His 'light' to shine through us. Moreover, Marcel insists, '[t]his, in spite of appearances to the contrary, is an active role' (MAMS 263). For the only effective resistance to the forces of evil must be to struggle with the evil within ourselves. If there is ever to be peace on earth man will have to be at peace with himself: each of us will have had to overcome his own temptations to evil through his own inner struggle.

For those who are sceptical that God's grace might save us from the destructive tendencies of modern society, Marcel's recommendations appear, at best, irrelevant. Similarly his diagnosis of the origin of these tendencies, couched ultimately in the language of sin and redemption, has little to say to those beyond his own community of believers. But what makes Marcel's discussion worth pursuing further is that, at a level between that of diagnosis and recommendation, at a level which we might call 'phenomenological' in a fairly loose sense of the term, Marcel's description of the manifestations of 'the spirit of abstraction' is insightful. Paradoxically, it also parallels and complements certain Marxist analyses of alienation. It thus contributes to a discourse which transcends the boundaries of distinctly Christian philosophy. It, like Marxism, offers a critique of modernity which does not call for 'post-modernity' but for the realization of the human potentiality immanent in the modern condition.

Marcel is, of course, critical of Marxism. He regards it as the source of Soviet 'totalitarianism' and as philosophically flawed. As a materialism Marxism is itself a philosophy of abstraction, and thus 'radically incompatible with the idea of a free man' (MAMS 20). Moreover, Marcel claims, Marxism is hostile to 'any philosophy centring on the idea of the "person"' (MAMS 230). Yet, Marcel's strictures notwithstanding, there are striking parallels between his notion of 'abstraction' and the Marxist notion of 'alienation'. For both, one of the most unacceptable dimensions of modernity is the reduction of human beings to 'things', and of human relations to uni-dimensional relations between 'things'. Of course, the explanation offered for this reduction is radically different – a moral 'desertion' for Marcel, capitalist production relations for Marx and subsequent neo-Marxists, such as Marcuse. Even so, we could well read Marcel's 'phenomenology of having' and his account of the insidious advance of the 'spirit of abstraction' and of 'technical man' as providing an extended meditation on the subjective experience of modern capitalist society.[32]

As we have seen, at the theoretical level, abstraction is linked to objectivist thought, to the realm of problem rather than mystery: abstract theories – be they scientific or philosophical – assume that the theorizer is a thinking subject detached from the object of theorization. Abstract thinking erroneously takes itself to be an *unsituated* thought. But abstraction, Marcel now argues, is not only a theoretical error. It is a much broader – and more dangerous – phenomenon. For abstraction, by denying our common situatedness, ruptures the bonds of fundamental participation, the mystery of 'I-Thou' communication, and thereby leaves open the way for violence against our fellows.

In its most extreme form, it was the 'spirit of abstraction' that enabled the Nazis to declare Jews and others to be non-human. But even in what appears to be a more benign form, namely the pursuit of universal principles, it is conducive to violence. For example, the principled egalitarianism of the French Revolution was, Marcel insists, intimately linked with the Terror (MAMS 2–3). While in contemporary France, 'the popular demand for equality' leads only to a 'levelling down' and to the predominance of feelings of 'resentment'. There is, says Marcel, 'a sort of moral blood-poisoning', in which each, instead of being satisfied with his own lot, covets that of his neighbour. In this dynamic, 'the other man becomes, for me, the person who covets my job, or, more subtly, who damages my inner esteem because he manages to get a better paid job than mine' (MAMS 30). In the name of the principle of equality, I reduce the other person to no more than one who threatens my ability to 'have' what I want. Once such resentment sets in, 'I-Thou' relations between us cease to be possible.

While Marcel's critique of the abstract principle of equality is mounted from the rather complacent assumption that everyone does already have a sufficiency in life, his description of the phenomenon of resentment remains powerful. And again we can find parallels with what Marx says about 'abstract right', as in the following passage from his 'Critique of the Gotha Programme'.

> Right by its very nature can consist only in the application of an equal standard; but unequal individuals (and they would not be different individuals if they were not unequal) are measurable only by an equal standard in so far as they are brought under an equal point of view, are taken from one *definite* side only, for instance, in the present case, are regarded *only as workers*.[33]

The application of abstract principles and the treatment of individuals as abstractions – from only 'one definite side' – involves for Marx (as for Marcel) a denial of full humanity. For Marx, of course, this denial could not be overcome through an intense personal struggle for moral improvement, but only through a radical social transformation such as Marcel deemed to be chimerical.

Technology and the spread of technical relations play, for both Marcel and Marx, an important role in heightening the tendency to treat human beings abstractly. 'Techniques', by which Marcel appears to mean mainly, but not exclusively, modern technologies, are bodies of objective and systemized knowledge which we may possess. We may easily enter into those kinds of relations of 'having' with them in which our possessions begin to possess us. A man may easily become 'the prisoner of his techniques' (MAMS 83) and identify himself with his products or possessions.

Over and beyond this individual self-objectification, there are wider social implications to the spread of technology. These include the depersonalization of those who come to be viewed by others as no more than their technical function. Machines have a function: they produce things which people desire to have ('use values'); and they are evaluated in terms of their efficiency in producing; by their *output*. In a society dominated by technology in the service of desire, human beings come to be regarded in a similar manner. As Marx had observed of mechanized factory production, there comes into being 'a lifeless mechanism independent of the workman, who becomes its mere living appendage'.[34] Marcel does not, of course, accept Marx's analysis of the emergence of this form of production as specific to capitalism, but he too abhors factory production and other kinds of non-creative work. For Marcel, such forms of work are but symptoms of a generalized tendency to depersonalization whose roots lie in the moral realm. With the development of technology it is very easy – it is a 'temptation' – to assess human beings by technical criteria:

> It is the man whose output can be objectively calculated ... who is taken as the archetype ... One might say that it is starting with the machine, and in some sense on the model of the machine, that man at the present time is more and more commonly thought of. (MAMS 179)

Furthermore, from this perspective, those whose 'output' is negligible will be regarded as an 'unprofitable charge' on society (MAMS 95). They will be seen – and may well come to see themselves – as worthless.

The predominance of the 'technocratic attitude of mind' (MAMS 203) is apparent also in the growth of bureaucracy. For bureaucracy too reduces people to abstractions, to accountable and classifiable properties. Nazi practices of forced labour and systematic extermination are but the logical extreme of bureaucratic depersonalization. It was perfectly *rational* that workers in the labour camps who became sick were exterminated, since they were considered as no more than labour units.

> If a man is thought of on the model of a machine, it ... conforms to the principles of a healthy economy that when his output falls below the cost of his maintenance ... he should be sent to the scrap heap like a worn out car . (MAMS 182)

But while such practices lie at the extreme end of a continuum, all bureaucracy depersonalizes, reducing concrete, situated individuals to abstract, classifiable characteristics. Moreover, the bureaucrat is as much depersonalized as his victims. His fellow-men become for him only 'problems', to be ordered according to technical 'solutions'.

'Mass society' [35] not only involves the development of depersonalized forms of production and bureaucracy, but also mass techniques of communication, ranging from means of transportation to the radio and press. While, in principle, increased means of communication could make for a more open world, this has not been the outcome. Instead, they have led to the development of greater conformity, the creation of 'a kind of lowest common denominator of well being' (MAMS 86). Accompanying this there has been also a destruction of community, an uprooting, a 'kind of return to nomadism' – literal in the lives of unskilled migrant workers, but no less real for many others whose sense of connection with their fellows has been broken. For such people, and they are a multitude, the sense of 'the reality of life' has been lost. '[L]ife', Marcel observes, 'is being less and less felt as a gift to be handed on, and more and more felt as a kind of incomprehensible calamity' (MAMS 94). It is their desire to escape from the anxiety and fear induced by such a condition that makes many people – those Marcel refers to as 'mass-men' – the easy victims of false prophets, capable of being whipped into a state of dangerous fanaticism.

Uprooted, unconnected, fearful, his own reality distorted by the media, the 'mass-man' is a willing prey to fanatical propaganda (MAMS 139).[36] While Nazism and Stalinism are the twin 'fanaticisms' which, for Marcel, stand at the end-point of abstraction, his concerns lie equally with postwar France. There, he warns, 'an atmosphere of latent fanaticism' threatens disaster (MAMS 151–2). And indeed much of his analysis of the destruction of traditional community, urban migration, the development of mass consumption and the mass media is more appropriate as a description of France – and other liberal capitalist societies – than of the Soviet Union.

But against the forces of depersonalization and the present 'crisis of man', political action of any systematic or organized kind does not, of course, provide the appropriate form of resistance. 'There can be no question here of my attempting to define anything resembling a political line of action. What we have to do with is rather an inner attitude' (MAMS 244). However, we cannot clearly demarcate an 'inner' from an 'outer' aspect of our thoughts, feelings, etc. This 'inner attitude' must thus find an 'expression' within each person's individual situation, and must include a personal response to on-going political events.

Freedom and situation

Marcel once described himself as 'a liberal who has become more and more painfully aware of the limits of liberalism'.[37] Since he regarded totalitarianism and liberalism as the only possible kinds of political systems in his era, and since totalitarian regimes attempt to destroy personal freedom, liberalism was the only hope. However, the central thrust of Marcel's thought runs counter to the very foundations of liberalism in so far as the notion of individual autonomy is central to the doctrine, in either its Lockean or its Kantian formulations. For the claim that individuals are autonomous, be it made on either 'possessive individualist' or on 'moral self-determination' grounds, runs directly counter to our participation in mystery. It involves, in Marcel's terms, making an abstraction of man, advocating an 'atomic individualism' (MAMS 191) of one kind or another; and it involves the failure to realize that subjectivity is never possible except as *inter*subjectivity.

For Marcel freedom is not to be confused with autonomy. On the contrary, freedom takes us *beyond* 'that tension between Same and Other' which predominates in 'the world of having' (BH 172) where autonomy is seen as a self-possession. In the fullest experience of freedom the very notion of an autonomous self is revealed to be an abstraction:

> In the scale of sanctity and of artistic creation, where freedom glows with its fullest light, it is never autonomy. For the saint and the artist alike, autocentricity and the self are entirely swallowed up in love ... Most of the defects of Kant's philosophy are essentially bound up with the fact that he had no suspicion of all this; he never saw that the self can and should be transcended without there being any need for heteronomy to replace autonomy in consequence. (BH 174)

Freedom, then, does not reside in the untrammelled possession of ourselves, or in having full control of our own actions. It is, rather, an experience of creative communion. Although freedom is most easily manifest in religious and artistic experience, it is however also attainable by ordinary people:

> There are modes of creation which do not belong to the aesthetic order, and which are within the reach of everybody; and it is in so far as he is a creator, at however humble a level, that any man can recognize his own freedom. It would be necessary, moreover, to show that the idea of being creative, taken in this quite general sense, always implies the idea of being open towards others: that openness I have called inter-subjectivity. (MAMS 24)

Freedom might perhaps best be called an open disposition for Marcel. It is neither an abstract capacity nor the possession of an untrammelled field of action defined by political rights, but a concrete way of 'being-in-situation' such that we are 'available', open to the 'mystery of being'.

It is still possible for freedom, conceived in this way, to be destroyed, but not by persecution or confinement *per se*. Martyrs die freely and a prisoner of conscience can be free. To destroy freedom is to destroy a person's inner spirit. What was most heinous about the regime in the Nazi concentration camps, Marcel believes, was not the extermination, the brutality, the forced labour, or the squalor, but the calculated attempt to induce *self*-contempt in the inmates. It was the employment of 'techniques of degradation' which required the inmates so to debase themselves in order to survive that they became worthless in their own eyes (MAMS 37 ff). In such a situation, a human being 'tends progressively to be reduced to the status of a mere *thing*', albeit a 'psychic thing' (MAMS 19).

But if this is the case, if the systematic attempt to objectify a class of persons can reduce them to a kind of thing-hood, then Marcel's crucial distinction between the orders of objectivity and existence surely collapses. For it is no longer a person's *own* 'act of desertion' – an act for which he or she is responsible – which destroys participation in the order of existence. It would appear that there are, after all, some situations which simply cannot be lived creatively. They operate as an objective conditioning force on the individual and can break a person's inner attitude. Moreover, if this is the case in the extreme situation of the concentration camp, it could also be so in many other situations in which there is a lesser degree of oppression. Marcel would not want to consider such a possibility, but might it not, for example, be the objective factor of grinding poverty which accounts, at least in part, for such phenomena as resentment and the search for security? These are not perhaps to be explained as purely spiritual ills.

Marcel had set out, from the *Metaphysical Journal* onwards, to reject Cartesian dualism by insisting on the embodied character of all human existence. He had tried to demonstrate that the lived experience of our 'being-in-situation' cannot be explained through the traditional dichotomies of consciousness and matter, subject and object, implied by the idea of the thinking subject. However, his demonstration was flawed by his refusal to recognize the power that objective aspects of our situation can exercise upon us. This power can operate independently of any moral failure or 'act of desertion' on our part. Indeed, it is Marcel's own observations on the destructibility of the inner attitude of freedom in extreme situations which urge on us the need to go beyond the dissociation of the orders of existence and objectivity upon which he had insisted.

By developing an account of situation as an intermingling, or even as a dialectic, of the orders Marcel called 'existence' and 'objectivity', Beauvoir, Merleau-Ponty and Sartre (in the *Critique*) were, as we shall see, able to elaborate a more adequate notion of the situated subject and a fuller account of social existence, including the domain of social action. By designating objectivity as outside existence, as fundamentally *extrinsic* to our situation and, generally, as entering existence only through our own individual moral failures, Marcel remained unable to make sense of significant areas of social existence, particularly those which involve collective action or those where conflict or oppression are pervasive. 'Evil', or 'sin', was the only explanation Marcel could finally offer for those ills of modern society which he so compellingly portrayed; Christian virtue the only possible means of resistance he could suggest. In spite of Marcel's insistence on a 'concrete' philosophy he ended up, paradoxically, in a kind of abstract Manicheism; there is no place in his world for the *ambiguity* of human life in which – as Merleau-Ponty, for example, would observe – good intentions can give rise to disastrous consequences and certain kinds of violence might, perhaps, promote a more fully human society. For Marcel, existence and objectivity remained unambiguously distinct orders. Thus the 'desertion' of the former for the latter was always a culpable, individual choice. Marcel refused, in the final analysis, to give us a social or political philosophy.

Yet, for all these limitations, Marcel's importance should not be underestimated. In his attempts to grasp the *situatedness* of human existence and to formulate ways of grasping it that avoid the dichotomies of objectivism and subjectivism, his work was pioneering. In his insistence that the concrete is the proper starting-point for philosophy and his opposition to abstraction and reductionism, he contributes in enduring ways to the discussion of fundamental issues in epistemology and social philosophy, including those of the relationship of embodiment to consciousness, of subjectivity to intersubjectivity and of individual existence to sociality. Through his treatment of these issues, he also set much of the agenda for the postwar generation of existentialists.

2

Sartre: individual constitution of situation

In Marcel's eyes, Sartre's was a philosophy wholly antithetical to his own. The product of a graceless atheism, it was no more than a distorted picture of 'an atrophied and contradictory world where the better part of ourselves is finally unable to recognise itself' (HV 183). The comment adequately captures some of the fundamental divergences between the two thinkers. For Marcel, despite the ills of modern society, God's grace is still the guarantee that the world is not inherently senseless. For Sartre, on the other hand, there is no meaning in the world except what we bring to it – and there is no assurance that each of us brings to it compatible meanings. On the contrary, our relations with each other are, according to Sartre, fundamentally conflictual.

However, Sartre's *Being and Nothingness*, my main focus in this chapter, also shares many of Marcel's preoccupations and assumptions. Moreover, it gives rise to similar difficulties to those we found in Marcel's work. These were to be more adequately addressed by the time Sartre published the *Critique of Dialectical Reason*, in 1960. But in *Being and Nothingness*, published in 1943, Sartre also set out to confront the problem of Cartesian dualism through an account of our 'being-in-situation', yet he too ended up paradoxically re-establishing a kind of dualism and privileging a radical subjectivity. This effectively precluded him from developing a concept of a shared, or intersubjective, or *social* situation. Indeed, it was for his excessive individualism that Sartre's orthodox Marxist critics of the time berated him. More recently, some commentators have claimed to find in *Being and Nothingness* a critique of capitalism and of bourgeois individualism. But although there is certainly a cultural critique of bourgeois society running through its many pages, my own view is that *Being and Nothingness* develops an essentially 'possessive individualist' notion of persons and, implicitly, an atomistic conception of society. For Marcel, because of his concerns with participation and religious community, radical subjectivism was not synonymous with a militant individualism. For Sartre, the atheistic recipient of a Protestant heritage, the one passed easily into the other.

Although it represents the culmination of a philosophical project begun in the early 1930s, most of *Being and Nothingness* was conceived and written between 1939 and early 1943. Over this period Sartre was a conscript in the French army, then a German prisoner of war and finally a resident of German-occupied Paris. It was through these experiences, Sartre later claimed, that he became a committed 'man of the Left', learning to recognize the interdependence of our lives and the need for collective action in the face of oppression. But it is striking that, for all its iconoclasm and hostility to bourgeois culture, *Being and Nothingness* remains a profoundly asocial and apolitical work. The insights Sartre was developing into what Beauvoir would later call *la force des choses* – the power of circumstances – did not leave their theoretical mark on his account of human relations. As he himself later observed,

> In a way, *L'Etre et le néant* itself should have been the beginning of a discovery of this power of circumstances, since I had already been made a soldier, when I had not wanted to be one... Then I was taken prisoner, a fate which I sought to escape. Hence I started to learn what I have called human reality among things: Being-in-the-world.[1]

But in *Being and Nothingness* human freedoms still appear as fundamentally autonomous and indestructible, subjectivity as absolute and individual. Even so, the work offers one of the most profound contemporary meditations on human subjectivity. Any attempt to rethink the notion of the subject and to develop an account of socially situated subjectivity must examine it.

Sartre subtitled *Being and Nothingness*, 'an essay on phenomenological ontology', and it both begins and ends with a discussion of the character of Being in general. However, most of the book is an inquiry into the character of that region of Being which Sartre calls 'being-for-itself': the region of human consciousness.

A central concern of the work is to examine how 'man', as consciousness, is (and is not) related to the world around him. Central to Sartre's examination of this matter is the issue of human freedom. Much of *Being and Nothingness* is an account of what Sartre takes freedom to be and of the ways in which freedom, which Sartre argues is a painful or 'anguished' experience, is evaded in what he calls 'bad faith'.

In describing man's relation to his own freedom, his evasion of it (or 'flight') and the relation of one person's freedom to another's, Sartre passes from discussing Being in general to discussing concrete human being at the level of the unique individual. Indeed, the whole structure of the book involves a development from general (abstract) Being to singular (concrete) human existence. At this latter level of analysis, which Sartre calls 'existential psychoanalysis', the aim is to reveal the fundamental choice by which each particular individual makes him- or herself what he or she is.

However, between the analysis of the individual and of Being in general, there lies an intermediate level – the level of 'phenomenological ontology'. Here Sartre seeks to elucidate the general features that pertain to the existential experience of any human being. Irrespective of who we are, human existence is always experienced as temporality and finitude, as freedom, as embodied, as a relation to others, etc. Although the particular manner in which these basic features are experienced will vary from person to person, they are invariable dimensions of all human existence.

Most of *Being and Nothingness* is concerned with elucidating this intermediate, phenomenological level. It is here that the relation of an individual subject to its situation – what Sartre also calls the relation of 'man' and 'world' – is explored. However, I will first briefly outline the main features of Sartre's ontology. Only then will I examine the relation of the individual subject to his or her situation, what this account leads Sartre to conclude about relations between individuals and, finally, those few sections of *Being and Nothingness* which suggest the embryo of a social philosophy.

Being 'in-itself' and Being 'for-itself'

Like Marcel, Sartre begins his inquiry by discussing the problem of dualism in the Western philosophic tradition. Modern phenomenology, especially the work of Husserl, provides, Sartre thinks, the most fruitful approach to this problem. Husserl, Sartre argues, makes an important advance over earlier analyses of consciousness by arguing that all consciousness is 'consciousness *of* something'. Yet he, like Descartes, still erroneously conceives consciousness as a relationship of *knowing*. If we conceive consciousness as knowing, then an object of knowledge is implied – and we immediately confront a radical separation of knower and known, of subject and object. Once we say that consciousness is knowledge of objects, we must either arbitrarily assign a constituting priority to one over the other, or we enter an 'infinite regress', in which each endlessly constitutes the other (BN lii–iii; liv–lv).

The way out of this dilemma, Sartre argues – and here his route is similar to Marcel's – is to conceive of consciousness as something other than knowledge of objects. Thus, prior to the kind of consciousness which is involved in knowing an object (Husserl's 'consciousness *of* something'), which Sartre calls 'positional consciousness', there is another kind of consciousness which is 'non-positional' and (Sartre uses the same term as Marcel here) 'immediate'. Immediate consciousness is a consciousness not of things but of 'consciousness (of) self' (*conscience (de) soi*). This consciousness is not a *knowing* of the self, since knowledge refers to objects and the self cannot be an object to itself.[2] Rather, what we have is what Sartre calls a 'pre-reflective cogito':

> It is the non-reflective consciousness which renders the reflection possible; there is a pre-reflective cogito which is the condition of the Cartesian cogito. (BN liii; lv)

Whenever we do something (count cigarettes in Sartre's example), a non-reflective consciousness of self is given with our consciousness of the thing we apprehend. This consciousness of self is not supplementary to our consciousness of something, but is inseparable from our having a consciousness of something. This consciousness of self, Sartre insists, is

> *the only mode of existence which is possible for consciousness of something.* Just as an extended object is compelled to exist according to three dimensions, so an intention, a pleasure, a grief can only exist as immediate consciousness of itself ... Pleasure [for example]

cannot be distinguished – even logically – from consciousness of pleasure. Consciousness (of) pleasure is constitutive of pleasure as the very mode of its own existence. (BN liv; lvi)

If consciousness (of) self is 'constitutive' of our consciousness (of) things, but not *vice versa*, then, Sartre argues, this means that consciousness is *absolute*. By this Sartre means that it is 'self-determining' and is in no way limited by the world around it. 'The very existence of consciousness comes from consciousness itself', he tells us (BN lv; lvii). In other words, nothing 'outside' it, nothing from the region of inert 'being-in-itself' can *cause* consciousness to come into being. Consciousness is thus – literally – *no thing*, or 'nothing' (*le néant*). It is, Sartre claims, a region of being radically distinct from that objective region, the region of things, in which causality operates. And since it is 'self-determined', we can also call it 'freedom' in an absolute sense.

Furthermore, if being-for-itself is, as opposed to being-in-itself, absolute freedom, this must imply that it can have no pre-given content or organization. For content and organization are, Sartre claims, elements only of the world of things. Thus consciousness is also 'nothing' in another sense: it is an emptiness. It is, says Sartre, 'like a hole of being [*un trou d'être*] at the heart of Being' (BN 617; also 78–9). But, as freedom, being-for-itself is not a passive emptiness. Although he does not discuss the point in detail, passivity and inertia are what, according to Sartre, characterize being-in-itself. Being-for-itself, as freedom, must be active nothingness. It negates or nihilates being-in-itself: it is the power to put the world of things into question, to alter, or to transcend it: 'The For-itself, in fact, is nothing but the pure nihilation of the In-itself' (BN 617).

However, it is only as individual human consciousness that this nothingness comes into being. Thus the discussion cannot remain with the 'abstract' analysis of Being (or ontology), but must shift to the study of the 'concrete' existence of man in the world (or phenomenology). In particular, since it is *man* who is the for-itself, that is, *man* who is consciousness, we need to understand man's 'forms of conduct' (BN 4) (his concrete ways of thinking, experiencing, acting, his ways of being with his fellow-men) in order to understand being-for-itself and its relation to being-in-itself and to Being in general. Thus general ontological questions become reformulated as questions of phenomenological analysis, and *Being and Nothingness* passes from an examination of ontology *per se* to the discussion, above all, of individual human freedom. Various commentators have pointed out that, although he designates the ontological and phenomenological levels of analysis as distinct, Sartre tends frequently to conflate them.[3] However, since being-for-itself can be apprehended only as individual consciousness, this slippage between levels would seem to be unavoidable. The main difficulty which results is that the formal attribution of freedom to being-for-itself – an attribution initially meaning only that it is not governed by causality of the kind which regulates being-in-itself – in practice spills over into the affirmation of the indestructibility of the freedom of all individual human existents, whatever their social conditions. If all that Sartre claimed was that, in any condition, a human is still a human and not a stick or a stone, his view would be unobjectionable. However, in slipping from the discussion of being-for-itself to the discussion of individual consciousness, Sartre goes on to make statements about the impossibility of the determination of individual freedom by *human* actions which are far more dubious. When he tells us, for example, that it is 'senseless to think of complaining since nothing foreign has decided what we feel, what we live, or what we are' and then goes on to exemplify this point by claiming that 'if I am mobilized in a war, this is my war; it is in my image and I deserve it' (BN 554), he has moved far beyond his initial formulation of the distinction between being-for-itself and being-in-itself.

Consciousness and freedom

'Man is the being through whom nothingness comes to the world' (BN 24). Man, in other words, *is consciousness*, the unconditioned power of negation. Like Marcel, Sartre has broadened the notion of consciousness beyond its more conventional meaning of the knowledge of things. Then, again like Marcel, he has argued that consciousness in this widened (indeed, infinite) sense is the source of all meaning in the world. However, Sartre's formulation implies an even more radical disjuncture of consciousness and materiality than one finds in Marcel's work. In the formulation, 'I am my body', Marcel had attempted to expand the notion of the self, to include its physical existence within its subjective unity. By contrast, Sartre defines man as first and foremost a consciousness, that is, a pure, empty power of negation. The encounter of the for-itself with the world is not given *fundamentally* as the encounter of an *embodied* self-consciousness. For

> the body, whatever may be its function, appears first as the *known*. We cannot therefore refer knowledge back to it or discuss it before we have defined knowing; nor can we derive knowing in its fundamental structure from the body in any way whatsoever. (BN 218)

Sartre makes the transition from ontology to the more concrete level of phenomenological analysis via a discussion of the activity of questioning. The way forward, he suggests, must be to examine the 'patterns of conduct' of the being that is 'man-in-the-world'. There are numerous patterns of conduct, but he suggests that one above all provides 'a guiding thread in our inquiry', that of *questioning* (BN 4 ff). Although the implication is that we could perhaps approach the question of man's relation with the world through an examination of some other conduct, Sartre's choice of questioning as the guiding thread is by no means random. For questioning does indeed involve a distancing of ourselves, a 'disengagement' from being (BN 24). But had Sartre chosen another kind of conduct for his guiding thread, it would certainly have been more difficult (perhaps impossible) for him to sustain his account of the absolute nature of consciousness and thus of human freedom.

Some years later, in the *Critique*, Sartre did choose a different starting place. He asserted that 'praxis' – meaning the intentional transformation of the material world by man to satisfy need – is the fundamental human conduct. From this new starting place, he developed a significantly different account of both consciousness and freedom than that elaborated in *Being and Nothingness*. But in *Being and Nothingness, questioning*, an interrogation of Being which aims at its comprehension rather than its transformation, is taken as the defining or archetypal human conduct. Questioning does not involve action of the kind that Sartre was later to call praxis. For although consciousness is always 'consciousness (of) something' and involves the nihilation of the in-itself, such nihilation need not involve the transformation of the material world, as praxis does.

The conduct of questioning (Sartre exemplifies it with his own activity of questioning in *Being and Nothingness*) involves 'on principle' the possibility of a negative answer to the question posed. Questioning thus brings into being the possibility of non-being, both as the possibility of the non-being of our knowing and as the possibility of the non-being of Being: 'The permanent possibility of non-being, outside us and within, conditions our questions about being' (BN 5). But then the further question we are left with is, 'where does nothingness come from?' (BN 11; also 22). Sartre's answer to this question is that nothingness must come from man. It is man's ability to withdraw, to 'nihilate' Being – epitomized in the question – which brings nothingness to Being: 'Man presents himself at least in this instance as the being who causes Nothingness to emerge in the world' (BN 24). Another way of describing the relation of the for-itself to the in-itself would be to say that it is through 'human freedom' that 'nothingness comes into the world' (BN 25).

The in-itself simply *is*. As a 'region of being', massive and inert, it is independent of the region of the for-itself which it does not need. However, in so far as the for-itself exists as a relation of individual human consciousness to the world, the in-itself can be 'modified' by the relations that human consciousnesses constitute with *particular* elements of it. Freedom, Sartre suggests in an initial formulation, involves man's relation to a 'particular existent'. He can put it 'out of circulation' by the relation he chooses to have with it. If he chooses to put it 'out of circulation', then 'it cannot act on him'. And, Sartre adds, 'this possibility which human reality has to secrete a nothingness which isolates it, Descartes, following the Stoics, has given a name to – it is freedom' (BN 24–5). We can say of a man both that he is consciousness (that he is a nihilating nothingness, or 'secretes' nothingness) and also that he is freedom. And just as consciousness is *self*-determined, so also is the freedom that is given with it: 'there is no difference between the being of man and his *being-free*' (BN 25). To be a man is to be free; that is, to be undetermined and uncaused, thus to make one's own existence and choose one's own 'project' in the world. Thus, in spite of his initial critique of Cartesian epistemology, Sartre still recapitulates Descartes in so far as he identifies freedom with consciousness and sharply delimits it from Descartes' *res extensa*, now being-in-itself. Sartre's own later self-evaluation is surely appropriate. 'My early work', he afterwards stated, 'was a rationalist philosophy of consciousness . . . *L'Etre et le néant* is a monument of rationality.'[4]

Of course, freedom always acts within certain givens which it has not itself created. As Sartre puts it, the for-itself cannot choose its 'position' although it can choose the 'meaning' of its 'situation'. I might have been born a worker or a bourgeois, a slave or a master; one of these contingencies will be my given position, yet it will not, for Sartre, *limit* my freedom; it will simply provide the situation in which I am free and must create the meaning of my life (BN 83–4). Sartre's initial account of the freedom of the for-itself leads to the discussion of what he calls 'bad faith' (*la mauvaise foi*). Consciousness (of) my freedom is not at all a happy experience; on the contrary, we experience it as 'anguish'. For at the moment of freedom, in which a choice is made, I am nothing, suspended between my past and my future. I have put my own past 'out of play', or nihilated it, since it in no way shapes my choice; but I am not yet the future that will be my act; I confront my nothingness and also my freedom wholly to nihilate *myself*.[5] Bad faith is the attempt to avoid the anguish of confronting my freedom, my nothingness. It often takes the form of 'flight', in which I attempt to alienate my freedom by treating myself as thing-like (BN 50 ff).[6]

Freedom is not only experienced as anguish, it also apprehends itself as 'lack'. Lack arises as the impossibility for the for-itself, as consciousness (of) self, ever fully to grasp or coincide with *itself* as an object of consciousness.[7] Equally, it arises in the inability of the for-itself ever fully to coincide with the being that it nihilates. Lack is the impossibility of completion, or 'totality'; it is 'the impossible synthesis of the for-itself and the in-itself. The being of human reality is thus a striving towards that which can never be realized; it is 'suffering' or, in Hegel's phrase, 'unhappy consciousness' (BN 90).

However, lack does not lead to a passive suffering. Instead, it is the source of the continual projection of freedom on to the world which Sartre calls 'transcendence', a projection in which also 'values' are created. Transcendence is a movement of continuous 'surpassing', for '(h)uman reality is its own surpassing toward what it lacks' (BN 89). And, since human reality exists for individual consciousness, it is always the movement of concrete individual freedom situated in the world. 'The self is individual', says Sartre, 'it is the individual completion of the self which haunts the for-itself' (BN 91). Man is, as Sartre puts it, a for-itself which seeks in vain to be also its own being, or in-itself. Man is 'a useless passion' (BN 615). He is the impossible desire to be 'God', or the 'self-cause' (BN 620–3). Although Sartre alludes in passing to the possibility of a 'self-recovery' that overcomes bad faith (BN 70, note 9), and to a 'radical conversion' which would involve abandoning the attempt to be God (BN 412, note 14), what remains fundamental to human existence, as Sartre portrays it in *Being and Nothingness*, is the useless pursuit of self-cause.[8] Not satisfied merely to be the free subjectivity which he is, man desires also to constitute his own being-in-itself and that of the world.

Since, as transcendence, freedom continually goes beyond *what is* in its vain striving for totality, it has to affirm ideals (i.e., non-existents) and values. 'Value', Sartre tells us, is 'what is lacked'. It is 'the beyond of all surpassings' (BN 93) and it is wholly inseparable from the freedom of the for-itself, for in its nihilating transcendence of the in-itself the for-itself can *never* avoid affirming values: '*nothing* makes value exist – unless it is that freedom which by the same stroke makes me myself exist' (BN 94). Like consciousness and freedom, value is *lived* (pre-reflective) before it is reflected upon. It is, as Sartre puts it, 'consubstantial' with the for-itself (BN 94). Thus, we can no more avoid affirming values of which we alone are the absolute source than we can avoid our absolute freedom. Since reflective consciousness refers us to lived consciousness (to the 'pre-reflective' *cogito*), Sartre goes on to argue that reflective consciousness also must always imply a disclosure of values, so that 'reflective consciousness can properly be called a moral consciousness' (BN 95).

A question that comes to mind at this point is what Sartre's notions of value and moral consciousness might contribute to ethics in the more traditional sense of the search for general precepts of good or right conduct. If all conduct affirms values, how are we to choose between conducts? Or do all conducts have an equal value? How also, somewhat more broadly, can we make political judgements? Sartre himself clearly had such questions in mind when, at the very end of *Being and Nothingness*, he raised as a question for further study the ethical implications of his work. 'Ontology', he remarked, 'cannot itself formulate ethical precepts' (BN 625), but it still leads to questions about human freedom that, 'can find their reply only on the ethical plane' (BN 628). Sartre concluded with a promise to 'address a future work' to these questions, but it never appeared. He did, however, write a quantity of preliminary material for it, some of which has been posthumously published as *Cahiers pour une morale*.[9] An examination of this material, written in 1947 and 1948, suggests that Sartre encountered grave difficulties in his attempt to elaborate an ethics from the premises of *Being and Nothingness*. Indeed, many of the more fruitful passages in the *Cahiers* anticipate the *Critique*, rather than elaborating on the arguments of 1943.

What is striking about Sartre's account of human existence in relation to the above remarks concerning the 'ethical plane' is the lack of any clear conception of a social or collective dimension to human reality. Although Sartre does discuss what he calls 'being-for-others' in the third part of *Being and Nothingness*, like Marcel, he examines primarily the relations possible between *two* individuals (a self and an other). As the foundation for a social philosophy *Being and Nothingness* would require us to conceive social groupings as aggregates of autonomous individuals, held together in some contingent manner – by fear perhaps, or interest – but with no ontological connection between them: social being is not given with human being; it remains secondary, contingent.[10] Thus language, culture, institutions, history, etc., are not relevant to individual freedom, except in so far as they happen to furnish its situation. But whatever the situation, individual freedom exists. It is hard to know what kind of ethical judgements we could ever make about this total freedom.

The result of Sartre's account of freedom is also to make individual actions intrinsically inexplicable to others. Since freedom is absolute and self-founded, it follows for Sartre that its choices cannot be explained; only phenomena in the realm of the in-itself, where causality operates, are open to explanation. At the level of the concrete individual, all those aspects of life which social scientists would look at to explain conduct – such as culture, class, past personal history, etc. – are irrelevant to freedom. For in the moment of free choice (that moment which is in fact a 'nothingness'), one's past is put out of play. One cannot talk even of the 'motive' for choice, for freedom is 'that *nothing* which insinuates itself between motives and act', and 'the structure of motives as ineffective is the condition of my freedom' (BN 34). We do have motives, but freedom, far from being bound by them, is their negation. Indeed, consciousness, as pure negation, Sartre argues, has no content. In the mode of not-being, consciousness is '*empty* of all content' (BN 34). It is empty of all motive, disposition, intention, all structures of apperception, all concepts.

Being and Nothingness is generally a closely argued book. If one is convinced by the central proposition that human being is nihilating consciousness, that it is free subjectivity which confronts inert being-in-itself, then most of Sartre's conclusions, paradoxical though they may seem, do follow. But need we accept this central proposition? As already suggested, Sartre arrives at his notion of negation by choosing questioning as his guiding thread. Even if we agree to go along with this choice of thread, it is not clear that it leads us to the claim that consciousness is pure nothingness as easily as Sartre assumes.

Firstly, the very activity of (even philosophical) questioning presupposes social existence and above all, as Merleau-Ponty was to point out, language. Language, for Sartre, does not 'pre-exist' the use which is made of it (BN 515ff).[11] It is not 'a Nature', an in-itself, which regulates us. While Sartre is undoubtedly correct not to grant full autonomy to a 'technique' such as language,[12] the fact remains that it must to some extent delimit – or 'structure' – what we can think. Plato, Descartes and Sartre *could not* question Being in the identical manner. Language would seem to be one of the areas of human existence which can least well be accounted for within Sartre's in-itself/for-itself dichotomy; and yet it is crucial to the activity of questioning, which Sartre places at the centre of his proof that consciousness is nothingness.

Of course, from the analysis of questioning, Sartre had proceeded not to the problem of language but to the discovery of the pre-reflective *cogito*. It is at the pre-reflective level, and not in questioning itself, that consciousness determines itself as pure nothingness. But at this level also we must ask whether the proposition of the radical separation of the for-itself from the world which it nihilates really can be sustained.

'Freedom-in-situation'

Having argued that the freedom of the for-itself is absolute and self-founded, Sartre is faced with a difficulty: the for-itself is not God, nor a Hegelian Absolute Spirit; it is *human*. As such it is individuated. It pertains to specific *persons*, embodied consciousnesses, each of whom is born in a particular time and place – that is, each of whom is born into and acts within a *situation* not wholly of his or her own making. The problem Sartre faces is the following: given its situated nature, how can one show that the absolute freedom of the for-itself exists irrespective of the constraints that its situation place on it?

Sartre makes it very clear that the absolute and unconditional nature of freedom which he defends is ontological. Thus he is not primarily concerned with the kinds of external constraints on action which arise from social life. Although it lurks in the background, the question of political and social freedom is not directly addressed in *Being and Nothingness*. Rather:

'To be free' does not mean, 'to obtain what one has wished', but rather, 'by oneself to determine oneself to wish' (in the broad sense of choosing). In other words success is not at all important to freedom. (BN 483)

The capacity to obtain the ends chosen is *not*, for Sartre, what defines freedom. However, that having been said, he promptly goes on to point out that although freedom concerns only 'autonomy of choice', choice is *de facto* impossible without action in the world. For freedom involves projecting ourselves toward ends from which we are separated by 'real existents'.

Since freedom involves a project which nihilates or transcends the in-itself, Sartre now points out that, 'choice being identical with acting, supposes a *commencement of realization* in order that the choice may be distinguished from the dream or the wish'. The freedom of the prisoner does not lie in his freedom 'to long for release' – that is, to dream – but in the fact that, '*whatever his condition may be*, he can project his escape and learn the value of his project by undertaking some action' (BN 484, my emphasis). Dreams are not actions; actions refer to a world which consciousness nihilates but which it does not necessarily choose. What Sartre now has to demonstrate is that, even in what appear to be the most constraining and adverse circumstances, a *project* is always possible. Freedom need not involve success in obtaining what we desire, but it does involve being able to have desires that are more than just dreams. The prisoner, the slave, the oppressed factory worker, even the torture victim, all must still be free, that is, able to sustain an active project in relation to their condition, if Sartre is right.

In order to sustain this position, Sartre sets out to explore the relations of the for-itself to that which it must nihilate at two levels. Firstly, at the level of ontology, it is necessary for him to work out the relations between being for-itself, as particular or individuated subjectivity, and being in-itself. Secondly, at the more concrete level of phenomenological analysis, he needs to explore the ways in which individual subjects constitute their own 'worlds' from being in-itself; the in-itself as a world of natural obstacles, of man-made instrumentalities and, yet more complex, as encountered in our relations to other people and to our own bodies. It is in discussing the relations of the for-itself to these various dimensions of the in-itself that Sartre develops most fully his argument for the simultaneously situated and yet absolutely free nature of the for-itself.

Sartre's argument at the level of ontology is complex, but the thrust of it can be summarized as follows. The for-itself is pure nothingness. But since the for-itself must be always a nihilating 'consciousness (of) something' it must have some kind of 'internal relation' to the in-itself:

> the for-itself without the in-itself is a kind of abstraction; it could not exist any more than a color could exist without form or a sound without pitch and a timbre. (BN 621)

Thus, far from being an impediment, the encounter with the in-itself has somehow to be co-given with the nihilating freedom of the for-itself. In addition, however, since the for-itself is not a universal, cosmic consciousness but *human* consciousness, it must also have a being, a manifest existence, in the world. The ontological paradox to be explained then, is how there can be a *being* of that which is *nothingness*.

Sartre argues that since it is nothingness, consciousness cannot be its own 'foundation' (*fondement*). Thus, if 'the for-itself *is*' (BN 79) – if it manifestly exists in the world – its being must come to it from elsewhere. Since it does not 'found' itself, its being must be accidental, or contingent, not 'necessary'. Sartre gives a special name to the contingency that causes the for-itself to have particular forms of being-in-itself, which it does not itself found. He calls it the *facticity* of the for-itself. Facticity involves the for-itself being 'thrown into the world' in a situation not initially of its own choosing, yet which it cannot deny is its own, and to which it is bound in a movement of internal negation. As Sartre puts it: 'Without facticity consciousness would choose its attachments to the world in the same way as the souls in Plato's *Republic* choose their condition' (BN 83).

Shifting abruptly from the level of ontology to that of individual human existence, Sartre goes on to point out that we cannot determine for ourselves whether 'to be born a worker', for example, or 'to be born a bourgeois'. What social class I am born into is an aspect of my facticity. Yet, at the same time, my relation to that factual condition must be freely constituted by me: 'facticity can not constitute me as *being* a bourgeois or *being* a worker'. I myself must choose my way of being within the class into which I have contingently been born. But I cannot avoid choosing: the for-itself is free to choose, but it is not free *not* to choose; it must choose to nihilate its contingently given situation in one way or another.

If the freedom of the for-itself is inseparable from its facticity, the question then becomes whether there are limits or constraints placed on my ontological freedom by my factual existence – by, for example, my class origin, or my physical constitution, my nationality, or race. With a tenacious rationalism that borders on *reductio ad absurdum* Sartre tries to show that even though such contingencies are given prior to choice, they do not ever limit the absolute freedom of the for-itself.[13] It is through exploring the concept of 'situation' that Sartre tries to develop his case.

Marcel treated the analysis of our situation as inseparable from the question of embodiment. This is one of the strengths of his philosophy: it is because 'I am my body' that I have a manifest existence and that I can say also that I am my situation. One might reasonably have expected Sartre to have made a similar argument. The facticity of the for-itself clearly must imply its embodiment, for what defines the for-itself as individual consciousness – and precludes it being Universal Mind – is its inherence in corporally distinct human beings. However, while he acknowledges this, Sartre tries instead to argue that the relation of consciousness to its situation is directly given. The body is only experienced secondarily, mediated through my relations with other people. For Sartre the for-itself merely happens, among other elements of its facticity, to exist as a particular body. Thus when Sartre starts to discuss how 'I' constitute 'my situation', what he discusses is above all the constitution of the meaning of the contingent in-itself by the free project of the for-itself.

'The concrete consciousness', Sartre tells us, 'arises in situation, and it is a unique, individualised consciousness (of) this situation and (of) itself in situation' (BN 91). It is through my project that I bring into being my situation. But I do it by acting on an in-itself which is an autonomous region of being. There is a 'brute given' of the in-itself, a 'coefficient of adversity in things', which we cannot change (BN 482). For example, one particular crag will be easier to scale than another, irrespective of my project. This autonomy of the in-itself is, not however, to be conceived as a limit on my freedom. Rather, it is its precondition. For the realization of my freedom must involve the transcendence of things, the nihilation of the in-itself. Pursuing the example of the attempt to climb a crag, Sartre describes the constitution of a situation through the relation of freedom to the in-itself in the following manner:

> Here I am at the foot of this crag which appears to me as 'not scalable'. This means the rock appears to me in the light of a projected scaling . . . What my freedom cannot determine is whether the rock 'to be scaled' will or will not lend itself to scaling. This is part of the brute being of the rock. Nevertheless the rock can show its resistance to the scaling *only if the rock is integrated by freedom in a 'situation'* of which the general theme is scaling. For the simple traveler who passes over this road and whose free project is a pure aesthetic ordering of the landscape, the crag is not revealed either as scalable or as not scalable; it is manifested only as beautiful or ugly. (BN 488, my emphasis)

In this example Sartre takes the simplest possible case: a clearly defined project of one individual with regard to an in-itself which is an inert natural object. In other instances the analysis becomes more complex: for example, if one is dealing with a project involving several people, or if the given to be transcended is a humanly created set of constraints or possibilities (anti-Semitism in one of Sartre's examples; a subway station in another, BN 523 ff; BN 424). However, it becomes clear in an extended discussion of what he calls the different 'structures' of situation[14] that Sartre takes the above example to express the fundamental relation of freedom to the external constraints it encounters in any situation.

It is important to note the active role of freedom in constituting the situation. The 'resistance' of the crag is possible only because freedom has already 'integrated' it into its situation by my choosing to climb it. Thus, even if the crag does, in the event, turn out to be 'not scalable' it will not, Sartre claims, constitute a limit to my freedom. For it is only by virtue of my freedom that it is not scalable. As the comparison between the 'simple traveller' and the would-be climber makes clear, it is my project which gives specific meaning, including quality, to the crag. It is my project which causes there to be what Sartre elsewhere calls 'an organization of things in *situation*'(BN 509).[15]

Although the concept of situation plays a central role in Sartre's argument, as a means of grasping the relation of the concrete for-itself to the contingently given in-itself, Sartre unfortunately offers several distinct and sometimes contradictory meanings to the term. The most common meaning of the term – and the one most consistent with Sartre's general objectives in *Being and Nothingness* – is the one just described. I will call this notion of situation, in which my free project constitutes my situation as its field of action, the notion of situation as *constituted field*. One can find, however, at least two other notions of situation in the book; one I will call the *common product notion*; the other the *condition notion*.

In situation as *common product*, consciousness continues to bring its situation into being, but the situation is conceived as having a greater degree of autonomy. The situation, as Sartre describes it, is a *third* kind of reality, neither for-itself nor in-itself but a common product in which 'it is impossible for the for-itself to distinguish the contribution of freedom from that of the brute existent'. (BN 488). The situation is 'neither objective nor subjective' and thus can be considered 'neither as the free result of a freedom nor as the ensemble of the constraints to which I am subject' (BN 551).

In so far as the situation as common product has a reality of its own and is a phenomenon distinct from either the for-itself or the in-itself, freedom runs the risk of losing itself in the situation. For example, discussing 'my past' as a structure of my situation, Sartre tells us that although we constitute our past in the light of our present project, once we have chosen it, our past 'imposes itself upon us and devours us' (BN 503). Once chosen, our past 'compels' us to act in certain ways and also to appear in certain ways for other people. Similarly, our situation always involves, as one of its structures, our 'being-for-others' and thus an 'outside' (BN 525 ff), an 'exteriority' which involves a loss of self, or 'alienation'. My 'being-in-situation' has certain characteristics which only the Other sees and thus imposes on me from without. There is, says Sartre, 'a weakness in the basic stuff [*pâte*] of freedom which causes everything it undertakes always to have one face which it will not have chosen, which escapes it and which for the Other will be pure existence' (BN 526).

The notion of situation as common product would seem to imply that certain limits do, after all, arise for my freedom through its situatedness. My past, the way others see me, etc., appear to condition my freedom. But with another twist of the argument, Sartre goes on to insist that these limits he has described do not after all impinge on my freedom! For although limits are placed on the common product – that is, on my situation – there still remains an

67

inviolate and absolute upsurge of freedom which has chosen this situation:

> my freedom by freely choosing itself chooses its limits; or, if you prefer, the free choice of my ends (i.e. what I am for myself) includes the assumption of the limits of this choice, whatever they may be. (BN 530)

Even though my situation may be alienated by an Other, I have chosen and constituted that situation, and thus I have *chosen* freely to assume my alienation. I cannot escape the 'exteriority of the situation', what Sartre calls my 'being-outside-for-others'. But if I have chosen freely to assume it, then I can transcend the objectifying Other. The Jew in the face of the anti-Semite, for example, still freely chooses his way of assuming the being-outside-for-others which is imposed upon him: 'whether in fury, hate, pride ... it is necessary for me to choose to be what I am' (BN 529).

Although Sartre insists that freedom is always 'in situation' and that the situation is 'neither objective nor subjective', nevertheless a core of radical subjectivity always remains and it is, finally, consciousness which constitutes even the situation as a common product. This becomes particularly clear in Sartre's discussion of the (Hegelian) example of relations between a master and his slave. '[T]he slave in chains is as free as his master'(BN 550), Sartre insists, *not* because freedom is a stoical resignation, a contemplation, or an inward movement, but because the slave is always a freedom-in-situation, choosing the meaning of his situation through his own choice of project. There is always a choice open to the slave. Furthermore, we have no means of making the judgement that the slave's situation is more constricting than that of the master; situations are wholly individual and thus incommensurable, as the following passage makes clear:

> To be exact, just because the life of the slave who revolts and dies in the course of this revolt is a free life, just because the situation illuminated by a free project is full and concrete ... the situation of the slave is *not comparable* with that of the master. Each of them in fact takes on its meaning only for the for-itself in situation and in terms of the free choice of its ends ... There is no absolute view-point where one could place oneself so as to compare different situations, each person realizes only one situation – *his own*. (BN 550)

Such solipsistic relativism must preclude the formulation of any generalizable principles of ethics or political conduct. Indeed, one cannot help thinking that Sartre was right when he later commented, '*L'Etre et le néant* traced an interior experience without any co-ordination with the exterior experience of a petty-bourgeois intellectual'.[16]

Ultimately, then, the notion of situation as a *common product* turns out to be underpinned by the notion of situation as *constituted field*. Furthermore, freedom does not only constitute the common product, it manages somehow to be simultaneously both absorbed into the common product and yet to remain the source of its constitution. In so far as freedom remains a pure for-itself, wholly unaffected by the intermingling of subjectivity and objectivity in the situation, Sartre's account of freedom remains fundamentally dualistic, even when he talks of a situation as a common product.

Further to compound the confusion, Sartre also uses in *Being and Nothingness* a third notion of situation – situation as *condition* – which is the direct opposite of the notion of situation as constituted field. This third notion is used only once, briefly, in the book. It appears as a rather puzzling aberration, since it runs wholly counter to the general thrust of Sartre's account of freedom. However, it is of interest since it occurs in a discussion of historical situation and is symptomatic of Sartre's inability to address the question of freedom within the context of social, rather than individual, existence.

Freedom involves putting the world 'out of circulation' in order to project other possibilities. In elaborating this theme, Sartre considers an example in which this simply *cannot* take place. A man 'immersed in the historical situation', he tells us, 'does not even succeed in conceiving of the failures and lacks in a particular political or economic organization' (BN 434). Considering the case of the workers of Lyon in 1830, Sartre tells us that they failed to build on their victory because they could not effect the nihilation which would have enabled them to project an alternative to their suffering. Their condition appeared to them 'natural', and thus not alterable:

> Their misfortunes do not appear to them habitual but rather *natural*: they *are*, that is all, and they constitute the workers' condition. They are not detached, they are not seen in a clear light, and consequently they are integrated by the worker with his being ... To suffer and *to be* are one and the same for him. (BN 435)

The point Sartre proceeds to make after this description is that the act of freedom by which the workers may perhaps finally transcend their oppression cannot be caused or motivated by their suffering; it must be a self-movement of the for-itself. However, the description of the workers' initial condition which Sartre gives us is one which simply should not be possible according to his general argument. For if 'to suffer and to *be* are one', this would mean that facticity has encroached on man to the point where it has, at least for the present time, in fact destroyed his freedom. Sartre is not here describing an example of bad faith; man simply *is* his condition; he *is* the passive product of external forces. Yet, in passage after passage elsewhere, Sartre has set out to argue that even in the most limiting conditions – those of slaves, torture victims, victims of anti-Semitism – human freedom remains indestructible. The example suggests that Sartre had not adequately worked out the relation of *social* situation to individual freedom in *Being and Nothingness*. Although his reading of history had suggested to him that social conditioning could form consciousness – and thus had implicitly raised the possibility that the for-itself is not impermeable – he could not yet integrate this insight into his philosophical framework.

My situation and the Other

The above discussion of condition notwithstanding, we have seen that Sartre's general argument is that freedom must always be situated and that it constitutes its own situation as its field of action, or transcendence. As he puts it: the 'paradox' of freedom is that 'there is freedom only in a *situation*, and there is a situation only through freedom' (BN 489). Sartre's archetypal example of this double-sided relation is that of the climber and the crag. But, as he himself acknowledges, human action does not generally take place only in relation to inert nature; it is invariably also action in a *human* world.[17] It is to Sartre's discussion of the fact that other people are always a structure, either directly or indirectly, of my situation that we must now turn. It is in this discussion that the inadequacies of his dualistic theory become most clearly apparent.

Situations are, for Sartre, fundamentally individual, each a synthetic field around the particular consciousness which constitutes it. Yet we also necessarily enter each other's situations. The central question Sartre addresses is the following: what is the relation that I, as a freedom in a situation which I have constituted, must have to another person, who is also a freedom in a situation which he or she has constituted? Given the self-constituted and self-centred nature of my situation, the arrival of the 'Other' within my field of action can only be an intrusion and a threat. For the Other is not a simple in-itself which I constitute or organize within my situation. He or she is another subject, a consciousness who is the focal point of a counter-organization. 'Thus', Sartre tells us, 'the appearance among the objects of *my* universe of an element of disintegration in that universe is what I mean by the appearance of *one* man in my universe'(BN 255).

Through his counter-transcendence, the Other threatens to incorporate my situation – and hence my freedom in so far as it is situated – into his situation. He threatens to reduce me to an object in his world. My only defence will be to attempt to perform the same operation upon his. Thus the fundamental relation between two freedoms must, according to Sartre's schema, be one of conflict: each attempts to transcend the freedom of the Other, to reduce the Other to thinghood, to an object within his own situation.[18] However, Sartre points out, the struggle must be one with no final outcome. For the indestructibility of freedom, (of what I have called ontological freedom, that is), implies that, short of death, no man can ever be reduced to pure objectivity, even though his situation can be destroyed.

'Being-for-others' cannot, however, be an ontological structure of the for-itself (BN 282). For it involves only the facticity – that is, the contingent in-itself – of the for-itself. My being-for-others arises on the ground of the Other's attempt to transcend my freedom. This he or she does by attempting to nihilate the visible exterior of my freedom: my being-in-situation. It is therefore through what Sartre calls the 'look'[19] that I encounter the nihilating freedom of the Other. It is when he or she *looks* at me that the Other steals my being-in-situation from me and incorporates it, object-like, within his or her own situation. What is implied also is that it is as visible (or otherwise sentient) existents that we encounter each other and struggle.

In a well-known example, Sartre describes the experience of being caught peeking through a keyhole (BN 259 ff). The Other sees me (or might see me) doing something I know I should not do. I experience 'shame' – that is, an awareness of myself from 'outside', as an object. 'By the mere appearance of the Other, I am put in the position of passing judgement on my self as on an object, for it is as an object that I appear to the Other' (BN 222; see also 261).

Although the example is extreme, Sartre's point is a general one. My encounter with the Other always involves my having a relation to myself as seen from outside, by another freedom. Shame and also fear (since I experience the Other as a threat to my freedom) and pride (a complex inversion of shame), are all fundamental reactions to my encounter with the Other. But, it must be stressed, they are *my* ways of recognizing my relation to the Other 'as a subject beyond reach'(BN 291). They are also the reactions on the basis of which I can try to reverse the relation and constitute the Other as an object for me: 'they include within them a comprehension of my selfness [*mon ipséité*] which can and must serve as my motivation for constituting the Other as an object' (BN 291). Thus, it follows that my freedom (my ontological freedom) cannot be wholly destroyed by the Other. The Other objectifies what we might call the manifestations of my freedom, but I remain free to choose my response to his or her transcendence, and I always retain the possibility of turning the tables. Conversely, if I objectify the Other's being-in-situation, I will fail to touch his or her ontological freedom, and the Other will remain always a potential threat, an 'explosive instrument' (BN 297), for me.

For Sartre there are, then, two fundamental human relations: the Other looks at me and I look at the Other. They are, above all, relations of conflict. 'Conflict', Sartre affirms, 'is the original meaning of being-for-others' (BN 364). It has been argued that Sartre is referring here only to relations in bad faith: that it is only in so far as I want to be God, the self-cause of my own being, that the Other is a threat to me.[20] Sartre himself perhaps hints as much in a short, enigmatic footnote,[21] but I think it is evident that if non-conflictual relations were to be developed this could only be through some kind of transcendence of original conflict. For as we have seen, conflict necessarily inheres in all human relations for Sartre because of the radically individual nature of consciousness. Since each consciousness constitutes its own situation, the Other can appear within it only as a locus of *counter*-constitution, as an objectifying power and threat. In the next chapter we will see Beauvoir arguing for the possibility of human relationships in which original conflict can be transcended. But her argument requires her tacitly to modify Sartre's ontology.

In explicating the idea that conflict is 'the original meaning of being-for-others', Sartre chooses to focus on the area of sexual conduct, which he describes as the 'skeleton' for other, more complex, kinds of conduct (BN 407). Lovers, in Sartre's bleak account, are engaged in the impossible attempt to possess each other *as freedoms*. For, in so far as I possess the Other, it is only as an object – as his or her facticity – and the Other's freedom escapes me. Sexual desire is not simply the desire to possess the Other's body but his or her transcendence (BN 392 ff). Yet the more I attempt to possess or control the Other as body, to make the Other by my look or touch a facticity, (instrument, object, thing, 'flesh'), the more the Other's transcendence evades me – and indeed threatens me.

In the most extreme case, sadism, the sadist tries to force the victim freely to identify himself 'with the tortured flesh', that is, to consent to being object. Yet in so far as the victim does have the freedom to consent – 'no matter what pressure is exerted on the victim, the abjuration remains *free*' (BN 403) – he has also the freedom to transcend the freedom of his torturer: 'The sadist discovers his error when his victim *looks at* him' (BN 406), and by doing so fixes him in the being-outside of sadism. The sadist, looked at by his victim,

> discovers that it was *that freedom* which he wished to enslave, and at the same time he realizes the futility of his efforts. Here once more we are referred from the being-who-looks to the being-looked-at; we do not get out of the circle. (BN 406)

Sartre's insistence that the 'circle' of looking and being-looked-at constitutes the central dynamic of human relations is, of course, wholly consistent with his ontology. Since man is 'the being through whom nothingness comes to the world'(BN 24), relations between men can only be those of mutual nihilation. However, this view of human relations raises numerous difficulties for Sartre's attempts to describe social and historical aspects of human existence – not to mention his desire to develop a politics of solidarity. Before turning to a consideration of some of these difficulties, it is however necessary to consider in more detail Sartre's analysis of the human body. For in dealing with the question of the body, Sartre finds himself caught in irresolvable problems which stem from any dualistic ontology, and which are also germane to his difficulty in accounting for social and historical life.

If Being must be either for-itself or in-itself, what are we to say about the human body? In Sartre's treatment, the body is clearly the facticity of a freedom which, short of death, remains indestructible. As facticities, Sartre argues, our bodies must exist for us through others. My body is given to me as an object by the look of the Other: 'the discovery of my body as an object is indeed a revelation of its being. But the being which is thus revealed to me is its being-for-others' (BN 305).

However, if the body were only this, I would not be able to account for internal experiences I have of it, such as pain. Nor would we be able to grasp, for example, the relation of the would-be climber, at the foot of the crag, to his body. For the would-be climber, his body is not a body for-others, but an integral part of his project of climbing. Thus, Sartre concludes, there must be two distinct aspects to the body. As well as my body 'for-others', there must also be what Sartre calls my body 'for-me', or the body 'as being-for-itself' (BN 305).

The body as for-itself is the body *as* consciousness. As we have seen, because the for-itself must exist in the world, it must be body: 'It necessarily follows from the nature of the for-itself that it be body' (BN 309). But although the body is indeed facticity, it is lived by the for-itself non-reflectively, as a movement of internal self-nihilation. The body for-me is 'the point of view on which there cannot be a point of view' (BN 329–30). We must simply say that 'consciousness *exists its body*'. From this it follows, for example, that pain is not a relation in which something (my body) hurts me (consciousness). Rather, pain is simply 'pain-consciousness' (BN 331 ff). Similarly, it is only as project that I have sense perceptions: 'it is the upsurge of the for-itself in the world which in one stroke brings into existence the world as the totality of things and the senses as the objective mode in which the qualities of things are presented' (BN 319). In other words, it is through my project that I constitute perceptions and feelings, just as I constitute my situation.

There are profound difficulties with Sartre's account of the body. First, with regard to the body for-itself, what Sartre has done is effectively to *reduce* the body to non-reflective consciousness. As soon as I have any reflective relation to my body, it must cease to be for-me. Thus, for example, I could not put a bandage on my cut hand without abandoning my body for-me and taking an external viewpoint on my injury. I would have to exist for myself as a body known to the Other before I could treat it. For it is impossible within Sartre's account that I could simultaneously grasp myself as both my body 'for-me' and my body 'for-others'. Either I *am* this cut hand; or my cut hand is an object for others, and exists for me as an object for others. These two 'aspects' of the body, Sartre insists, are on '*different and incommunicable levels of being*' (BN 305, my emphasis). But if this is so, then

Sartre is unable to give us a coherent account of the embodied self. We would appear to be condemned to an endless oscillation between pure subjectivity and pure objectivity, with no way in which the 'self' can link them.[22] The division of being into the two 'regions' of being-for-itself and being-in-itself results in the affirmation that – somehow, in some inexplicable manner – two incommunicable aspects of being pertain to one and the same bodily existent. Thus Sartre's account of the body is far weaker than Marcel's or, indeed, Beauvoir's or Merleau-Ponty's. It sunders the unity-in-tension of subjectivity and objectivity which they, in varying degrees, attempt to capture in the concept of the 'body-subject'.

The problem of social relations

Returning now from the body to the issue of relations between selves, we can see more fully why they must be fundamentally relations of conflict for Sartre. Not only does the Other, in constituting his or her own situation, attempt to destroy my situation; he or she must also transform my body for-me into an object. Furthermore, the Other also causes me to apprehend *myself* as an object, as a being-for-others. The Other's look does not only constitute a direct assault on my freedom, it also causes me to alienate myself, to apprehend my own body as an object, and to objectify my own situation. Self-alienation comes to me through the look of the Other.

Sartre's analysis centres mainly on the relations of two individuals, the dyad of a Self and an Other. As recently suggested, what Sartre develops in *Being and Nothingness* can best be described as an account of 'interpersonal relations', rather than of 'social relations'.[23] Yet social existence – meaning relations between multiplicities of human beings and also the emergence from these relations of common contours to the world in which individuals constitute their own situations – was also of profound importance to Sartre. Practically, through his growing political engagement as a man of the Left, and as a theoretical problem, Sartre was obliged during and after the writing of *Being and Nothingness* to grapple with the question of social relations. Indeed, in the immediate postwar period, during which Sartre was becoming a public figure, issues of social – and political-relations became increasingly the focus of his work.[24] Even in *Being and Nothingness*, the question of *social* relations is obliquely dwelt upon. It is not subjected to the same systematic analysis that Sartre gives, for example, to temporality or the body, but it is the focus of a multiplicity of sub-discussions and observations.

Surveying these, one can identify two somewhat different accounts of social relations. One, most consistent with the general argument of *Being and Nothingness*, accounts for relations of more than two people as being simply extensions of the relations of the Self-Other dyad. The other, more muted, but anticipating in embryo the *Critique*, involves a notion of the emergence of social relations through the mediation of what Sartre calls 'instruments' and 'techniques'. I will consider each of these accounts in turn.

For Sartre, as we have seen, situations are intrinsically individual. It would seem then that within his analysis there could be no place for a *social* situation. For a social situation would have to involve a common field of action, constituted through a shared project. This, strictly speaking, would be impossible unless it also involved some form of shared consciousness, an intersubjectivity. What Heidegger had called a *Mitsein* (a 'being-with') would have to be possible and Sartre – quite consistently – denies such a possibility. There could not be, contrary to what Heidegger – or indeed Marcel – had argued, 'a being which in its own being implies the Other's being' (BN 247). Such a notion would have to imply a 'collective consciousness', or an 'inter-subjective consciousness' (BN 414), and these are by definition impossible for Sartre; consciousness is the individual upsurge of nihilating freedom in the world.

However, having ruled out the possibility of an intersubjective constitution of situation, Sartre is left with the problem of explaining how *any* social relations are possible. For if one extends the analysis of the fundamental Self-Other relation and takes it to be the basis of all and any human relations, the logic of such an extrapolation would be to give us an account of the human world that is similar to Hobbes' state of nature. The world would be Hobbesian not only in the sense of being fundamentally conflictual, but in the sense of being necessarily random, unstructured and anarchic. For the main features of Hobbes' state of nature are not only fear and conflict, but the lack of stability, of order, of institutions, of common linguistic meaning – of all those regularities that permit human culture to develop and which are made possible for Hobbes only by the contract to end the state of nature. However, for Sartre, even though there is no contract, such a state of nature is self-evidently not the world into which mutually hostile individual freedoms are 'thrown'. On the contrary, the world into which individual freedoms are contingently born is one which *already* has order and regularity. It has such 'collective techniques' as language;[25] it has cultural identities (for example, skiing in the 'French' as opposed to the 'Norwegian' style); it already has what Sartre is later to call 'practical ensembles' – that is, relatively stable and identifiable social groupings, such as nationalities and social classes; and it already has history, a degree of perceived continuity over time. How is one to account for all these social aspects of life on the basis of Sartre's account of Self-Other relations, unless one appeals to those modes of objectivist social explanation that Sartre would reject?[26]

Although Sartre is emphatic that the only ontological basis for relations between any number of people must be the mutually nihilating relations of Self and Other, he does briefly suggest that some collective experiences are possible at the psychological level. These are derivative, secondary kinds of experience, yet, Sartre suggests, they can form the basis for certain kinds of social relations. The most common experience is that of what Sartre calls an 'Us-object' (*le «Nous» objet*) (BN 415 ff). This arises when I and the Other, locked in confrontation, and each attempting to transcend the being-in-situation of the Other through the look, are suddenly *over*-looked by a third person – the 'Third'. With the arrival of the Third on the scene, both my situation and that of the Other are simultaneously transcended and organized within the situation of the Third. Then, when I accept responsibility for my now alienated situation, I cannot avoid also accepting responsibility for the Other as part of *my* situation. For the Third has organized us into one and the same situation: 'I suddenly experience the existence of an objective situation-form in the world of the Third in which the Other and I shall figure as *equivalent* structures in *solidarity* with each other' (BN 418).

The Us-object is a common psychological experience. It is found, for example, where several individuals work under a common supervisor, who functions as a Third to them all. It is also the main explanation Sartre offers for class relations. These are not primarily a matter of exploitation and resistance, as Sartre describes them, but of who is in a position to be a nihilating Third to whom. Working-class consciousness – the solidarity of class resistance – is thus an adoption of the alienated Us-object experience:

> The 'Master', the 'feudal lord', the 'bourgeois', or the 'capitalist' appear not only as powerful people who command, but also and

above all as *Thirds*; that is, as those who are outside the oppressed community and *for whom* this community exists. It is therefore *for them* and *in their freedom* that the reality of the oppressed class is going to exist. They cause it to be born by their look ... This means that I discover the 'Us' in which I am integrated or 'the class' *outside*, in the look of the Third, and it is this collective alienation which I take up when saying 'Us'. (BN 421)

In this account Sartre offers us some explanation of not only the existence of classes but also of actions of class solidarity – that is co-operative social relations – without abandoning his account of being-for-others as a conflict of individual consciousnesses. But it is not a sufficient explanation. For, if we keep within Sartre's framework of analysis, it is not possible to explain why some people are – and *remain* – masters, lords, capitalists, while others are members of the oppressed (looked-at, objectified) class. For as looks people are equal. What Sartre's account cannot include (even though he recognizes it exists) is the inequality of power and of access to means of material production which preclude workers from transcending their masters as a class through transcending the masters' looks. If we imagine an old-fashioned confrontation between a factory owner and a group of striking workers at the factory gate, the strikers might well turn a common nihilating gaze on the owner and, in Sartrean terms, alienate his freedom. But this would not mean that the man ceased to be the factory owner, nor that he ceased to have power over the workers, whose means of resistance would have to be more than those of the look to alter the relations of *power*. If the human world is structured into such social ensembles as classes, in which men have relations of co-operation as well as conflict, we cannot explain this on the foundation of being-for-others alone.

Sartre seems implicitly to recognize this in so far as he intermittently suggests another possible basis for social relations, the mediation of 'instruments' and 'techniques'. Discussing 'my fellowman' (*mon prochain*), not as a directly encountered, hostile Other, but as evidenced through the humanization of the world in which 'I' am situated, Sartre writes as follows:

> To live in a world haunted by my fellowman is not only to be able to encounter the Other at every turn of the road; it is also to find

myself engaged in a world in which instrumental complexes can have a meaning which my free project has not first given them . . . I, by whom meanings come to things, I find myself engaged in an *already meaningful* world which reflects to me meanings which I have not put into it. (BN 509–10)

By 'instrumental complex', Sartre means a created object, as diverse as 'a station, a railroad sign, a work of art, a mobilization notice'. Meanings are also given in a set of 'general techniques', such as speaking and walking, which we all share, though each of course integrates these into his or her own project. Indeed, 'belonging to the *human race* is, in fact, defined by the use of very elementary and very general techniques' (BN 512). We can do nothing without encountering our engagement in a humanly created world – presumably even the would-be climber at the foot of the crag will have chosen a sound pair of boots for his feet if he aims to get to the top!

Sartre suggests also that certain kinds of *social* relations can be directly constituted through things and techniques – those of what he calls a 'We-subject' (BN 423 ff). A We-subject is also only a psychological experience. It arises when I and others pursue one and the same end across an instrumental-complex. For example, in a work crew I freely make a rhythm which is *also* a common rhythm, and indeed 'it gets its meaning only through this general rhythm'. However, such an experience of a We-subject is not in any way to be confused with intersubjectivity, or *Mitsein*. Although 'it seems in fact that it overcomes the original conflict of transcendences by making them converge in the direction of the world'(BN 425), it does not do so. Although we are engaged in a common task or field of action, our subjectivities remain radically distinct. Through things and through my body, I can temporarily apprehend my own transcendence 'as extended and supported by other transcendences'. But this is an 'unstable' and 'fleeting' experience, 'a purely subjective impression which engages only me'. Thus, even where a shared task would appear to give us a common constitution of one situation as 'ours', this is not in fact the case. Each continues to constitute his own individual situation, even though each does so in relation to the 'same' instrumental complex. The fundamental, dyadic relation of Self-Other is not thereby overcome. On the contrary, Sartre ends his discussion of the We-subject by reaffirming: 'The essence of the relations between consciousness is not the *Mitsein*; it is conflict' (BN 429).

In these discussions of the Us-object, of instruments and techniques and of the We-subject, Sartre goes some way towards indicating how social relations, those wider than Self-Other relations, are possible. However, in so far as he treats these as derivative and reaffirms the primacy of conflictual relations between individuals, the existence of social relations is not adequately accounted for in *Being and Nothingness*. The existence of social groups of various kinds, of social organization and structure and of the relative continuity of social forms that make it possible to talk of history cannot, finally, be explained within Sartre's account as more than random individual situations. Sartre is faced with the problem of what Beauvoir later called 'the contingent absurdity of the discontinuous'(EA 122) – the impossibility of discovering a common sense or coherence in a multiplicity of situations, each of which is intrinsically discrete. Yet, its radical individualism notwithstanding, one already glimpses in *Being and Nothingness* some of the insights which were later to bear fruit in Sartre's major work of *social* ontology, the *Critique*. It was, however, to take the confrontation between Sartre's radical individualism and that most profoundly social theory, Marxism, to bring these to full visibility.

Part Two
Social Situations

3

Beauvoir: the weight of situation

In her autobiography, Simone de Beauvoir describes a damp, dreary evening in the Spring of 1940, when she and Sartre wandered around the streets of Paris discussing philosophy. Sartre, briefly in Paris on leave from the army, sketched out for her the main lines of the argument of what was to become *Being and Nothingness*. It was an argument which he had been working out in his notebooks during the several months of enforced idleness thrust upon him by life as a conscript during the 'phoney war'; but it was, of course, the culmination of many years of prior study and reflection.[1] Their discussions over the next few days, Beauvoir tells us, centred above all on the problem of 'the relation of situation to freedom'. On this point they disagreed. Since this disagreement was one that continued for several years – and was, I will argue, only resolved by Sartre gradually abandoning his own views of situation and subjectivity for ones much closer to Beauvoir's – it is worth quoting Beauvoir's account of their conversation in full:

> I maintained that, from the point of view of freedom, as Sartre defined it – not as a stoical resignation but as an active transcendence of the given – not every situation is equal: what transcendence is possible for a woman locked up in a harem? Even such a cloistered existence could be lived in several different ways, Sartre said. I clung to my opinion for a long time and then made only a token submission. Basically, I was right. But to have been able to defend my position, I would have had to abandon the terrain of individualist, thus idealist, morality, where we stood.[2]

As we have seen, Sartre continued in *Being and Nothingness* to maintain the view he had pushed Beauvoir to accept in 1940: torture victims, he insisted, can objectify the torturer and the slave is as free as his master. Since each individual subject constitutes his situation as the unique field of his own project, no comparison between two situations, from which we could judge one to be more free than the other, is possible. These views are the eminently consistent conclusions that must follow from Sartre's ontology, in which the for-itself, as pure nothingness, is unfounded and uncaused. In so far as Beauvoir questioned such conclusions, there was in her questioning at least an implicit challenge to Sartre's ontology.

The issue of Beauvoir's intellectual relation to Sartre is complex. She is best known (from her volumes of autobiography) as the chronicler of their interlinked lives; she is known as a novelist and, particularly in the anglophone world, for her treatise on women, *The Second Sex* (1949). The latter was acclaimed as a work of origin by the women's liberation movement of the late 1960s, especially in the USA. However, most commentators, even feminist ones, have generally treated Beauvoir as a derivative thinker, a kind of footnote to Sartre: her novels exemplify *his* philosophy, her essays offer marginal clarifications or, in the case of *The Second Sex*, at best a creative application of *his* main ideas. There is some truth in such an interpretation: Beauvoir did consciously work within Sartre's framework and she made no claim to be a philosopher of Sartre's stature.[3] Even so, their intellectual relationship was clearly very much a two-way process. As both of them have pointed out, Sartre modified ideas and even rewrote works at Beauvoir's instigation.[4] When, in the postwar period, Sartre began seriously to confront Marxism and to consider the question of social existence more fully, Beauvoir had preceded him. Although she engaged in a more muted and less direct conversation with Marxism than Sartre, Beauvoir was the one who first pointed the way beyond Sartre's dyadic account of human relations, sketching in its stead an account of socially mediated subjectivity.

Although Beauvoir said she worked within Sartre's framework, she did so rather unfaithfully. While beginning from Sartrean premises, by which I mean those of *Being and Nothingness*, her tenacious pursuit of her own questions led her at times to some most unSartrean conclusions. This is particularly the case with her treatment of the question of the situated nature of subjectivity. In *The Second Sex* especially, she came to conclusions – already presaged in the 1940 conversation cited above – which were clearly opposed to Sartre's account, in *Being and Nothingness*, of the autonomy of the subject.

Where, however, she stopped short was at the point of formulating the alternative ontology which her concrete analyses called for. If, as she argues, situations do indeed fundamentally modify the freedom of the individualized for-itself, then Sartre's radical disjuncture between being-for-itself and being-in-itself is put into question. In many ways Merleau-Ponty's ontology – the topic of the next chapter – offers a better foundation than does Sartre's for Beauvoir's account of the subject and of the modification it undergoes in certain kinds of situation.

I will focus in this chapter on three works by Beauvoir, written over the period 1943–9. These are: two essays on ethics, *Pyrrhus et Cinéas* (written in 1943) and *The Ethics of Ambiguity* (written in 1946),[5] and *The Second Sex* (begun in 1946, but written mainly in 1948 and 1949). As a clear line of intellectual development links these three works, I will treat them chronologically. Over much the same period, of course, Sartre himself was beginning to encounter the inadequacies of *Being and Nothingness* as a foundation for social philosophy and ethics and gradually to attempt to modify some of his arguments. But, starting in 1943, Beauvoir was the one who first deepened and fleshed out Sartre's notion of *situation*, beginning to develop it into a tool for analysing social as well as individual existence; social as well as ontological aspects of freedom.[6]

Pyrrhus et Cinéas

Early in 1943, when *Being and Nothingness* had been completed but was not yet published, Beauvoir was invited to contribute to a series of books on existentialism. Her first reaction, she tells us, was that Sartre had already said all there was to say in *Being and Nothingness*.[7] Then she decided that there was a set of issues about which she had something fresh to say: issues she had already touched upon in her recently completed novel about the Resistance.[8] They concerned the interdependence of freedoms and the problem of violence. Working consciously within Sartre's framework, she produced *Pyrrhus et Cinéas*.[9]

Beauvoir begins her argument from two Sartrean propositions. Firstly, her doubts of 1940 notwithstanding, she still contends, with Sartre, that freedom, that is, subjectivity, is indestructible: whatever our condition we are free to choose. When we act on each other, we can act only on each other's exteriority: on each other's *situation*. Thus, with Sartre, she concludes that ultimately I can neither help nor harm another in his freedom. If we try to be generous, our action 'only reaches the exterior [*les dehors*] of the other' (PC 83). Violence too acts only on another's facticity (PC 86), and not on his freedom. 'In one sense', she tells us, 'violence is not an evil, since one can do nothing either for or against a man' (PC 116).

Beauvoir secondly follows Sartre in initially asserting the radical separateness of freedom: each individual is for her a free subject, a unique transcendence, a Sartrean for-itself:

> Men do not to begin with depend on each other, because to begin with they *are* not: they must become. Freedoms are neither united nor opposed: they are separated. It is in projecting himself into the world that a man situates himself in situating other men around him. (PC 48)

This far Beauvoir's argument is familiar. However, from the indestructibility of individual freedom and the separate constitution by each subject of its unique situation, Sartre had proceeded to argue that relations between freedoms are inherently conflictual: each freedom encounters the other as a threat. The other is the constitutor of an alternative situation which is not mine, and in which I am now merely an object for him. While Beauvoir does not challenge Sartre head-on, she does not proceed to replicate this last part of Sartre's argument. Instead, she explores some startlingly different alternatives, involving such unSartrean notions as generosity and equality.

I have already suggested that Sartre was faced with a difficulty in the 1940s. The social philosophy implicit in *Being and Nothingness* was one in which society was conceived as a quasi-Hobbesian state of nature – as not only conflictual but also contingent and structureless; as an anarchic aggregate of freedoms in random conflict. Thus Sartre's philosophy was not able to provide a theoretical foundation for his growing commitment to the project of socialist revolution. Sartre was, of course, aware of the problem – it was implied in the questions concerning ethics with which he ended the book and which he explored in his abandoned *Cahiers*. But apart from the vague notion of an individual 'radical conversion', he did not address the problem in *Being and Nothingness*. In *Pyrrhus et Cinéas* Beauvoir attempted to show that there is a connection between Sartre's account of ontological freedom and the commitment which they both shared to bringing about a different social order. To make this case, however, she had to modify Sartre's account of interpersonal relations, demonstrating that they need not be relations solely of conflict. For Sartre, it will be recalled, Heidegger's idea of *Mitsein*, that man is 'a being which in its own being implies the Other's being', must be rejected (BN 247 ff). For Beauvoir also, 'men' are radically separate freedoms. Yet, she goes on to point out, paradoxically, they are also interdependent. If I try to imagine a world in which I am the only person in existence, the image is truly horrifying, for nothing I did would have any point to it. 'A man alone in the world would be paralysed by the self-evident vanity of all his goals; he undoubtedly could not bear to live' (PC 65; also 110). Although I freely create my own project, its meaning *for me* depends on the existence of other people and their willingness and ability to confirm its significance. Above all, they must be willing and able to take up my creation and give it a future that goes beyond my present. Thus, Beauvoir insists, it is only from others that we can obtain an affirmation of our existence. For although others do indeed nihilate or objectify me, it is they alone who also can give my being the necessity I seek. I can to some degree escape the contingency which threatens to devour my actions through the recognition of others.

'Man'[10] for Beauvoir, as for Sartre, is a useless passion, a nothingness which seeks in vain to be. Man wishes to be a self-cause, a for-itself-in-itself and he experiences his inevitable failure as an anguish which he generally attempts to avoid in 'bad faith'. What Beauvoir now suggests is that a certain partial escape from nothingness, a certain degree of being, can be achieved through the recognition of my project by others.

> Only the other can create a need for what we give him; all appeal, all demand comes from his freedom; in order for what I have established to appear as a good, the other must make it his good: then I am justified in having created it. Only the freedom of the other is able to give necessity to my being. (PC 95–6)

Above all what I am able to obtain through others is a future: my project remains open beyond the end of my act, even beyond my death, if others take it up and use what I have created as the starting-point for their projects. It is important to point out that it would not be sufficient if only *one* other person were to take up my project. I require it to be taken up by a *multiplicity* of others. One other freedom could not give sufficient necessity to my project, since in isolation each individual freedom remains finite. It is only a multiplicity of freedoms, each supporting the others, which can overcome individual finitude (PC 120).

But not all relations with others involve such mutual affirmation. There has to be a *choice* of such relations – what Beauvoir calls a choice of 'generosity' on the part of the persons concerned.[11] Moreover, for such a choice to be possible, a certain objective condition also has to be met: there must be *equality* between them. By equality Beauvoir means, above all, social equality: equal power and equal access to those material means which are necessary for the projects we choose to undertake.

In relations of generosity, the Sartrean conflict of consciousnesses is not abolished, but it is transcended by the willingness of each freedom also to recognize the subjectivity of the other. Instead of each attempting to make an object of the other, each recognizes that the other, even though apprehended in exteriority, as an object, is *also* a subject; and each agrees to respect the subjectivity of the other:

> In lucid, agreed recognition, these two freedoms which seem to exclude each other must be able to hold themselves face to face: mine and that of the other; I must grasp myself as at the same time object and freedom; I must recognise my situation as founded by the other, even while affirming my being beyond the situation. (PC 83–4)

Even though Beauvoir herself is more concerned with the social preconditions for such relations of generosity than with analysing the relations themselves, this account implies a fundamental reworking of Sartre's account of relations with others. In arguing that the main precondition is *social* equality, Beauvoir attempts for the first time to create a link – however inadequately still – between Sartrean ontology and the ethical and political domain.

If I am to have relations of reciprocal generosity with others, and if my existence is to be given meaning through others taking up what I create, they must be my equals (*mes pairs*). This is to say, in the first instance, they cannot be *less free* than I am. For if I experience myself as transcendent over the other, then I simply cannot avoid objectifying him (PC 113) and he will not then be able to take up and give transcendence to my creation for me.

> The other's freedom can do nothing for me unless my own goals can serve as his point of departure; it is by using the tool which I have

invented that the other prolongs its existence; the scholar can only talk with men who have arrived at the same level of knowledge as himself; only then can he suggest his theory as a basis for further work. The other cannot accompany my transcendence unless he is at the same point on the road as me. (PC 114)

Thus, in order to extend my own freedom, I need others to be able to attain my own level of creation. This in turn, Beauvoir next argues, requires me, for the sake of my own freedom, to struggle to make all men my equals with regard to their material well-being. For otherwise they will not be able to accompany my skills, my intellectual endeavours, etc. In other words, the social situation of my fellows has an effect upon my freedom, upon the meaning I am able to give my own project, and thus it is my concern.

I must therefore endeavour to create for all men situations which will enable them to accompany and surpass my transcendence. I need their freedom be available to make use of me, to preserve me in surpassing me. I require for men health, knowledge, well being, leisure, so that their freedom does not consume itself in fighting sickness, ignorance, misery. (PC 115)

Beauvoir emphasizes that her argument must apply to all human beings; in either perpetrating violence or failing to oppose its perpetration against anybody, I work against my own need to be surrounded by subjects who will be able to recognize me and be capable of taking up my projects: 'Even if I oppress only one man, all humanity appears to me as a pure thing in him' (PC 116).[12] The insoluble nature of political problems arises, however, from the fact that, given also the separateness of human projects and the conflicting interests that must arise, I cannot avoid doing violence to others. Violence is always a scandal and always self-defeating; yet we cannot avoid it. In struggling to create situations in which my fellow men no longer consume their freedom in a fight for mere physical survival, I may have to do violence to their oppressors; it is justified violence but is no less self-defeating for that. Beauvoir was to explore this paradox further in *The Ethics of Ambiguity*, written three years later. But before turning to that work, let me examine what the argument for the interdependence of freedoms in *Pyrrhus et Cinéas* implies for Sartre's account of individual subjectivity.

In *Being and Nothingness*, it will be recalled, freedom refers not to efficacy in completing our projects, but to a free choice of project: 'by oneself to determine oneself to wish' (BN 483). Furthermore, while subjectivity is always situated, situations are constituted by the subject. Situations are not only individual but incommensurable, and we could not – except by assuming the role of an objectifying Third – judge that a master is more free than his slave, or the torturer more free than his victim. From the point of view of freedom, all situations are equal.

Already in 1940, as we saw, Beauvoir was doubtful about this view. Reflecting on *Pyrrhus et Cinéas* in 1960, Beauvoir described the work as one in which she attempted to 'reconcile' her own conviction that situations are 'graded' (*hierarchisées*) with the Sartrean notion of freedom as the indestructible upsurge of the for-itself, or transcendence.[13] In order to attempt this, she adopted the Cartesian distinction between *freedom* (*liberté*), which has no external limits, and *power* (*puissance*), which can be restricted.[14]

> Power is finite, and one can augment or limit it from without; one can throw a man in prison, take him out of it, cut off an arm, lend him wings; but in all cases his freedom remains infinite. (PC 86)

However, as we will see, this is not a distinction which she was able consistently to sustain.

Since anything that I do affects only the 'exteriority' (*les dehors*) of another, Beauvoir's argument concerning the interdependence of freedoms must initially refer to what in this distinction she calls *power*. It is my *power* (what we might call my *effective freedom*, as distinct from my *ontological freedom*) which depends on the power of others. If others do not take up the tool I have invented, or the theory I have developed, it would seem at first consideration that the limit involved must be a limit only on my effective freedom and not on my ontological freedom, or transcendence; for the latter is untouchable and infinite. However, as Beauvoir's argument concerning the interdependence of freedoms *qua* transcendences proceeds, the distinction between the two kinds of freedom begins to break down.

Transcendence is the upsurge of the for-itself in the world, but it becomes concrete; it particularizes itself in the specific projects of individuals. When it does this, it of course encounters the limits of the situation of the individual. The slave has transcendence and a project, like any other person, but the specific content of the projects open to him is circumscribed by his situation as a slave, a situation which is not of his own making. Thus his effective freedom is more limited than that of his master. His choices can be made only within narrow confines, not of his choosing. We might say that he cannot choose his situation, although he remains free to choose *within* it. Moreover, his *future* is more closed than that of his master. It is this lack of an 'open' future which begins, in Beauvoir's account, to imply that there is a qualitative modification of transcendence itself. This is to say also that the lack of an open future implies a modification of the for-itself, of ontological freedom.

If poverty, sickness, ignorance, as well as slavery, are to be opposed, it is because they preclude projects that open on to the future. They condemn human beings to 'consume' their freedom in a dreary cycle of repetition. A transcendence which so consumes itself lacks a project which enables it to appeal to other men to accompany it into the future: it is qualitatively different from a transcendence which appeals to others and can open into a future that extends beyond itself. It has, in comparison, a circular quality. Beauvoir was later to develop the notion of *immanence* to describe such an entrapped transcendence. In *Pyrrhus et Cinéas* we are simply left with the still undeveloped idea that although all men have freedom, in the sense of transcendence or ontological freedom, it has a different quality depending on the situation – the field of effective freedom – of the person concerned. A consistent Sartrean position would not, of course, permit one to speak of such qualitative differences; as a pure upsurge of nothingness, the for-itself could not in any way be qualified for Sartre. Thus the ideas which Beauvoir begins to develop in *Pyrrhus et Cinéas* involve a radical, though only implicit, modification of Sartre's account of the autonomous subject.

The Ethics of Ambiguity

In *The Ethics of Ambiguity*, written some three years later, Beauvoir returned to the questions she had treated in *Pyrrhus et Cinéas*. Her use of the word 'ambiguity' in the title of the work is of considerable significance. Ambiguity for her refers to a paradoxical reality, in which each of two contradictory aspects of a single existent carries equal weight. For Sartre, the for-itself precedes and constitutes the meaning of its own facticity. My body, others, relations with others, are merely facticities of the for-itself. For Beauvoir, however, human existence is ambiguous because these facticities appear in her account to be of equal weight with consciousness: man *is* thing, body, as well as consciousness. He is object as well as subject; and he lives a continual tension between these equal and contradictory aspects of his existence. Life, she begins by saying, is the building of death. And it is only man who 'knows and thinks this tragic ambivalence which the animal and the plant merely undergo'. Thus, man is both 'a pure internality against which no external power can take hold' and, at the same time, 'he also experiences himself as a thing crushed by the dark weight of other things' (EA 7).

Body and consciousness, object and subject – man's relations with other men must include this paradoxical dual reality. Separate, yet interdependent, men both threaten and empower each other; they both negate and extend each other's freedom. Taking these ambiguities as her starting-point, Beauvoir sets out to address the problem of ethics: what precepts, if any, can we develop that should govern our conduct towards each other, given who and what we are? My concern here, however, is not directly with the precepts she develops, but with the account of freedom-in-situation and its limits which she elaborates *en route* to the ethical precepts.

As in *Pyrrhus et Cinéas*, Beauvoir refrains from directly criticizing the account of conflictual relations with others of *Being and Nothingness*, but she argues that we can in some conditions transcend them. An 'ethics of ambiguity', she tells us, 'will be an ethics which will refuse to deny *a priori* that separate existents can at the same time be bound to each other' (EA 18). She reiterates the argument from *Pyrrhus et Cinéas*: freedom needs an 'open future' and only others can give it to me (EA 72). Thus, Hegel's description of the struggle between consciousnesses in which 'each seeks the death of the other'[15] – a description which was closely paralleled by Sartre – is incomplete. While my first response to the arrival of the other is indeed to feel that he is stealing the world from me and to hate him accordingly, this hatred is 'naïve' (EA 70 ff). For '[i]f I were really everything there would be nothing beside me; the world would be empty'. The other in fact steals the world from me for Beauvoir only to give it back again enriched, and I would be foolish not to realize this and to overcome my initial hatred: 'One can reveal the world only against a background of the world revealed by other men. No project can be defined except by its interference with other projects.' Subjectivity, in short, cannot exist without intersubjectivity.

Projects in this account are separate, yet they also require each other. From this paradoxical insight Beauvoir develops both an initial notion of *society*, not to be found in *Being and Nothingness*, and an account of violence and oppression which introduces a *social* dimension. Violence and oppression are not only dyadic relations of self and other for her. They are embedded in the logic of a world of *multiple* projects and their complex 'interferences'(EA 71). This is a logic which Sartre, like Marcel, had not attempted to examine, at least in *Being and Nothingness*.

Society

Beauvoir's notion of society in *The Ethics of Ambiguity* is sketchy and underdeveloped. However, it still offers a considerable advance in overcoming the atomistic notion implicit in *Being and Nothingness*. Beauvoir begins from a critique of Hegelian and Marxist notions which, in her view, erroneously attribute more substance to the state or to society than to individuals. 'If the individual is nothing, society cannot be anything', she insists (EA 106). Yet she is also anxious to avoid the random and structureless conception of society which, she realizes, could be the result of such a radical individualism – and which I have argued was the outcome in Sartre's case. 'Separation does not exclude relation', she insists; on the contrary, it implies it. And since I need not one but many others to take up my project and give it necessity, there is the possibility that multiple relations can cohere into intelligible forms with a degree of temporal permanency:

> Society exists only by means of the existence of particular individuals; likewise, human adventures stand out against the background of time, each finite to each, although they are all open to the infinity of the future and, thereby, their individual forms imply each other without destroying each other. A conception of this kind does not contradict that of a historical intelligibility; for it is not true that the mind has to choose between the contingent absurdity of the discontinuous and the rationalistic necessity of the continuous; on the contrary, it is part of its function to make a multiplicity of coherent ensembles stand out against the single background of the world and, inversely, to comprehend these ensembles in the perspective of the ideal unity of the world. Without raising the question of historical comprehension and causality, it is enough to recognize the presence of intelligible sequences within temporal forms so that anticipations and consequently action may be possible. (EA 12a)

In this passage, Beauvoir raises the questions which Sartre did not, and could not, raise in *Being and Nothingness*. Although, with Sartre, she begins from the separateness of freedoms, she realizes that unless we can also demonstrate some coherence emerging from them, some social forms with a temporal continuity, we are condemned to a kind of solipsism in which comprehension of and reasoned action in relation to a multiplicity of men would be impossible. We would, as she puts it, be locked into 'the contingent absurdity of the discontinuous'. But since projects can be shown to be interdependent as well as separate we can, at least to some extent, escape such absurdity. There are 'coherent ensembles'[16] which can be distinguished. Beauvoir implies that such ensembles are not mere intellectual constructs, although she does not explain how they are objectively constituted. Nor does she discuss how such ensembles are connected to each other.

In another passage, however, Beauvoir raises the startling possibility that a *common situation* can give rise to a *common project* – in other words that a joint action is what creates ensembles. A social class, she claims, has a comparable freedom to an individual and, like an individual, can evade it in a collective 'bad faith'. Like an individual, a class chooses the meaning of its situation through its project:

> The proletariat, taken as a whole, as a class, can become conscious of its situation in more than one way. It can want the revolution to be brought about by one party or another. It can let itself be deluded, as happened to the German proletariat, or can sleep in the dull comfort which capitalism grants it, as does the American proletariat. It may be said that in all these cases it is betraying; still, it must be free to betray. (EA 20)

Unfortunately, Beauvoir does not go on to explain or develop this idea; nor does she explore its philosophical implications. But once again, what she is saying implies a non-Sartrean account of social existence. For Sartre, the nearest the proletariat could come to a collective choice of the meaning of its situation would be through experiencing itself as an Us-object, collectively objectified by the capitalist as Third. But what Beauvoir says in this passage would imply that a collective freedom is possible which is its *own* source, and which is not constituted from outside by a Third.

Oppression and violence

Although Beauvoir mentions such instances of collective freedom and talks more generally of the interdependence of freedoms, these are intimately linked in her analysis with oppression and violence. The ambiguity of freedoms, interdependent yet separate, makes possible not only generosity and collective freedom, but also the possibility of attacking another's freedom by denying it the recognition it needs: 'It is this interdependence which explains why oppression is possible and why it is hateful'(EA 82). Beauvoir distinguishes two levels of violence in human relations. The first simply is given in the ambiguity of freedom and is ineradicable. The Sartrean conflict of consciousnesses might at times be transcended, but it is not thereby eliminated. As transcendences, men 'concretely compete with others for being... The truth is that if division and violence define war, the world has always been at war and always will be' (EA 118–19). Conflict, resulting in violence, can arise even when our projects aim to increase the field of human freedom. It can happen 'that one finds oneself obliged to oppress and kill men who are pursuing goals whose validity one acknowledges oneself' (EA 99). For example, she says, anti-fascists in Europe during the Second World War rightly opposed liberation movements in the British colonies even though the goals of these movements were valid. For their effect at the time was to weaken Britain in its yet more important struggle against fascism. Political judgements have always to be made in situations of complexity, where conflicting goals, even legitimate ones, make violence unavoidable.

While Marxism and revolutionary politics are not explicitly the focus of *The Ethics of Ambiguity*, Beauvoir's meditations on violence clearly arise from her preoccupation with the question of revolutionary violence and the Marxist debate over ends and means. No 'science of history' can resolve these dilemmas, she points out, for 'at each particular moment we must in any case maneuver in a state of doubt' (EA 123). But, however imperfect our knowledge, we still must act; and we must try to do so in such ways that the means we choose do not contradict and undermine the ends we aim at. 'The means, it is said, will be justified by the end; but it is the means which define the end, and if it is contradicted in the moment that set it up, the whole enterprise sinks into absurdity'(EA 124). Thus, in the name of a mythical future liberation of the international proletariat, Stalinism has erroneously elevated the triumph of the Soviet Union from a means to an 'absolute end' – an end in whose name it in fact undermines international revolution and carries out what have become unjustifiable acts of violence. The best that can be done in politics is to be honest with ourselves and others about what we are doing, and to consider whether the violence we do in the name of a specific goal is likely to further or to undermine it. Violence 'must be legitimised concretely' (EA 148).[17]

Violence, then, is inherent in social existence and it cannot be avoided in even the most liberatory politics. However, over and above this fundamental level of violence, Beauvoir describes relations of violence of a second degree: oppression. Oppression, for Beauvoir, can include dyadic relationships, but it is generally a wider, social relation. Oppression is usually practised against particular social groups – workers, but also women, blacks, colonial peoples, Jews. It involves not merely the attempted objectification described in the Hegelian struggle of consciousnesses or Sartre's conflictual looks, but a systematic attempt to modify the social situation of a group of people so as to prohibit them from developing a free transcendence which will compete with that of the oppressors. As such, oppression involves the establishment and maintenance of relations of social inequality.

Oppression divides humankind into two 'clans': those capable of free transcendence, and the oppressed 'who are condemned to mark time hopelessly in order merely to support the collectivity'. They pay for the freedom of the elite and 'the oppressor feeds himself on their transcendence' (EA 83). The 'consumption' of the transcendence of the oppressed is, however, a concrete and material process in Beauvoir's analysis. Her use of the idea of consumption is clearly associated with Marx's account of the consumption of labour power in the capitalist labour process, and the concomitant reduction of human beings to abstract labour. Life, she says, involves two kinds of action: basic, material reproduction – what she calls life 'perpetuating itself'– *and* the movement of free transcendence towards an open future. It is of course the latter kind of action which distinguishes the uniquely human. As Marx had written, 'the realm of freedom actually begins only where labour which is determined by necessity and mundane considerations ceases; thus in the very nature of things it lies beyond the sphere of actual material production'.[18] If a life can do nothing but maintain itself at the material level, says Beauvoir, 'living is only not dying, and human existence is indistinguishable from an absurd vegetation' (EA 82–3). Oppression, then, involves shutting off a group from transcendence and condemning it to a life of vegetation so as to increase the field of freedom of the oppressors.

Of course, oppression is in the final analysis self-defeating. For the oppressor undermines his own freedom in so far as he needs it to be supported by a world of free men. But the self-defeating nature of his project is not acknowledged by the oppressor, who always evades responsibility for his actions in 'bad faith'(EA 96). Since, for this reason, we cannot count on a 'collective conversion' (EA 97) of the oppressors, the only way forward towards a society of equal freedoms has to be through resistance and revolt on the part of the oppressed.

Turning, however, to the experiences of the oppressed, Beauvoir points out that many of them are not, in practice, capable of revolt. For their transcendence is not merely cut off from its future; it ceases even to be able to project a future. Yet more sharply than in *Pyrrhus et Cinéas*, Beauvoir's analysis diverges at this point from the Sartrean view of freedom. Some of the oppressed are complicitous in their oppression and, in bad faith, evade the revolt that alone could open the way to freedom for them. But others simply do not have that choice. Their situation has so penetrated even their ontological freedom, so modified it, that not even the commencement of a transcendent project is possible. The very withdrawal of consciousness which, for Sartre, is the origin of transcendence and which enables freedom to choose its way of taking up its situation (for example, whether or not to give in to the torturer) has ceased to be possible.

The most severely oppressed live in what Beauvoir, following Sartre, calls the condition of 'seriousness'; their lot appears to them so natural, so immovable, that no choice of how to live their situation appears possible. For example, the present distribution of wealth is made to appear so natural that it is unquestionable. Yet far from being a moral fault of the oppressed, or an evasion of freedom in bad faith, seriousness is inflicted upon them. 'One of the ruses of oppression is to camouflage itself behind a natural situation since, after all, one cannot revolt against nature' (EA 83). This is the condition which Sartre had briefly described in passing in *Being and Nothingness* in the example of the workers of Lyon. For Beauvoir, however, such a condition is central to the issues of ethics and politics. The oppressed man 'can fulfill his human freedom only in revolt' (EA 87), yet his situation may have been made such that he is unable even to recognize that he is oppressed. The oppressed live in an 'infantile world', immediate, with no sense of future, or any alternative. They have 'no instrument, be it in thought or by astonishment or anger, which permits them to attack the civilization which oppresses them' (EA 38). Since they are human beings, they still retainn an ontological freedom, but it is made 'immanent', irrealizable, by the situation others have imposed upon them (EA 102–3). For Beauvoir, unlike Sartre, oppression can permeate subjectivity to the point where consciousness *itself* becomes no more than a passive registering of the oppressive situation. Although it cannot be definitively eliminated – and can always re-erupt should oppression start to weaken – freedom can be reduced to no more than a suppressed potentiality.

Social inequality is, above all, what brings about this condition: 'The less economic and social circumstances allow an individual to act upon the world, the more this world appears to him as given' (EA 48). Mystification and ignorance, deliberately perpetuated by those who have power, compound the grip of seriousness on the freedom of the oppressed (EA 98). Thus the struggle for a world of free and mutually confirming transcendences must aim to alter the situation of the oppressed. For those of us who already have freedom, yet whose transcendence is still limited by the oppression of others, the struggle must be to change the situation of the oppressed; we must intervene, not to help them directly, but to enable them to become themselves capable of choosing to resist their situation. Beauvoir sharply distinguishes such support from charity. For charity is always 'practiced from the outside' and is a form of objectification (EA 86). Similarly, of course, an overly objectivist vanguardism must be rejected as a form of objectification. We cannot liberate other people. All that we can hope to do is to act on their situation, to re-shape their exteriority, so that their freedom ceases to be closed in on itself and can assume its own transformative project.

In the course of her analysis Beauvoir frequently criticizes contemporary, 'orthodox', Marxism for its objectivism, for claiming that there are autonomous laws of historical development which act independently of individual human action. For Beauvoir, Marxism at its best is a 'radical humanism' which 'rejects the idea of an inhuman objectivity' (EA 18). But orthodox Marxists have frequently attempted to deny freedom and suppress subjectivity.

Neither *Pyrrhus et Cinéas* nor *The Ethics of Ambiguity* is a work explicitly about Marxism or socialism. But the call for a 'radical humanism' which is the unifying theme of both works provides the standpoint from which Beauvoir elaborates important elements of an existential critique of orthodox Marxism. Even more significantly, she also develops an argument concerning the interdependence of freedoms and the necessarily intersubjective character of subjectivity which supplies the missing link between Sartre's philosophy and Marxism. In *Materialism and Revolution* (1946), Sartre made some similar objections to orthodox Marxism to those Beauvoir made in *The Ethics of Ambiguity*. But it was she alone, starting in *Pyrrhus et Cinéas*, who began to make the case for that interdependence of freedoms which a synthesis of existentialism and Marxism must be able to demonstrate. She indicated the most crucial transformations that the philosophy of *Being and Nothingness* would have to undergo before it could be linked not only with ethics or political and social philosophy but, also and above all, with humanistic Marxism. Beauvoir's work must thus be seen as a prolegomenon to Sartre's later 'Marxist existentialism'.

The Second Sex

The Second Sex, published in 1949, offers us a painstaking case-study of oppression – that of women by men.[19] Once again, Beauvoir begins from within Sartre's framework, but ends by offering us an analysis which bursts out of the confines of Sartreanism. Most evaluations of *The Second Sex*, even feminist ones, have uncritically accepted Beauvoir's claim that her work was philosophically derivative. Most assume that, as one author has recently put it, Beauvoir simply used Sartre's concepts as 'coat-hangers' on which to hang her own material, even to the point where it can be said that 'Sartre's intellectual history becomes her own'.[20] However, such a view is grossly misleading. For although Beauvoir doubtless tried to work within a Sartrean framework, she did not wholly succeed. Indeed, many of the inconsistencies in *The Second Sex* reflect the tension between her formal adherence to Sartrean categories and the fact that the philosophical implications of the work are in large measure incompatible with Sartreanism. It is, once again, on her divergences from Sartre that my discussion will focus.

The book begins on firmly Sartrean ground. 'What is a woman?' asks Beauvoir, and answers initially that woman is defined as that which is not man – as other:

> She is determined and differentiated with reference to man and not he with reference to her; she is the inessential as opposed to the essential. He is the Subject, he is the Absolute: she is the Other. (TSS 16; xvi)

In the Sartrean struggle between consciousnesses, man consistently attempts to confirm his own subjectivity through the objectification of woman. Much of Volume I is taken up with describing the various facets of this objectification – from the reduction of woman to male property in marriage, to the way man conceives her as Other in myth and literature.

However, very early in the book Beauvoir introduces a distinction into the notion of otherness which is not found in *Being and Nothingness*. Extending the argument of her 'ethical essays', she points out that there can be relations of otherness between *equals* in which conflict, though not eliminated, is relativized by 'reciprocity': the recognition by each of the Other's freedom as equal to his or her own (TSS 17; xvii).[21] If, however, the situation of the protagonists is, to begin with, *unequal*, then instead of a reciprocal relation of tension being created, otherness will be of a second kind, involving oppression. Where there is a conflict of equals, 'there is created between them a reciprocal relation, be it in enmity, be it in amity, always in tension'. However, '(i)f one of the two [groups] is in some way privileged, has some advantage, this one prevails over the other and undertakes to keep it in subjection'(TSS 93; 61). The notion of otherness alone cannot explain woman's oppression for us. The problem is to explain why woman's otherness has not resulted in 'reciprocity', but has enabled man to objectify her. Why have men been able effectively to deny women their subjectivity, and to impose upon them conditions in which free transcendence is not possible?

Woman's man-made 'destiny'
Today it is unexceptionable to argue that women are not 'naturally' destined for marriage and motherhood above all else. In the France of the 1940s it was, as Beauvoir describes in her autobiography, a view which provoked widespread hostility.[22] Woman's condition, she argued, has been humanly created; it cannot be explained as a biological 'destiny'. We must look rather to human relations for an explanation. With Sartre, Beauvoir holds that only things, the in-itself, are subject to causality. Man, on the other hand, makes himself as a free project; the for-itself is *uncaused*. Thus we can never describe any human condition as inevitable. To claim that a condition is unchangeable is to commit the error of seriousness and it is in general a form of bad faith. We cannot then explain woman's condition as inevitable, however universal it appears. What is called the 'eternal feminine', the behaviour and character which seem to distinguish women from men, is humanly created and thus alterable. Woman could have a different future, her biological constitution notwithstanding.

However, this point having been made at some length, Beauvoir goes on to diverge even more widely from Sartre than she had done in the ethical essays. Although the eternal feminine is humanly created and not natural, it is created by *man* (the male), through the situation which he imposes on woman. From woman's perspective, this situation *is* generally experienced as a destiny, as inevitable and not alterable. Moreover, such an experience of her situation is not necessarily a choice of bad faith on the part of woman. For although her situation is indeed humanly created, *she* is not the one who has made or chosen it: 'the whole of feminine history has been man made' (TSS 159; 128). If woman is oppressed to the point where transcendence is no longer possible, then her situation *is* effectively her destiny; it acts upon her like a natural force. Beauvoir had already described such a condition in her ethical essays. Now she elaborates the notion of *immanence* (introduced only in passing in *The Ethics of Ambiguity*) as a philosophical grounding for her description.

Extending from her earlier argument that freedoms, because they are interdependent, need to maintain an open future for each other, she writes as follows:

> Every subject continually affirms himself through his projects as a transcendence; he realises his freedom only through his continual transcendence toward other freedoms; there is no other justification for present existence than its expansion towards an endlessly open future. Each time that transcendence falls back into immanence there is a degradation of existence into the 'in-itself', of freedom into facticity; this fall is a moral fault if the subject agrees to it; it takes the form of a frustration and an oppression if it is inflicted upon him. (TSS 28–9; xxviii-ix)

Woman is locked in immanence by the situation *man* imposes upon her – and she is not necessarily responsible. As has been pointed out, a consistent Sartrean position would make woman responsible for herself, no matter how constrained her situation.[23] But for Beauvoir, women's acceptance of this imposition runs along a continuum. Some do choose to accept it in bad faith, because of the security and privilege it brings. Others, unable to conceive of real alternatives, accept it while engaging in forms of passive resistance and 'resentment'. But for yet others, as for the oppressed whom Beauvoir had described in *The Ethics of Ambiguity*, freedom is suppressed to the point where they cease to be capable of choice or resistance. Beauvoir shifts, sometimes rather arbitrarily, between these alternative accounts of women's relation to their oppression. But what is of interest is that, at the most oppressed end of the continuum, Beauvoir breaks even more sharply from the Sartrean notion of the subject than in her earlier essays. For many there is no 'moral fault' because there is no possibility of choice. In the notion that freedom can 'fall back into the "in-itself"', that the for-itself can be turned, through the action of other (i.e. male) freedoms, into its very opposite, Beauvoir has finally and definitively broken from the Sartrean notion of the absolute subject. Indeed, one might even formulate her position, albeit only at this extreme end of the spectrum, in the terms Foucault used: woman is a historically constituted, not a constitut*ing*, subject. Not only does woman fail to *constitute* her situation in any way, she is in fact its *product*: 'when an individual, or a group of individuals, is kept in a situation of inferiority, the fact is that he *is* inferior ... yes, women on the whole *are* today inferior to men, which is to say that their situation gives them less possibilities' (TSS 24; xxiv).[24]

Although it is of human origin, the condition imposed on woman by man is analogous in its power over her to the rule of natural forces over other kinds of objects. As the young girl grows up she discovers that she *already* has been given inferiority as 'a fixed and preordained essence' (TSS 324; 297). A girl is twelve – 'and already her story is written in the heavens. She will discover it day after day without ever making it' (TSS 325; 298). Woman, says Beauvoir repeatedly, is 'doomed', 'destined', through the action of male freedom, to her condition. Beauvoir's notion of the falling back of freedom into the in-itself is not to be dismissed as a mere metaphor. It describes the real condition of a human life that lacks the freedom which normally characterizes human existence. Yet, from a Sartrean perspective, one cannot take the statement as wholly literal either. Strictly speaking, within Sartre's usage of the terms, the degradation of an existence into the in-itself would have to mean that oppressed woman has actually ceased to be human. For Sartre, either the for-itself, the uncaused upsurge of freedom, exists whatever the facticities of its situation, or else it does not exist. In the latter case one is dealing with the realm of inert being. In so far as Beauvoir's account of woman's situation as one of immanence involves the claim that the for-itself can be penetrated and modified by the action of others, it implies another notion of the subject than Sartre's. Beauvoir is trying to describe human existence as a synthesis of freedom *and* constraint, of consciousness *and* materiality which, finally, is incompatible with Sartre's notion of the subject.

However, Beauvoir also refuses to go as far as Sartre's structuralist and post-structuralist critics were later to go in wholly discarding the notion of free subjectivity; even when it is suppressed, reduced to immanence, subjectivity remains as a distinctly human potentiality. Thus while, for example, much of her detailed account of the young girl's 'formation'[25] could well be retold in the Foucauldian mode of 'the political technology of the body', of 'discipline' and 'dressage', Beauvoir would never have agreed to abandon the notion of a *repression* of freedom.[26] However suppressed, however disciplined, it is still freedom-made-immanent which distinguishes even the most constituted human subject from a well-trained animal.

Immanence is a condition which must be continuously inflicted on woman. As long as it is inflicted it is, for her, her destiny. There is no way she can choose to live the condition of immanence as a free choice. Unlike Sartre's example of the oppressed Jew, who can choose how he lives the otherness imposed on him by the anti-Semite (BN 523 ff), Beauvoir's most oppressed woman has no way of living her otherness as a free choice. Those women who try – through narcissism, all-consuming love, or mysticism – to assume their immanence as a choice can never succeed. Theirs is 'this ultimate effort – sometimes ridiculous, often pathetic – of imprisoned woman to transform her prison into a heaven of glory, her servitude into sovereign liberty' (TSS 639; 628). But such choices are no more than fantasy. They involve relations with an 'unreality' (her own double in narcissism, God in mysticism), or else (in all-consuming love), 'an unreal relation with a real being' (TSS 687; 678). These fantasies never permit woman to gain the 'grasp on the world' which freedom requires.

If woman is to escape from immanence she cannot then do so by an act of individual choice alone. Given her condition of immanence, any 'choice' she might make could be only a choice of immanence. Thus, Beauvoir argues, the liberation of woman must come, in the first instance, from the outside. As in the case of the slave who must be put 'in the presence of his freedom' (EA 87) before he can choose it, woman's *situation* must be altered before she can effectively struggle for her own freedom. Thus, we must now examine in more detail Beauvoir's account of woman's situation.

Woman's situation: institutions
Volume II of *The Second Sex*, 'Lived Experience',[27] begins with the following statement: 'One is not born a woman: one becomes one' (TSS

295; 267). From cradle to grave the female will be treated differently. Man creates for her a *situation* of otherness. Living her life in this situation, she experiences herself as other, and indeed she is other. There is a broad male consensus on the female 'character'. Across the ages woman has been described as emotional, irrational, amoral, devious, vain, as weak, helpless and passive. Beauvoir admits, perhaps far too readily, that all these qualities are generally to be observed in women.[28] However, she insists, they are not to be explained as an 'essence'. They are manifestations of woman's immanence, the product of her situation.

In painstaking detail, beginning with the different treatment received by young children according to sex, Beauvoir shows us how young girls and women are made to feel and to be non-agents; how horizons are cut off, the experiences of choice and responsibility denied to them. She traces, at least for her own era, society and class, woman's experience through all ages – childhood, puberty, sexual initiation, adulthood and old age – and she explores the interlinked aspects of the adult woman's situation; from marriage to childbirth and social life. The latter barely extends beyond the home: economic activity, politics, the high arts – all realms of significant action beyond the home – are barred to her. Prepared from birth only to catch a man – that is, to make herself his 'prey' (TSS 361; 337) – and to bear children, dependent on man, confined as his property in his house, it is not surprising that woman has no 'grasp on the world'. The 'eternal feminine' is to be explained then not as an essence, but as a synthesis of 'economic, social, historical conditioning' (TSS 608; 597).

If we compare Beauvoir's account of woman's situation with Sartre's discussion of situation in *Being and Nothingness*, we are struck by several divergences. Most obviously, situation has become in Beauvoir's analysis above all *condition*, external force. We are no longer in the realm of the free constitution of the meaning of its situation by an autonomous subject. But there are also other important, though related, divergences. These concern, above all, the greater emphasis on various social aspects of situation in Beauvoir's analysis and her claim that we can talk of a situation as *general*, as being an objective reality which is experienced in similar ways by the members of a certain category of human beings.

In Sartre's discussion of the structures of my situation (BN 489 ff), other people are present (unless they attempt to nihilate me) indirectly, via the humanly produced instruments I use and the general techniques such as language which I have in common with them. They are also present as my being-outside-for-others but this too is an indirect presence. For Beauvoir, however, others are *directly* involved in my constitution of the meaning of my freedom-in-situation. In contrast to Sartre's solitary rock climber Beauvoir had described, in *Pyrrhus et Cinéas*, a solitary walker experiencing his relation to nature – but as soon as the walk is over needing to tell his experience to a friend in order to confirm it (PC 68–9). For Beauvoir, we have seen, my situation is always mediated for me by others – hence her argument that I need freedoms equal to mine in the world. However, for women (and other oppressed groups), such a confirmation through others is impossible. The social constitution of her situation entails the suppression of woman's freedom, not its confirmation.

To begin with, woman lacks relations of equality with man. To the significant figures in her world – father and husband especially, but also priest, doctor, etc. – she is an inferior, not an equal. Subtending these direct, personal relations in which she experiences her objectification, woman also encounters as a major structure of her situation what we might call a set of social institutions. It is these institutions which function analogously to natural forces in perpetuating her immanence. If all that took place between man and woman was a Hegelian (or Sartrean) struggle of consciousnesses between two human beings, one of whom happened to be male and the other female, we could not anticipate which one of them would win and remain a subject, making the other an object. However, if we examine the relations of a *husband* and a *wife*, then it is very different. For the institution of marriage in all its aspects – legal, economic, cultural, etc. – has formed in advance for the protagonists their own relation of inequality. As Beauvoir points out in a strikingly unSartrean passage,

> it is not as single individuals that human beings are to be defined in the first place; men and women have never stood opposed to each other in single combat; the couple is an original *Mitsein*; and as such it always appears as a permanent or temporary element in a larger collectivity. (TSS 67–8; 35)

The relations of any particular couple are embedded in the relations of the larger collectivity and they are delimited by it. Thus, as Beauvoir also points out, although woman's situation and history are 'man made', *individual* men may be as much the victims of what has become an impersonal system of forces as are women:

> A colonial administrator has no possibility of behaving well towards the natives, nor a general towards his soldiers; the only solution is to be neither a colonist nor a military chief; but a man could not stop himself from being a man. So there he is, guilty in spite of himself and oppressed by this fault which he himself has not committed... The evil does not originate from individual perversity... it arises from *a situation against which all individual action is powerless.* (TSS 732–3; 723–4, my emphasis)

In other words, the result of multiple, free (male) human action throughout history has been to create a set of institutions which function as a real limit on freedom, of either men or women. The process of change will thus have to commence from the radical modification of the institutional aspects of woman's situation. Marriage, motherhood, her exclusion from economic and other kinds of activity, all will have to be extensively transformed. What the Soviet Union once promised still offers a vision of such a world of equality (TSS 733–4; 724–5), and Beauvoir is optimistic that, should women attain economic and social equality, in time an 'inner metamorphosis' will also take place (TSS 738; 729). Liberation is not a matter of individual choice to begin with, but of complex social processes which modify woman's situation until the point is reached where a free – but not wholly autonomous – subjectivity can come into play.

Towards the end of the book, Beauvoir examines the 'independent woman' (TSS 689–724; 679–715). She is the new professional woman, who has no need of a man to support her. In some ways she is the harbinger of the free woman of the future. But in fact she experiences her life as a series of irresolvable conflicts between her 'human' freedom and her 'feminine' destiny. For finally, Beauvoir concludes, woman's oppression cannot be overcome except within the framework of the fuller abolition of human oppression. Thus, although she criticizes the orthodox Marxist account for its overly economistic explanation of woman's oppression (TSS 84–91; 53–60),[29] Beauvoir concludes *The Second Sex* with an extended quotation from Marx's 'Economic and Philosophical Manuscripts'[30] concerning the relations between the sexes, followed by an appeal 'to establish the reign of liberty in the midst of the world of the given' (TSS 741; 732).

In so far as woman's oppressive situation is not simply individual but is an impersonal complex of social institutions, we can talk of woman's situation as a *general* one. From a Sartrean perspective this raises certain difficulties. For Sartre, since situations are uniquely constituted, we could not talk of a general situation; nor could we judge one situation to be more free or to be preferable to another. Like Sartre, Beauvoir also wishes to start from individual experience. The 'lived experience' of woman's situation, examined in Volume II, is, of course, *individually* lived. Extensive citations from women's memoirs, novels, etc., give her account an intensely personal and subjective foundation. Yet, at the same time, Beauvoir wants also to be able to evaluate that experience as a whole. The very isolation to which women are condemned precludes each from seeing the generality of her situation. But, Beauvoir insists, not only can we generalize about woman's situation, we can also *judge* between her situation and that of man:

> all comparisons are idle which purport to show that woman is superior, inferior, or equal to man: their situations are profoundly different. If we compare these actual situations, we see clearly that the man's is far preferable; that is to say, he has many more concrete opportunities to project his freedom in the world. (TSS 638; 627)

In *The Ethics of Ambiguity* Beauvoir had already posed more clearly than Sartre the problem of the intelligibility of social existence and the same problem is posed, yet again, by the position she now takes in *The Second Sex*. Human experience is individual experience but it also has *generality* – as becomes especially clear in the experience of immanence. We thus need a theory which can encompass both subjectivity and the objective givens of human existence – a theory of socially mediated subjectivity such as is precluded by Sartre's disjunction of being in-itself and being for-itself and the autonomy he grants to consciousness. In so far as Beauvoir's account of woman's situation as one of immanence involves the admission that free consciousness, the for-itself, can be penetrated by the objectivity of the in-itself, it implies a notion of the subject as socially embedded and intersubjective, and not as autonomous. It implies also a notion of embodied subjectivity which is significantly different from Sartre's account of embodiment in

Being and Nothingness, and which puts into question Sartre's division of being into two different and incommunicable regions.

Woman's situation: the body

Beauvoir's description of the institutions which constitute woman's situation is impressively thorough. But by itself it does not answer the question she had posed at the beginning of the book: *why* has man been able to impose such an oppressive situation on woman? She has shown us how woman's inequality and otherness are sustained, but this does not explain why they are possible in the first place. To explain why, she argues, we need also to look at the biological differences between the sexes, even though these differences do not in themselves constitute a 'destiny'.

Mortality, as Sartre had pointed out, is one of the necessary structures of human existence. 'Were he immortal', Beauvoir paraphrases, 'an existent would no longer be what we call a man' (TSS 39; 7). Yet, she again adds, each individual man, though mortal, requires an infinite future – a future which only other free men can give him. Concretely what this means is that each individual freedom requires 'the perpetuation of the species'. Thus, she concludes, 'we can regard the phenomenon of reproduction as ontologically founded'. Human existence is no more possible without reproduction than it is without death, and a society which ceased to reproduce itself would be a society in which individual projects would be meaningless.

Individual women, especially today, may have the choice not to reproduce; and reproduction is as much a social as a biological process. But even so, it is an inescapable fact, a basic 'given' of any woman's situation, that she has a different physiology from a man's, a physiology geared to the role of her sex in the perpetuation of the species. Beauvoir repeatedly stresses that biological facts have no significance beyond the values which man chooses to give them. For example, although woman *is* physically weaker than man, having 'less muscular strength', her weakness only has a meaning in a humanly created context (TSS 66–7; 34). Yet this is not to deny that woman's biology does perhaps predispose her for immanence: her physical powers are less than those of man and, Beauvoir concludes, woman consequently tends to have a less firm 'grasp on the world'. Furthermore, through her reproductive function itself, she is the victim of natural forces over which she has no control. Although woman's body is not by itself sufficient to 'define' her as woman, it is 'an essential element of the situation she occupies in the world' (TSS 69; 37). Biological givens do not necessarily condemn woman to subordination, but they 'play a part of the first rank' in woman's history and 'are one of the keys to the understanding of woman' (TSS 65; 32).

Through her body, Beauvoir argues, woman is condemned to experience a conflict which man does not experience, 'the conflict between species and individual' (TSS 63; 30). Woman, a human existent capable of transcendence, is condemned to consume a significant amount of her time and energy in 'natural functions'.[31] These are necessary for the perpetuation of the species and for there to be freedoms which open on to an infinite future, but according to Beauvoir they involve no *project*. Menstruation, pregnancy, childbirth and lactation are not *activities*, she insists; woman cannot affirm her existence through them. 'Her misfortune is to have been biologically destined for the repetition of Life' (TSS 96; 64), while man's role in perpetuating the species as a producer and a defender has always involved more than 'vital process', and has required of him 'actions which transcend his animal condition' (TSS 95 ff; 63 ff). Here, claims Beauvoir, is the 'key' to the mystery of woman's Otherness. Production and risking one's life in warfare are free affirmations of existence, but the animal function of reproducing the species is not.

There is then, according to Beauvoir, a biological differentiation which provides a basis for the social construction of inequality between the sexes. Women, of course, are not only wombs. They are capable of free existence. But the fact that they must affirm their freedom beyond or in spite of their reproductive function puts them at a disadvantage – a disadvantage upon which men have capitalized. Man has taken advantage of woman's partial immanence to impose upon her a condition of greater immanence. Woman, having submitted passively to her 'biological fate', has found herself also condemned to incarceration in the endless cycle of domestic labour, which is the kind of activity most compatible with maternity. Across the centuries she has been condemned to the cycle of household tasks, effectively unchanging, which have excluded her from creative and transcendent activity. Thus, in Beauvoir's account of woman's situation, the female body is seen as a real and general obstacle to freedom, an objective 'given', upon which man has been able to construct the institutions that constitute her oppression.

As an explanation of the origin of woman's oppression, Beauvoir's analysis is not wholly compelling. For, as later feminists have pointed out,[32] she repeatedly undervalues that element of freedom which can be present in parenthood and the activities associated with it. In so doing, she also tends to valorize the male-biased dualisms in Western thought which identify the masculine with the active and the rational, and the female with the passive and the corporeal. However, the importance of Beauvoir's account lies less in its adequacy as an explanation of woman's oppression *per se* than in what it implies more generally about the relation of freedom and subjectivity to embodiment. For while much of her discussion focuses on the female body, it also implies a more general reformulation of the account of the body which Sartre had offered.

For Sartre, it will be recalled, there are two primary 'aspects' to the body, involving two different and 'incommunicable' levels of being. These are my body-for-others (my body as object), and my body-for-me (my body as consciousness). In so far as my body has objectivity, for Sartre, its objectivity comes to me through other freedoms. It is only through the mediation of the Other – prototypically through the look – that I grasp my body as an objective structure of my being. Without such mediation I simply live my body-for-me as my point of view, as integral to my project. Although Beauvoir describes the body which concretely exists as 'the body lived by the subject' (TSS 69; 38), this is not identical with Sartre's body-for-me. Woman's relation to her body cannot be subsumed under Sartre's two aspects. For woman encounters her lived body as having an objectivity which is not mediated by another consciousness. She discovers her body as 'an obscure alien thing', from which biological processes obtrude without her consent:

> She is of all mammalian females at once the one who is most profoundly alienated and the one who most violently resists this alienation; in no other is the enslavement of the organism to reproduction more imperious, or more unwillingly accepted. (TSS 64; 32)

Although shame, modesty, etc., arise from woman's relation to her body in the presence of others, what Beauvoir is describing is an objectivity that the body has irrespective of such interpersonal or social experiences. Woman's body *is* nature, the demands of the species; it is, in short, Sartre's in-itself, as well as a body for-others. Furthermore, woman's body cannot have the non-reflective quality of Sartre's body-for-me. Woman cannot simply live her body as her point of view, for she continually encounters it as other than herself. 'Woman, like man, *is* her body: but her body is something other than herself' (TSS 61; 29). If woman says, 'I am my body',[33] the statement is complex. For she would surely have to say also, 'I am partly other than myself'. Beauvoir's woman is not a Sartrean freedom, a for-itself for whom the particularities of the body are merely facticities. She is a real compound of materiality and consciousness. At various points in the text Beauvoir states this very clearly, although she does not attempt to elucidate the ontological implications of such a view. For example, she writes

> To be present in the world implies strictly that there exists a body which is *at the same time* a thing in the world and a point of view on this world. (TSS 39; 7, my emphasis)

Although woman experiences the thinghood of the body more profoundly than man, much of Beauvoir's account of woman's body describes more generally the 'ambiguity' of all human existence as materiality *and* consciousness, necessity *and* freedom. As she puts it in one passage,

> man is, like woman, flesh, therefore a passivity, the plaything of his hormones and the species, the restless prey of his desires. And she is, like him, in the midst of carnal fever, consent, voluntary giving, activity; they live out, each in their own manner, the strange ambiguity of existence made body. (TSS 737; 728)

Woman's greater predisposition to immanence lies in her more pervasive subordination to the exigencies of the body – a subordination which man has built upon in constructing her oppression. Yet men also are not free of such ambiguity.

Beauvoir does not, unfortunately, work out the broader philosophical implications of such a notion of ambiguous existence. It is to Merleau-Ponty's philosophy (itself frequently described as a philosophy of ambiguity), that we must turn for an ontology which will support her descriptions. Beauvoir herself perhaps recognized as much. For citing Merleau-Ponty's view that, 'the body is generality' at one point, she expands on it in the following unSartrean manner:

> Across the separation of existents, existence is all one: it makes itself manifest in analogous organisms; therefore there will be constants

in the relation of the ontological to the sexual. At a given epoch, the techniques, the economic and social structure, of a collectivity will reveal an identical world to all its members: there will also be a constant relation of sexuality to social forms; analogous individuals, placed in analogous conditions, will take from what is given analogous significations. This analogy does not establish a rigorous universality, but it does enable us to rediscover general types within individual histories. (TSS 78; 46–7)

Through the notion of the generality of the body, not only the question of woman's oppression but the philosophical difficulties which Sartreanism had raised for Beauvoir can be addressed. The problem of the radical separation of situations and the concomitant problem of social and historical intelligibility – problems with which we have also seen Beauvoir struggling in her ethical essays – become less acute if, through the generality of the body, we each encounter an 'analogous' condition. Moreover, it becomes possible to address more fully the question of the simultaneous separateness and interdependence of freedoms. It becomes possible to rethink the notion of the subject in full recognition of what 'encumbers' it, and yet to do so without reducing it to a mere 'effect'.

4

Merleau-Ponty: situation and social world

Merleau-Ponty was born in the same year as Beauvoir (1908), and also studied philosophy at the Ecole Normale Supérieure in the late 1920s. Like Beauvoir and Sartre he developed an interest in phenomenology as an alternative to the dominant idealist philosophy of Brunschvicg. It was, however, only during the German Occupation that he came to know Sartre and Beauvoir well: all three, pushed by events into an attempt at activism, participated in a rather short-lived intellectuals' Resistance group, 'Socialisme et Liberté'.[1] Thereafter they remained in close contact and planned to found a journal together after the War.

That journal, *Les Temps Modernes*, began monthly publication in October 1945, with Sartre as its editor, Merleau-Ponty its political editor and Beauvoir an active member of its small editorial board. The journal treated issues of politics, culture and philosophy. Its editorial policy was defined as socialist and (from 1946) anti-colonialist, while remaining firmly independent of the French Communist Party. To the latter it offered a 'critical support' which was not received with gratitude.[2] Later, in the cold war atmosphere of the early 1950s, a quarrel took place. Merleau-Ponty left the journal in 1952, rejecting as now impossible, in such a polarized world, a continued commitment to even a 'humanist' Marxism. Three years later, in making public his rejection of Marxism,[3] he trenchantly attacked not only Sartre's politics (which were at this time more firmly in support of the communists), but also the philosophy which, he claimed, underlay those politics. But although the quarrel became heated only in 1955 and in a primarily political form, the philosophical divergences were present from the very start. We can already see them in Merleau-Ponty's work of 1945, the *Phenomenology of Perception*, the work which will be the main focus of this chapter.

Although Sartre is not frequently mentioned by name, much of the final third of the *Phenomenology* should be read as critique of *Being and Nothingness*. Beauvoir appears to have recognized this. For in her review of Merleau-Ponty's book, published in the second issue of *Les Temps Modernes*, she described their divergences as follows:

> While Sartre, in *Being and Nothingness*, emphasises above all the opposition of for-itself and in-itself, the nihilating power of consciousness in the face of being and its absolute freedom, Merleau-Ponty on the contrary applies himself to describing the concrete character of the subject who is never, according to him, a pure for-itself ... For Merleau-Ponty my history is incarnated in a body which possesses a certain generality, a relation to the world anterior to myself, and this is why this body is opaque to reflection, and why my consciousness discovers itself to be 'engorged with the sensible'. It is not a pure for-itself, or, to use Hegel's phrase which Sartre has taken up, a hole in being; but rather 'a hollow, a fold, which has been made and which can be unmade'.[4]

In this comparison, Beauvoir comes to the heart of the divergence between Sartre and Merleau-Ponty. Against Sartre's opposition of for-itself and in-itself Merleau-Ponty argues for what has been described as a 'monistic ontology'.[5] There is, for Merleau-Ponty, no fundamental bifurcation of Being into the 'regions' of consciousness and the inert. There is, rather, an undifferentiated or 'general' Being, a 'primordial layer where both things and ideas come into being' which is 'on this side of the ideas of subject and object' (PP 219). Thus for Merleau-Ponty, unlike Sartre, a 'pure for-itself', with an 'absolute freedom' is an impossibility. Moreover, since all human action is rooted in this primordial layer, philosophizing itself can never be an autonomous activity. Philosophical questioning is not, as Sartre had claimed, the proof that man is the unique source of nothingness. On the contrary, Merleau-Ponty describes a good philosophy as one which reflects on its *own* inescapable embeddedness in primordial Being; one whose efforts 'are concentrated upon again finding a primitive contact with the world, and endowing that contact with a philosophical status' (PP vii).

In 1945 Beauvoir put her finger on the fundamental divergence between the philosophies of Sartre and Merleau-Ponty. She refrained, however, from making any public judgement between the two in her review. In a loud silence, she passed on to other matters. A decade later, replying to Merleau-Ponty's attack on Sartre,[6] Beauvoir's main defence of Sartre at the philosophical level was simply that Merleau-Ponty had misread him. Against Merleau-Ponty's reading, Beauvoir now claimed that Sartre's was not 'a philosophy of the subject',[7] but a philosophy of embodied subjectivity, of intersubjectivity, of situation. Merleau-Ponty, Beauvoir insisted, had created a 'pseudo-Sartrism' and attacked it for political purposes – as a means of discrediting Sartre's support for the Communist Party and of justifying his own new position of 'a-communism'.

What Beauvoir's argument implied was not that Merleau-Ponty's own philosophy was flawed, but that Sartre's was defensible because it was so *similar* to Merleau-Ponty's on all the important points. But although Beauvoir quoted numerous passages from *Being and Nothingness* to show that Merleau-Ponty had wilfully misread Sartre, her case is not a convincing one. As we have seen, Beauvoir herself had already reformulated Sartre's thought in radically new ways in the 1940s, and she had borrowed considerably from Merleau-Ponty in doing so. Thus her 1955 defence of Sartre against Merleau-Ponty involved, ironically, a reading of Sartre refracted through the lenses of her own prior reading of Merleau-Ponty. As will become apparent, those elements of Beauvoir's theory which cannot be adequately grounded in Sartre's early philosophy – the 'interdependence of freedoms' or *Mitsein*, immanence, social institution, the generality of situations and of the body – in short what we might call a philosophy of the socially situated subject, can be better anchored in Merleau-Ponty's phenomenological ontology. Furthermore, Sartre himself was to take up certain aspects of Merleau-Ponty's thought as he became increasingly concerned with problems of social existence and history in the late 1950s.

There are, of course, profound 'family resemblances' between the French existentialists. But Merleau-Ponty's philosophy remains distinct not only from Sartre's but also from Marcel's. However, at first glance his philosophy appears to share much with the latter's, to which he explicitly acknowledged an intellectual debt.[8] It was, he suggested, especially in Marcel's treatment of the theme of 'incarnation' – the notion that 'I am my body' – that his generation found the central premise for their attack on the dominant 'idealism', epitomized by

Brunschvicg. For the idea of incarnation involved, Merleau-Ponty claimed, 'a new way of thinking'. In particular, it implied that the philosopher could not conceive of himself as a detached 'spectator' of reality, but was always a situated participant. It also raised as a central problem the relationship of the self with the other and it raised the question of 'history' since, 'the theme of history is ... at bottom the same as the theme of the other'.

Marcel's treatment of the other and of history is, we saw, far from adequate. Merleau-Ponty's meditations on these themes are richer by far. They involve what can best be viewed as a creative transcendence of Marcel's notions of embodiment and situation. Like Marcel, Merleau-Ponty begins by distinguishing man's relation to his body from the relation of a consciousness to an object. An external object 'stands before me', he says, 'but I am not in front of my body, I am in it, *or rather I am it*'(PP 150, my emphasis). For Merleau-Ponty, as for Marcel, to exist is to be one's body; and to be one's body is to be a body-subject, a unity which precedes the dichotomies of mind and body, subject and object, being for-itself and being in-itself.

However, we should not let these affinities mask the significant divergences in their thought. For Marcel, to say that I participate in Being as a body-subject is to say that my relation to Being is immediate and that it is destroyed if I try to subject it to the *mediating* activity of rational scrutiny: my participation in Being is simply 'mystery'. For Merleau-Ponty, in contrast, the inquiry must begin where Marcel leaves off. It will not suffice simply to posit a mysterious harmony between myself and the world which is beyond scrutiny. Such a harmony can be posited only on the basis of Catholic faith, which implies a dogmatic closure of inquiry (SNS 74 ff). The concept of the 'body-subject' involves, for Merleau-Ponty, not a mysterious harmony with Being, but a *paradoxical* and *ambiguous* relationship, in which consciousness and materiality, subjectivity and the world of 'things' are co-extensive. Moreover this relationship is open to scrutiny and to philosophical investigation.

It will not do, according to Merleau-Ponty, to dismiss what Marcel called the order of 'objectivity', the world of causally ordered things, as something which intrudes upon us only through our own failures, through what Marcel had called acts of 'desertion'. Nor should the world of things be conceived as self-sufficient being in-itself, nihilated by an antithetical being purely for-itself. Because, Merleau-Ponty argues, our existence is inseparable from our inherence in the world of things, subjectivity and objectivity are to be distinguished only as differentiations *within* one 'primordial being'. As a body-subject man is not a consciousness 'in' an objective body, but another kind of being, *neither* for-itself nor in-itself. The body, says Merleau-Ponty, 'forms between the pure subject and the object *a third genus of being*', in which 'the subject loses its purity and its transparency' (PP 350, my emphasis).

It is in elaborating this notion of an 'impure' subject that Merleau-Ponty, without ever wholly abandoning the notion of the subject as the centre of effective action, overcomes the individualism of the Cartesian (and Sartrean) subject and initiates a philosophy of the social subject. In so doing, as we shall see, he develops a profound, if uncomfortable, synthesis of the philosophy of the subject with Marxism.

Embodiment and the 'Primacy of Perception'

In order to elucidate our existence as impure, embodied subjects, Merleau-Ponty begins from our experience of the sensible world, particularly from perception. For perception itself is what he calls a 'third' or intermediate experience, neither objective nor subjective, and which neither empiricism nor idealism has been able to grasp in its irreducibilty.[9] When, for example, I see that a patch of the carpet is 'red'(PP 4 ff), my perception is not explicable simply as a physico-chemical response to visual stimuli; for I see the patch *qualitatively*. It is 'an element in a spatial configuration'; it is textured ('woolly') and 'the meaning of the word "patch" is provided by my previous experience'. In other words, perception is not, as empiricist theory would have it, only a passive reception of external stimuli; it is, rather, 'a process of integration in which the text of the external world is not so much copied as constituted' (PP 9).[10]

On the other hand, idealism – Merleau-Ponty also calls it 'intellectualism' – fails equally to explain what is involved in such a perception. For the possibility of 'constitution' does not involve, as Descartes thought, an act of judgement or a mental hypothesis on the part of a 'constituting consciousness'. Descartes tells us (in his second 'Meditation'), that when I look out of my window, strictly speaking, what I see passing in the street are 'hats and coats', and it is only by an act of *judgement* that I say 'I see men' (PP 32 ff). In this account, perception *per se* does not give us access to truth. For 'intellectualists', such as Descartes, '[p]erception becomes an "interpretation" of the signs that our senses provide in accordance with the bodily *stimuli*, a "hypothesis" that mind evolves to "explain its impressions to itself"'. Against this explanation, Merleau-Ponty argues that intellectualism, like empiricism, implies an overly dualistic ontology. For both there is a world of objects and qualities which I passively receive as sense stimuli. For empiricism these directly give me truth, while for intellectualism mind, God-like, interprets the stimuli to create truth. But what neither is able to grasp is perceptual truth as something neither passively received nor actively constructed, but *sui generis*, a *real phenomenon* which is not reducible to any other.

Merleau-Ponty does not, of course, wish to deny *all* reality to Sartre's (and Hegel's) distinction between being for-itself and in-itself. Rather, what he wishes to show is that these concepts grasp reality in an abstract, one-sided manner. It is impossible to think of one aspect without the other, for both imply the unity of Being which precedes them. For Sartre, being in-itself simply is, while being for-itself, as 'the pure nihilation of the in-itself', is self-determining. For Merleau–Ponty, however, not only do they inhere in one Being; they are in everyday experience generally indistinguishable. It is only from the perspective of intellectualism, the 'high-altitude' thinking of a 'constituting consciousness', that they have the appearance of being radically distinct. In our everyday perceptual experience of the world, perceiver and perceived are not being for-itself and being in-itself, nor subject and object. They form, rather, a kind of 'gestalt' or a 'system' in which each calls the other into being:

> In perception we do not think the object and we do not think ourselves thinking it ... In this originary layer of sense experience which is discovered only provided that we really coincide with the act of perception and break with the critical attitude, I live the unity of the subject and the intersensory unity of the thing, and do not conceive them after the fashion of analytical reflection and science. (PP 238–9)

The 'subject of sensation' is neither a Cartesian *cogito*, nor a Sartrean for-itself. For, writes Merleau-Ponty:

> he need not be a pure nothingness with no terrestrial weight. That would be necessary only if, like constituting consciousness, he had

to be present everywhere at the same time, co-extensive with being, and in process of thinking the truth of the universe. (PP 215)

But if the 'subject of sensation' is not a 'pure nothingness', neither can he perceive 'pure being'. For each of us brings to what we perceive 'sediments' from our previous experience, which preclude us from ever grasping it as a pure, unmediated, in-itself. It is through my own intentionality that I create 'the spectacle perceived'. But this intentionality is not to be confused with a traditional constituting consciousness. Rather, it is an 'operative intentionality' (PP xviii), in which I am a kind of conduit for a more general perceptual experience. As a *sentient* subject I am, says Merleau-Ponty, 'a repository filled with natural powers at which I am the first to be filled with wonder'. He concludes with the words Beauvoir cites in her review, 'I am not, therefore, in Hegel's phrase, "a hole in being", but a hollow, a fold, which has been made and which can be unmade' (PP 215).

Perception implies always a point of view, thus that I am *situated* in Being. Since I am immersed in what I perceive, I do not wholly control the field which 'my' perception organizes around me. What I perceive has always a certain autonomy, a 'generality' which escapes me. There is an 'anonymity' to perception and to other sensory experiences which means that they are never completely 'mine'. Rather, in the experience of sensation I discover 'a modality of general existence ... which runs through me without my being its author'(PP 216). Merleau-Ponty uses the term the One (*L'On*) to describe this anonymous Being which runs through my own embodied being. But although this would appear to be a translation of Heidegger's notion, *das Man*, its connotations are very different: the *One* does not designate an inauthentic submersion in the collectivity, but the generality of Being which grounds intersubjective communication. Strictly speaking, Merleau-Ponty tells us, 'I ought to say that *one* perceives in me, and not that I perceive' (PP 215). The perceiving self, he insists, 'is not myself as an autonomous subject, but myself in so far as I have a body and am able to "look"'(PP 240). But if such a self is not a Sartrean for-itself, neither is it a 'constituted' self, or an 'effect', as for example Foucault or Lacan would argue.

Ontology of situations

The body, we saw, is 'a third genus of being', neither for-itself nor in-itself but irreducible. Situations are also, for Merleau-Ponty, a third genus and, as such, situations are real entities. They are not in the last instance reducible to material milieux or to conjunctures of structures. But nor are they constituted by consciousness. Sartre, it will be recalled, had played with the possibility of such a third genus of being in *Being and Nothingness*, when he described situations as a *common product*. But he did not sustain this line of exploration, and ultimately he gave priority to consciousness in the constitution of situations. For Merleau-Ponty, however, situations are, like the body, irreducible expressions of 'primordial being'.

Perception, we have already seen, implies both an embodied and a situated subject. It is my situation, even in the most minimal sense of the spatial location of my body, that gives me my particular viewpoint on things. This viewpoint does not, however, give me objective space or size. Lived, situated perspective, for example, does not conform to the rules of geometry, but involves also my perception of the thing within my particular field of vision (PP 48).[11] However, even if we try to hold aside for now (as far as is possible) what Merleau-Ponty calls the 'human setting'(PP 136), situated perception implies far more than mere spatiality. For the things that we perceive also have such qualities as colour, texture, weight – all of which we 'perceive' together in the thing.

As with spatiality, these qualities are neither subjective nor objective: colours, for example, are not autonomous qualities. 'A colour is never merely a colour, but the colour of a certain object' (PP 313); and in seeing the woolly colour of the carpet, I will also 'see' it as soft. In addition, my perceptual situation will always include a world of both personal and social meanings. For example, the woolly softness of the carpet may signify comfort, perhaps also luxury. Even to perceive a non-humanly made thing is to bring to it social meanings. For Merleau-Ponty, Sartre's would-be climber at the foot of the crag would bring to his situation not only the individual project of climbing the crag but also *social* values, such as perhaps the healthiness of the outdoor life, or the virtue of endurance.

When, in addition, we examine the social dimensions of a primary perceptual situation we also see very clearly, intertwined with them, its temporal dimensions. 'Recollections' and 'sediments' – habitual ways of perceiving, originating in my prior perceptual experience and my general social existence – are part of what I bring to any situation. I also bring a future. For my perception involves my own movement towards a future, my project. Merleau-Ponty describes the drawing together of these multiple dimensions of a perceptual situation in the notion of an 'intentional arc' which 'subtends' perception. It is such an arc, he says, 'which projects round about us our past, our future, our human setting, our physical situation, our ideological situation, and moral situation, or rather which results in our being situated in all these respects' (PP 136). The arc metaphor suggests that situations are not rigid entities, but are always in flux. Forming and re-forming, each is in part structured by the sediments of prior situations, while also merging into and structuring future ones. It follows that for Merleau-Ponty situated action can never be wholly free action. Situated action involves a complex relation of freedom and necessity, in which situations are transcended and yet, as we will see, also impose their own significations on those who transcend them.

Merleau-Ponty remarks at one point that, 'ambiguity is of the essence of human existence and everything we live or think has always several meanings' (PP 169).[12] Because it synthesizes past and future, perceiver and perceived, self and social world, etc., there can be no *one* determinate meaning – or *sens*[13] – to the situation. But ambiguity can also involve more than the presence of multiple or indeterminate meanings in a situation. In the above passage Merleau-Ponty uses the word *équivoque* to denote ambiguity. Elsewhere, however, he uses the term *ambiguïté*, and this implies *contradictory* meanings. It is this latter kind of ambiguity which leads Merleau-Ponty also to talk of the 'tension' of human existence, and to develop not merely an ontology of situations but a *dialectical* ontology of situations.

There is a paradox in human existence which is central to Merleau-Ponty's philosophy. On the one hand, Being is One, and it runs through us. Individual existence inheres in a unitary, primordial Being. On the other hand, Being is not a static plenum which engulfs us in passive harmony. Although man is not, for Merleau-Ponty, a 'hole in being', he is still a 'hollow'. In less metaphorical language, while not pure consciousness man still has a capacity to differentiate himself, to stand out from the Being which runs through him. In man, Being ceases wholly to coincide with itself. Man is, as Merleau-Ponty puts it in an essay on Hegel, 'a place of unrest' (SNS 65–6).[14] For man transcends Being and yet is transcended by it. He is, in short, the point of origin of a tension, of a movement of contradiction, or a dialectic, in Being. In this dialectic, both human transcendence and finitude are revealed.

For Merleau-Ponty (as for Beauvoir and Sartre) human existence is transcendence: we take up and transform situations through our own projects. However, since there is no pure for-itself, transcendence is a *reciprocal* movement between man and world; and it is, contrary to Sartre's notion of nihilation, only a partial movement, what we might call an internal disturbance, within the primordial unity of Being. Since it is a reciprocal movement, transcendence may be described, for Merleau-Ponty, beginning from either pole, from man or world.

Beginning from the pole of embodied subjectivity, of the project, Merleau-Ponty writes as follows:

> Existence ... is the very process whereby the hitherto meaningless takes on meaning ... We shall give the name transcendence to this movement through which existence takes up for its own purposes and transforms [an actual] situation. Precisely because it is transcendence, existence never utterly outruns anything, for in that case the tension which is essential to it would disappear. (PP 169)

From the gestures of the body, to language, to cultural artefacts, ways of producing and institutions, all that pertains to human existence is transcendence; it perpetually creates meaning, meaning which is never complete but which opens on to the future.

However, such a movement of transcendence also perpetually encounters limits. It is here, at the other pole, emphasizing the transcendence of the world over the project, that Merleau-Ponty's account of the project diverges most radically from Sartre's. For Sartre facticity is not a limit on freedom, except in so far as I attempt in bad faith to become 'self-cause'. For Merleau-Ponty, the limits I encounter in the world do not arise from the futile attempt to be self-cause. Nor – although they indicate our finitude – are they necessarily to be encountered as tragic. While the transcendence of the world perpetually delimits individual existence and reveals its finitude, such delimitation may be experienced in two ways: either as an enrichment of individual existence, or as its alienation or negation.

'My life', says Merleau-Ponty, considering the first of the possibilities, 'is constantly thrown headlong into *transcendent things* and passes *wholly outside me*'. Discussing his own project – writing the *Phenomenology* – he continues: 'This book, once begun, is not a certain set of ideas; it constitutes for me an open situation ... in which I struggle blindly on until, as if miraculously, *thoughts and words become organised by themselves*' (PP 369, my emphases). Our finitude is, in such an instance, the source of our inherence in a world which, while transcending us, furthers our transcendence.

However, it is also possible to encounter the transcendence of the world as a threat. This occurs when I withdraw into consciousness and attempt to take a de-situated, spectator's view: the more I define myself as a pure subjectivity, the more I become threatened by the objectivity of the world which I then confront. There *is* a problem of the 'genuine-in-itself-for-us'. But it appears only when we step back from our 'ordinary preoccupations'. The 'thing' is then 'hostile and alien, no longer an interlocutor, but a resolutely silent Other' (PP 322; also SNS 28–9). Thus Sartre's account of the relations of being for-itself and in-itself is not wholly erroneous; but it tells only half the story. The relation of man and world is one of reciprocal affirmation and negation, a relation which we may call not only ambiguous or paradoxical, but also *dialectical* – because it involves a movement of contradictory yet mutually supporting transcendences. 'The dialectic', Merleau-Ponty writes in the *Phenomenology*,

> is the tending [*la tension*] of an existence towards another existence which denies it, and yet without which it is not sustained [*elle ne se soutient pas*]. (PP 167–8)

In other words, what is at issue here is not a mere *identity* of opposites, but a movement whose source lies in a relation of interdependence and opposition.

For Merleau-Ponty dialectics are multiple, present in all facets of human existence. Even the simplest perceptions are dialectical movements, for at a minimum, my perceptual encounter with the thing perceived brings past and future into a relation in which each both 'denies' and 'sustains' the other and in which new meanings are brought forth: '[b]y taking up a present, I recover possession of and transform my past... But I do so only by committing myself somewhere else' (PP 455).

Moreover, for Merleau-Ponty perception must always carry *social* meanings. In the *Phenomenology*, Merleau-Ponty makes a distinction for purposes of exposition between the 'natural world', that is, the world of perceptible 'things', and the 'social' or 'human' world. But in reality, he insists, we never experience these worlds as distinct, for there is a social context which we bring to any perception. We are, at any moment, situated in both the natural and the human worlds, and we not only perceive but also act in various ways on and in these inseparable worlds. Thus existence is dialectical in many and complex ways. Accordingly, in the next sections, I will cease trying to hold the human world in abeyance and will deal more fully with Merleau-Ponty's account of human relations.

Intersubjective situations

As body-subjects, we each inhere in the generality and anonymity of Being, in the One. It follows, for Merleau-Ponty, that some kind of general relation between us must be a given of human existence. The interrelation of human existences does not have to be created from a position of initial separation: it is part of what it is to be human. However, in so far as we are each a 'place of unrest', a nihilating movement within Being, it is also open to us to engage in mutual self-nihilation, of the kind Sartre had described. Social existence is, *par excellence*, the realm of the dialectic for Merleau-Ponty: men cannot but always have the possibility both to deny and sustain each other.

In encountering another person I can experience both a shared, or 'intersubjective' existence *and* a negating Other. Intersubjectivity (which I will discuss first) exists in so far as I and another are both situated in, perceive and can communicate about the same natural and social world. We cannot ever have the identical perception, since we are separate existences, each a body-subject with its own unique situation. Yet there can be such overlap between our perceptions as to create between us an 'interworld'(PP 357), a primordial communication. Thus intersubjectivity need not presuppose a 'collective consciousness', such as Sartre had argued must be implied by the notion of *Mitsein*.

Merleau-Ponty exemplifies this notion of intersubjectivity as born of a common inherence in Being in a discussion of two people looking at a landscape. When my friend Paul and I look at the landscape, must we suppose 'that we each have private sensations, a knowledge of things that is for ever incommunicable?' Merleau-Ponty replies that this is not the case. We can communicate, and the basis for our communication is not only our speech, our gestures, but a shared *vision* of the landscape:

> When I think of Paul I do not think of a flow of private sensations indirectly mediated to mine through interposed signs, but of

some-one who has a living experience of the same world as mine, as well as the same history, and with whom I am *in communication through that world and that history*... It is precisely because [it]... is my own view of the landscape, that I enjoy possession of the landscape itself, and the landscape for Paul as well as me. Both universality and the world lie at the core of individuality and the subject. (PP 405–6, my emphases)

In this account, far from the other person threatening to make my situation disintegrate around me, he (or she) enriches it, and is experienced as confirming my own perceptions. In this relationship we are *equals*, such as Beauvoir had described in her account of interdependent freedoms.

The question of intersubjectivity also takes us beyond our shared perceptions of the natural world to 'the perception of other people'. Here, language plays a crucial role – and especially dialogue:

In the experience of dialogue, there is constituted between the other person and myself a common ground; my thought and his are interwoven into a single fabric, my words and those of my interlocutor are called forth by the state of the discussion, and they are inserted into a shared operation of which neither of us is the creator ... We are collaborators for each other in perfect reciprocity. Our perspectives merge into each other, and we co-exist through a common world. (PP 354)

In this example, intersubjectivity involves an experience of being transcended, but by our common creation. In a dialogue we actively produce that which transcends us: neither of us is, finally, the 'creator' of this new 'fabric'; it creates itself through us, just as sensation 'runs through us'. Moreover, the transcendent here is not a threat to our own personal transcendences – it is rather their prolongation. In this prolongation our reciprocity comes to have real existence: there comes into being a *third* existent – the dialogue – which escapes us both in its generality. Thus Beauvoir's problem – that 'two freedoms which seem to exclude each other must be able to hold themselves face to face' (PC 83) – is not a problem for Merleau-Ponty because he does not start with pure freedoms.

The generality of Being which runs through us mediates our individual perceptions and thoughts. It transcends them in new existents, which we have launched together and to which we both share access. Intersubjectivity does not involve a total identity of perceptions or thoughts, but the possibility of sharing – each from our own particular situation – a 'common ground' because we both pertain to the generality of Being. As Merleau-Ponty summed up these ideas, shortly after the *Phenomenology* was published:

> I will never know how you see red, and you will never know how I see it; but this separation of consciousness is recognised only after a failure of communication, and our first move is to believe in an undivided being between us. *There is no reason to treat this primordial communication as an illusion* ... In the perception of another, I find myself in relation with another 'myself', who is, in principle, open to the same truths as I am, in relation to the same being as I am.[15]

Merleau-Ponty points out in the *Phenomenology* that the 'problem' of intersubjectivity is only a problem which we encounter in adult life, when we can come to attain the self-consciousness of the Cartesian *cogito*. The child 'has no awareness of himself or of others as private subjectivities'. For the child, the 'intersubjective world' is 'unproblematic'. We would be mistaken to view the child as wholly in error, or to view the divide between childhood and adulthood as absolute. On the contrary, Merleau-Ponty suggests, our 'unsophisticated' childhood assumptions continue to underlie our adult experience. Indeed, we cannot make any sense of the Hegelian – or Sartrean – 'struggle between consciousnesses' if we ignore the fact that struggle must always be preceded by an intersubjectivity which it negates:

> For the struggle ever to begin, and for each consciousness to be capable of suspecting the alien presences which it negates, all must necessarily have some common ground and recall their peaceful co-existence in the world of childhood. (PP 355)

It is conflict, rather than 'peaceful co-existence' which is initially the problem to be explained. Given our co-existence in the unity of primordial Being, why should conflict, rather than harmonious intersubjectivity, arise at all? To put it another way, why was Marcel mistaken when he excluded from his notion of human relations 'proper' those relations which involve conflict and objectification?[16]

To answer these questions, we must begin by recalling the different possible relations I can have to transcendent things – either as taking up and prolonging my own project for me and tending to overcome my finitude, or else as a threat, as 'hostile and alien'. Similarly, it is my ability to effect at least a partial withdrawal into my inner consciousness which leads me to encounter the other person as a threat. 'With the *cogito* begins that struggle between consciousnesses, each one of which, as Hegel says, seeks the death of the other' (PP 355).

The experience of myself as a *cogito* or pure subjectivity is, for Merleau-Ponty, real but one-sided. Since 'we are born into the world', we have two contradictory, yet interdependent, kinds of experience of other people. One, discussed above, is that in which my being 'interweaves' harmoniously with that of others. But *also*, says Merleau-Ponty:

> in so far as I am born and my existence is already at work and is aware that it is given to itself, it always remains on the hither side of the acts in which it tries to become engaged... This self, a witness to any real communication, and without which the latter would be ignorant of itself, and would not, therefore, be communication at all, would seem to preclude any solution to the problem of the other. There is here *a solipsism rooted in living experience* and quite insurmountable. (PP 357–8, my emphasis)

Solipsism is, then, not necessarily an error or a fault. It is a significant aspect of my relation to other people – a point which has been ignored by commentators who have emphasized the centrality of communication in Merleau-Ponty's social and political thought. But in so far as I experience myself solipsistically – as an infinite subject, the constitutor of all meaning in the world – difficulties do present themselves concerning the nature of other people. Of course, in solipsism I appear to transcend other people: they only exist for me because I experience them. But even so, I still cannot avoid recognizing them as 'people' – that is, as having a consciousness something like my own.[17] But then, that being recognized, solipsism presents me with 'the absurdity of a multiple solipsism' (*le ridicule d'un solipsisme á plusieurs*; PP 359).

The way beyond this difficulty is not to ignore solipsism, but to realize that the experience is only one aspect, one 'moment', of my relation to the world. 'Solitude and communication cannot be two exclusive alternatives', Merleau-Ponty writes, 'but two moments of one single phenomenon, since in fact other people do exist for me'. Indeed, he continues, 'my experience must in some way present me with other people, since otherwise I should have no occasion to speak of solitude, and could not begin to pronounce other people inaccessible' (PP 359).

However, if I choose to emphasize for myself only the moment of my own subjectivity, then I am able to suspend the interworld which exists between myself and the other. Here, for Merleau-Ponty, lies the error in Sartre's account of interpersonal relations. Sartre claims that the fundamental relation is one in which each attempts to objectify the other. But such an operation is possible only in so far as we ignore our common inherence in Being – an inherence which is necessarily revealed in any action we undertake. Even objectification has to be a form of communication:

> In fact the other's gaze transforms me into an object, and mine him, only if both of us withdraw into the core of our thinking nature, if we both make ourselves into an inhuman gaze... But even then, the objectification of each by the other's gaze is felt as unbearable only because it takes the place of possible communication. A dog's gaze directed towards me causes me no embarrassment. The refusal to communicate is still a form of communication. (PP 361)

The inseparability of communication and conflict, the inevitable *reciprocity* given in a dialectic in which each of these moments implies the other, is a theme on which Merleau-Ponty meditated extensively in his essays of the 1940s. For example, in 'A Note on Machiavelli' (1949, S 211–23), he explored the question of violence in politics, arguing that when I do violence to another, I discover that I do violence also to myself. For – as Beauvoir also pointed out – my victim is not a wholly distinct other, but one whose freedom is intertwined with my own.[18] Were I a pure subject, my violence against the other would not rebound against myself, for I would be untouchable. But to exist is to be an embodied and situated subject: to exist 'without being or doing anything is impossible, since existing is being in and of the world'(PP 361). As soon as I act – and violence involves action – it is evident that I am not a pure subjectivity. My subjectivity 'is a *revealed* subjectivity, known to itself and to others, and for this reason, it is an *intersubjectivity*' (PP 361), my emphasis . Violence, then, is a self-contradictory movement.

It originates from my withdrawal into pure subjectivity, from which standpoint I define the Other as pure object. But it can complete its trajectory as an act only by abandoning the stance of pure subjectivity and engaging with the other in a relation of incarnate existences.

In *Humanism and Terror*, Merleau-Ponty's most sustained treatment of the world of politics, he again returns to Hegel's 'struggle to the death' between consciousnesses, re-interpreting it more explicitly in terms of embodiment. Beginning by again citing Hegel's claim that 'each self-consciousness aims at the destruction and death of the other', Merleau-Ponty continues as follows:

> But consciousness can do nothing without its body and can only act upon others by acting on their bodies. It can only reduce them to slavery by making nature an appendix of its body, by appropriating nature to itself and establishing in nature its instruments of power. (HT 102)

Since we are body-subjects and not pure consciousnesses, conflict *cannot* remain at the level of the 'gaze'. Oppression and power are general, *social* relations which are possible only because of the finitude of our embodied existence. With this insight, Merleau-Ponty's analysis – unlike Sartre's – easily extends itself from interpersonal relations (those of Self and Other) to the broader field of society and history, and to our situation within it.

We can also see why Marxism was of such profound significance for him. For Marxism too, with its privileging of productive activity over consciousness, can be read as calling for a fundamental reworking of the notion of the subject. For Marx, at least as Merleau-Ponty interprets him, 'the subject is no longer the epistemological subject but is the human subject'. Consequently, 'this subject is no longer alone, is no longer consciousness in general or pure being for-itself. He is in the midst of other consciousnesses which likewise have a situation' (SNS 134).

Social and historical situations: intersubjectivity

At the level of social existence, the relations of co-existence and conflict take on yet greater complexity. I will begin, once again, at the pole of co-existence, or intersubjectivity. Here, Merleau-Ponty introduces the notion of *institutions* as the bearers of intersubjective significations and mediators of individual actions. Even the simplest perception of an object, we saw, always takes place in a human setting. Indeed, '[o]ur relationship to the social is, like our relationship to the world, deeper than any express perception or any judgement' (PP 362). Intersubjectivity is always present because we inhere in a world of *already* given collective meanings, in principle accessible to all of us.[19] We could say of sociality, like sensation, that it 'runs through us'.

Collective meanings are not, however, universal, in the sense of being identical for all human beings irrespective of time or place. Languages, cultures, ways of producing, are distinct and continually changing institutions. Thus, another dialectic of human existence is the movement through which collective meanings cohere into those institutions which individuals encounter as transcendent, yet which they also perpetually transcend. In the *Phenomenology*, Merleau-Ponty further develops and exemplifies this idea through a discussion of *class*. To 'be a proletarian' is not to be the product of an objective economic 'condition'; nor, of course, is it purely a matter of conscious choice. Rather, it is a question of how the individual takes up and lives his or her condition:

> What makes me a proletarian is not the economy or society considered as a system of impersonal forces, but the society or the economy as I carry them within me and experience them ... *It is my way of being in the world within this institutional framework* (PP 443, my emphasis).

Institutions are encountered by us as 'pre-given'; but *only* in relation to a project which will transcend them and yet whose possibilities they shape. They come into being and alter in a dialectic of transcendence and sedimentation in which the past is not a mere 'residue', a dead weight which determines the future, but an opening for individual action on to the future.[20] To be a proletarian is not to be a victim of circumstance, the passive product or effect of social structure, but to have a particular kind of opening on to the future. Freedom is embedded in a dialectic in which institutors and instituted are inseparable.

Merleau-Ponty's notion of 'institution' brings to the fore the question of his relationship to structuralism. It has quite often been suggested that Merleau-Ponty should be considered a proto-structuralist since, unlike Sartre, he gives so much weight to the power of the pre-given natural and social world over the individual.[21] It is true that Merleau-Ponty does frequently talk of structure, as well as institution. He also was very enthusiastic about Saussure's structural linguistics for some years in the 1950s,[22] and hailed the early work of Lévi-Strauss as a major achievement. But for Merleau-Ponty, structures are not the *autonomous* bearers of meaning or of social functions that, broadly speaking, they are for structuralism.

Structures, according to Merleau-Ponty are, like institutions, 'neither things nor ideas' (S 117). They are elements of an 'interworld' which organize the field of possibilities for new projects. Thus, to describe the structured nature of the human world is not, for Merleau-Ponty, to eliminate the subject or to reduce it to an effect. Unlike some later interpreters, Merleau-Ponty reads Saussure as *rescuing* the study of linguistics from the objectivist perspective of causal explanation. With Saussure, he tells us:

> the very conception of language as pure object was again called into question... Saussure's linguistics legitimates, in the study of language – beyond the perspective of causal explanation which links each fact with a previous fact and thus spreads language before the linguist like a natural object – the perspective of the speaking subject who lives in his language (and who may in some cases change it). (SNS 87)[23]

Linguistic structure is not for Merleau-Ponty an autonomous entity of which individual speakers are merely the passive recipients and transmitters. Nor is language a 'prison'. Rather it is a field of structured possibilities. Similarly, Merleau-Ponty reads Lévi-Strauss's account of kinship structures as an attack on objectivist social science of the Durkheimian variety. Discussing Lévi-Strauss's early work on kinship,[24] Merleau-Ponty insists that the structuralist social scientist develops only 'models', and that 'there is no question for him of substituting the model for the reality' (S 117). One can indeed discover regular correlations, even elementary 'laws of exchange' in kinship relations. But the significance of an anthropology such as that of Lévi-Strauss lies, according to Merleau-Ponty, not in the establishment of such laws themselves but in the exploration of the relation of these laws to 'the other end of the anthropological field', where 'structures burst apart'. There, 'exchange, symbolic function, and society no longer act as a second nature which is as imperious as the other and effaces it. Each person is invited to define his own system of exchange' (S 124).

For Merleau-Ponty, structuralism calls upon us to rethink the subject as a cultural and symbolic self within the complex interchange of individual and general encompassed in the notion of institution. Structure, according to Merleau-Ponty, shows us

> how we are in sort of circuit with the socio-historical world, man being off-centre from himself [*excentrique à lui-même*], and the social finding its centre only in man. (S 123)

A self not properly centred on itself, an 'impure' subject, an 'institutor' but not a conscious 'constitutor' of his world: Merleau-Ponty's 'man' is no longer a Cartesian *cogito*. Yet, however 'off-centre' it is, Merleau-Ponty's subject remains also an *acting* subject, the initiator of a project.

Merleau-Ponty died in 1961. In 1962 Lévi-Strauss published *The Savage Mind*, dedicated 'To the Memory of Maurice Merleau-Ponty'. But had Merleau-Ponty continued to live, one cannot imagine that he would have seen his own thought mirrored in that of Lévi-Strauss. For far from wanting to restore the other end of the anthropological field, where structures burst apart, *The Savage Mind* revealed Lévi-Strauss's aim to be a single-minded reductionism. The final goal, he declared, should be to reduce the human sciences to the natural sciences, to succeed finally, 'in understanding life as a function of inert matter'. The 'ultimate goal of the human sciences', he insisted, was 'not to constitute but to dissolve man'.[25]

It is not fortuitous that Merleau-Ponty first introduced the notion of institution in the *Phenomenology* in the context of a discussion of social class. While the centrality of dialectical thought in the *Phenomenology* can be traced to the influence of Hegel,[26] it perhaps owes more to Marx. In the first issue of *Les Temps Modernes*, which appeared only a few months after the *Phenomenology* was published, Merleau-Ponty described the War as not only a radicalizing experience, but one through which his generation came to 'rediscover' certain of the 'truths of Marxism'(SNS 148). Marxism was not, of course, to be confused with orthodox Marxism, the doctrine of the communists. In the face of the War experience, Marxism 'had to be taken up anew'. What this meant for Merleau-Ponty was a reading of Marx – especially the 'young' Marx – in which he discovered close affinities between Marx's account of man and society and his own.

1940s orthodox Marxism, like its more recent structuralist relative, denied that Marxism could in any possible way involve a philosophy of the subject; consciousness was simply the reflex of external material forces. Yet Marx's own texts – even his late ones – are, to say the least, ambiguous on this point. While orthodox and structuralist interpretations resist acknowledging any possible convergence between Marxism and what is brusquely dismissed as idealism, there is arguably what we could call a Cartesian 'moment' that is crucial to Marx's thought. Merleau-Ponty both recognized and explored this possibility.

But the central issues in his debate with orthodox Marxism were ones of agency, as much as epistemology. If, as Marx said in *The Eighteenth Brumaire*, 'men make their own history',[27] the question is whether they do so merely as the passive or inadvertent carriers of objective forces, or whether they do so as *agents* of some kind. Although the form of Louis-Napoleon's regime can be explained by reference to the particular balance of class forces of the time, Marx also argues that not 'anyone' could have fulfilled his role. Louis-Napoleon's blood relationship to the original Napoleon gave him a unique mantle of legitimacy in the eyes of the French peasantry – a legitimacy which he very consciously *chose* to exploit. In this example, and others in Marx's historical writings, the individual emerges as a unique and goal-pursuing agent, as far more than the passive bearer of class interests.

Moreover, in the description which Marx gives in *Capital* of the labour process, he posits agents who are engaged in a purposive transformation of the means of production:

> what distinguishes the worst architect from the best of bees is this, that the architect raises his structure in imagination before he erects it in reality. At the end of every labour process, we get a result that already existed in the imagination of the labourer at its commencement. He not only effects a change of form in the material on which he works, but he also realises a purpose of his own that gives the law to the modus operandi, and to which he must subordinate his will.[28]

But if, for Marx, the worker has and applies to the labour process 'imagination', 'purpose' and a 'will' (albeit a 'will' which must submit itself to the requirements of the particular labour process in order to produce), then we are surely entitled to ask what kind of a consciousness Marx attributes to such a person. Is he or she not in some sense — a sense which Marx does not clearly specify — a subject? It is this possibility which Merleau-Ponty explores, arguing that Marx effected a radical transformation, but not a total elimination, of the Cartesian *cogito*. Merleau-Ponty draws mainly on Marx's early writings in making this claim, but my above observations would suggest that his remarks are pertinent also to Marx's late work.

In so far as the *cogito* involves for Descartes 'exclusive reference to the interior' and remains contemplative (SNS 78–9), Merleau-Ponty agrees that it gives an erroneous priority to a subject who is conceived as a pure consciousness. But all the same, he insists, 'no man can reject the *cogito* and deny consciousness, on pain of no longer knowing what he is saying and of renouncing all statements, even materialist ones' (SNS 79–80). The very project of Marxist theory itself must assume thinking, knowing subjects who produce it and to whom it is addressed. And if 'men' are to be the agents of revolutionary transformation, class consciousness must be more than a passive reflection of an objective situation; it must be a way of living and transcending it.

Where, however, Marxism surpasses the *Cartesian* notion of the subject is in denying that consciousness is, to begin with, wholly 'interior' or contemplative. Reformulating Marx, Merleau-Ponty writes:

> The *cogito* is false only in that it removes itself and shatters our inherence in the world. The only way to do away with it is to fulfill it, that is, to show that it is eminently contained in interpersonal relations. (SNS 133)

If, for Marx, consciousness can be said to inhere in the world and to be contained in interpersonal relations, then Marxism implies something like Merleau-Ponty's own notion of an impure subject. It implies a consciousness that exists only in and through the generality of Being and which thus is also inherently intersubjective. But while such an intersubjective notion of the subject is to be found in Marx, Merleau-Ponty claims, it is not sufficiently developed. In such works as *The Eighteenth Brumaire*, Marx's analyses tacitly use such a notion of the subject, but his own theoretical formulas and 'above all those of his commentators' do not adequately explicate it. '[T]he Marxist discovery of social existence as the most "interior" dimension of our life', Merleau-Ponty claims, 'not only admits but demands a new conception of consciousness on the theoretical plane which would establish a basis for both its autonomy and its dependence'. Since it is above all 'existentialism' that can bring this 'new conception' to Marxism, 'a [living] Marxism should "save" and integrate existentialist research instead of stifling it' (SNS 82).

Merleau-Ponty is surely right in saying that Marxism needs to develop its notion of the subject more fully. But his claim that existentialism, by which he means his own philosophy, can provide Marxism with the proper means for 'fulfilling' the *cogito* encounters difficulties. In the *Phenomenology*, as we saw, Merleau-Ponty takes sensation, especially perception, to be that 'third genus' which reveals our inherence in Being and which reveals Being also to be intersubjective. However, in his writings on Marx, Merleau-Ponty shifts the discussion to *praxis* as if it unproblematically grounds intersubjectivity in the same way as perception. 'For Marx', he tells us, 'the vehicle of history... is man involved in a certain way of appropriating nature in which the mode of his relationship with others takes shape; it is concrete human intersubjectivity' (SNS 129, emphasis removed). But enjoying a landscape with my friend Paul, for example, and 'appropriating' it as a means of production with which, say, to produce food, do not give us the experience of intersubjectivity in the identical manner.

In the first case, although we are each the centre of our own distinct perception, the overlap of perceptions which makes our communication possible is ensured by our inherence in virtually one and the same perceptual situation – an inherence in which we share approximately the same experience as two *equals*. But as an object of *praxis* the 'same' area, no longer contemplated as a landscape but as a means of production, can be viewed in radically different ways by each of us, depending on our goals and interests. Furthermore, the relation between us might cease to be that of two mutually perceiving and sharing equals. If, to extend from Merleau-Ponty's example, Paul is a tenant farmer and I am his landlord, what each of us brings to the perception of the 'same' landscape will be very different. We may well stand side by side, looking, but Paul will look with the eye of a cultivator and a tenant. He will perhaps notice the degree of slope as suggesting the danger of soil erosion; the presence of shade-giving trees along one edge as cutting out necessary sunlight; both signify that the land will not yield as much for his labour as an acre elsewhere would. I, the landlord, will probably be less aware of such details. For me the land perhaps signifies family continuity, the inheritance that I will pass on to my children (who will also stand here and appreciate the magnificence of the very same row of trees); or perhaps above all it signifies my economic security, my ability to derive a steady income from its rent. But if our perceptions are organized by such different and even opposed *practical* goals, then it could be that the degree of overlap between them is no longer sufficient to ground the experience of intersubjectivity between us. Practical experience cannot be reduced to perceptual experience, if only because it takes place always in the context of material constraints of a kind which do not effect perception.

Merleau-Ponty does not sufficiently elucidate the relation between perception and praxis. A hiatus remains between his account of the impure subject of perception in the *Phenomenology* and the equally impure subject of praxis in his political writings of the 1940s. Even so, Merleau-Ponty still develops a significant account of *situated* action which, like situated perception, is immersed in the ambiguous generality of Being. Furthermore, he looks to Marx to find not only a surpassing of the individual Cartesian *cogito* in intersubjectivity, but also a profound sense of the weight or 'inertia' of the general *social* being in which the impure subject of praxis is situated.

Marxist 'materialism' is not, Merleau-Ponty claims, a form of reductionism. Rather it is a recognition of the weight of sedimented prior praxis, of *institution*, on new praxis. 'Economic life' is not 'a separate order to which the other orders may be reduced.' Instead,

> it is Marxism's way of representing the inertia of human life; it is here that conceptions are registered and achieve stability ... Economic life is at the same time the historical carrier of mental structures, just as our body maintains the basic features of our behaviour. (SNS 108)

Economic life is, then, the expression of that generality of social being in which individual praxis is immersed. As such it appears above all as the carrier of *meanings*. The economy, he tells us, is the 'schema and material symbol of the cultural order' (SNS 112).

In this reading the economy emerges as an expression of the One, as the guarantor of intersubjectivity and the manifestation of a basically harmonious human sociality. One might well be inclined to accuse Merleau-Ponty of rosy romanticism and a seriously distorted reading of Marx. But there is a second thread which runs – albeit more intermittently – through some of the essays in *Sense and Non-Sense* and which is taken up more fully in *Humanism and Terror*. This thread takes production to be also the point of origin of human conflict, and history to be a far from harmonious or predictable process of development: the 'conflict' pole of the dialectic of social existence moves back into view.

Social and historical situations: generalized conflict

If it is Marxism that is best able to give us a theory of 'concrete human intersubjectivity', it is also Marxism that shows us most clearly why there is what Merleau-Ponty called 'the discordant functioning of human intersubjectivity' (SNS 97). Although in the *Phenomenology* Merleau-Ponty had examined the source of such discord in what I have called interpersonal relations, it was mainly through his reading of Marxism that he examined its place in wider social relations, and considered the related question, whether history has a *sens* – a meaning or direction.

In *Humanism and Terror*, Merleau-Ponty suggests that what he there calls 'struggle' is 'a necessity of the human condition'. As we saw in the discussion of interpersonal conflict, struggle cannot remain at the level of the gaze but, between embodied subjects, must take material forms. What Marxism shows us is that

> what accounts for there being a human history is that man is a being who externalizes himself, who needs others and nature to fulfill himself, who individualizes himself by appropriating certain goods and thereby enters into conflict with other men. (HT 102)

Since human existence is social existence, conflict does not remain at the level of the dyad of Self and Other; nor is it wholly explicable on the basis of dyadic conflict. It takes on the more general social forms which Marxism explores under the rubric of class and class conflict.

But if conflict is intrinsic to embodied human existence, then the Marxist assumption that the end of class society would put an end to any significant social conflict is put into question. In *Humanism and Terror* Merleau-Ponty simply leaves the question open: we cannot know the answer, but neither do we need to know in order to make today's political choices. 'For the moment', he tells us, 'the question is not to know whether one accepts or rejects violence, but whether the violence with which one is allied is "progressive" and tends towards its own suspension or toward self-perpetuation' (HT 1).

In the late 1940s Merleau-Ponty thought that communism, for all its flaws, still exhibited a tendency towards the suspension of violence. While there was no reason to assume that it would *end* violence, he considered it at the time more likely than capitalism to reduce violence at the global level.[29] On this basis, Merleau-Ponty pursued a policy of 'critical support' for the Soviet Union and the French Communist Party, while also emphasizing the risks that the 'humanist' project of Marxism was being 'derailed' by the concatenation of unforeseen events. In issuing these warnings Merleau-Ponty claimed that he was in no way refuting Marx or rejecting Marxism, 'since Marx himself pointed out that chaos and absurdity were one of the possible ways for history to end' (SNS 163).[30] Although odd remarks in Marx's work might justify such a reading, Merleau-Ponty's interpretation was not an obvious one, nor one that was widely accepted at the time. In discussing the ways in which *sens* transforms itself into *non-sens*, 'humanism' into 'terror' – in trying, in short, to integrate a notion of *contingency* into the heart of Marxism – Merleau-Ponty once again read Marx very much through his own lenses. In so doing he raised issues about Marxism as a theory of historical progress and about the ambiguity of political action and socially situated human freedom.

'My freedom', as Merleau-Ponty had put it in the *Phenomenology*, 'is not distinct from my insertion in the world' (PP 360). Thus freedom, for Merleau-Ponty, can never be absolute. We can talk only of a qualified and ambiguous freedom:

> The world is already constituted, but also never completely constituted; with respect to the first relation we are impelled, with respect to the second we are open to an infinite number of possibilities. But this analysis is still abstract, for we exist both ways *at once*. There is, therefore, never determinism and never absolute choice. (PP 453)

But action in the sphere between determinism and absolute choice is action whose outcome is always uncertain, particularly at the social and political level, where a multiplicity of individual projects can randomly come into play and where institutions may, instead of supporting our projects, resist, deflect, or transform them. Hence, Merleau-Ponty's insistence that Marxism cannot predict the future shape of history with any certainty, that the Marxist project may well become 'derailed'. While multiple individual projects or praxes can at times cohere through a common situation, to ensure a 'line of development' or a *sens* of history, it is equally possible that *sens* will dissipate into *non-sens*, and that the outcome of what appear to be rational and humane projects will be chaos and even violence. There is, as Merleau-Ponty puts it in *Humanism and Terror*, 'a sort of maleficence in history' (HT 94; also S 224–43) which undermines our aims, leaving us the authors of that which we had never intended. Beyond the conflict directly engendered by the 'discordant intersubjectivity' of the class struggle itself, and beyond the kind of violence that stems from what Marcel had called moral 'desertion'(BH 165), there is something else: an element of irreducible conflict which stems from the very being of social existence.

Beauvoir had expressed the same idea when, in *The Ethics of Ambiguity*, she suggested that, beyond the violence of oppression, those forms of action opposed to oppression could themselves be the source of further violence. But what Merleau-Ponty explores more extensively than Beauvoir is the *irreducibility* of conflictual social – and especially political – relations to those of dyadic interpersonal conflict. Both Sartre and Marcel had, in their opposed yet symmetrical ways, taken the inter-individual dyad to be the central human relationship. What Beauvoir suggested, and Merleau-Ponty further explores, is the notion that there is an autonomous dynamic to those general and conflictual relationships which take place at the level of politics and what Merleau-Ponty also calls 'public' history. These relationships cannot be explicated on the 'interpersonal' model because the ambiguous mediation of social institutions and the play of contingency are irreducible aspects of politics and of history.

A double dilemma is posed for Merleau-Ponty by these insights: the problem of scepticism (or irrationalism), and what we might call the problem of political judgement. If politics is, *par excellence*, the realm of impure action, where individual projects lose their meaning in the encounter with other projects and with institutions, if *sens* so easily gives birth to *non-sens*, it might seem that we should give up the attempt to detect any coherence or direction to history. And would it not also appear to follow, if history is going nowhere, that any kind of political action, any kind of regime, is as good and as bad as any other? In short, is not political judgement impossible? Merleau-Ponty tries to steer a course between a vulgar Marxism, for which the direction of history and political values are taken to be wholly unproblematic, and the apparent alternative of scepticism and amoralism.[31]

The sceptic's position, Merleau-Ponty argues, is one of false objectivism. It claims that, in the face of the apparent irrationality of the social world, no judgements are possible. But such a claim can only be made by assuming a false posture of detachment which denies our situatedness in the social world. However irrational the social world might appear (or however discontinuous, in a later terminology), we cannot avoid expressing meaning or values in everything we do or say. As Merleau-Ponty wrote in the preface to the *Phenomenology*: 'Because we are in the world, we are *condemned to meaning*, and we cannot do or say anything without its acquiring a name in history' (PP xix). Thus scepticism simply fails to admit to its own values which, since it offers no reason to try to change anything, must be a defence of the status quo:

> historical skepticism is always conservative ... Under the pretext of objectivity it freezes the future and eliminates change and the will of men from history. When it believes it is simply facing facts ... it is really making a bet, expressing a preference and a wish, and assuming a responsibility. (SNS 168)

But if neither scepticism nor the demonstration that there is a clear *sens* of history is possible, what is left for us? Two things are left, Merleau-Ponty suggests. First, a careful and 'open' reading of our present, 'which even recognizes chaos and non-sense [*non-sens*] where they exist, but which does not refuse to discern a direction [*sens*] and an idea in events when they appear' (SNS 169). Such a reading cannot, of course, be made from an orthodox Marxist perspective, any more than from a position of scepticism. But a humanistic, or existential, Marxism, one which acknowledges the role of both men and circumstances and their ambiguous interplay, offers us an orientation for such an open reading.

Secondly, Merleau-Ponty suggests, we need to be guided in our political judgements by neither a blind faith nor cynicism, but by what he calls 'good faith'. Good faith implies the willingness to choose and to act in uncertainty, but only where there are reasonable grounds for doing so. 'If commitment goes beyond reasons, it should never run contrary to reason itself', he tells us (SNS 179). His own position of 'critical support' for communism and action in the Resistance during the German Occupation would both be examples of good faith. In neither case could action be undertaken with any certainty; yet in both, one course of action would seem to promise more space for human freedom than the other possible options. Even if there are no grounds for great optimism, Merleau-Ponty's insistence that there remain grounds for at least a sober good faith is still salutary. The basis for this claim lies, of course, in his account of human existence as necessarily intersubjective as well as conflictual, and in the claims that subjectivity is impure and freedom always situated.

Freedom in situation

It is, for Merleau-Ponty, only because we are both situated in the world and able to transcend it that we can talk of freedom. Freedom is always one aspect of a dialectic in which freedom and situation both 'deny' and 'sustain' each other. In the final chapter of the *Phenomenology* Merleau-Ponty draws out his own conception of freedom through an extended discussion and critique of *Being and Nothingness*. For Sartre, as we saw, even the obstacles which freedom encounters (as in the crag climbing example) are obstacles only through freedom's own choice. Thus, as Merleau-Ponty remarks:

> There is then ultimately nothing that can set limits to freedom except those limits that freedom has determined for itself through its own initiatives, and the subject has only the exterior which it gives itself... There is no action of things on the subject. (PP 436) [32]

Such an ubiquitous notion of freedom gives us no basis to discriminate between actions, Merleau-Ponty complains. '[I]f the slave displays freedom as much by living in fear as by breaking his chains', then, he argues, 'it cannot be held that there is such a thing as a *free action*'. Freedom has become, in Sartre's account, 'as it were our state of nature' (PP 437). By contrast, Merleau-Ponty argues that not any choice is a choice of freedom. For example, for Sartre, collaborating during the Occupation was just as free a choice as resisting. But Merleau-Ponty wants to be able to distinguish between the two: one was a choice which diminished the realm of freedom, whereas the other implied an act of good faith in the possibility of sustaining freedom. We need to talk not of freedom as a 'region of being', but of particular choices and actions as being ones conducive (or otherwise) to freedom.

But freedom is more than a matter of subjective intention. The cripple who wants to rescue a drowning person and the strong swimmer who actually does it 'do not have the same experience of autonomy'. What is at issue is the reasonably anticipated (though never guaranteed) outcome invited by an action. 'The very notion of freedom demands that our decision should plunge into the future, that something should be done by it, that the *subsequent instant should benefit from its predecessor*' (PP 437, my emphasis). Thus *openness* becomes for Merleau-Ponty the hall-mark of free action. The choice of collaboration was the choice to close down the field of future action, to support oppression and diminish freedom.

But for an action to open on the future and support further free action, the situation in which it takes place has to be relatively stable. In Merleau-Ponty's view, a further problem of Sartre's account is that since freedom effectively constitutes the meaning of the facticities of its own situation, it is free at any instant to change that meaning. Since time, for Sartre, is essentially conceived as a series of instants held together only by consciousness, situations lack the stability which allows each action effectively to shape the next. Thus, Merleau-Ponty protests:

> if freedom is doing, it is necessary that what it does should not be immediately undone by a new freedom. Each instant, therefore, must not be a closed world; one instant must be able to commit its successors... Unless there are cycles of behaviour, open situations which call for a certain completion and are capable of constituting a background to either confirmatory or transformatory experience, freedom never takes place. (PP 437–8)

But this means that situations cannot be constituted – temporally or otherwise – by an untranscended freedom. Merleau-Ponty agrees with Sartre that freedom brings into being obstacles for freedom; however, these obstacles, Merleau-Ponty insists, are in their specific qualities *independent* of our projects, and must be experienced as such:

> Whether or not I have decided to climb them, these mountains appear high to me because they exceed the grip of my body... In so far as I have hands, feet, a body, I sustain around me *intentions which are not dependent upon my decisions and which affect my surroundings in ways which I do not choose.* (PP 440, my emphasis)

In other words, certain general relations to the natural world are given with our embodiment. These are independent of our specific intentions and projects, and thus their significance for us is not brought into being by freedom alone. But, of course, these should not be construed only as *limits* on freedom; they are, equally, evidence of freedom's inseparability from our insertion in the world and of the prolongation of our projects by the world which transcends them.

Moreover, in the human world freedom is situated in a mesh of social significations which it does not directly constitute itself. Both the personal and the social past continue to exercise influence on future action. Thus, against Sartre's claim that I am 'free' at any moment to abandon the inferiority complex which I have had for twenty years, Merleau-Ponty retorts that this is not 'probable'. 'Generality and probability are real phenomena', he insists (PP 442). Once we recognize that our existence is situated, that it is inseparable from our body, our surroundings, our past, etc., we do not have to accept Sartre's 'either/or'. Probability exists as the 'weight' of the past, of institutions or other circumstances, upon us.

We can now see how Merleau-Ponty's thought bears on Beauvoir's difficulties. In her discussion of woman's immanence (and that of other oppressed groups) Beauvoir had wanted to say that woman is both the product of her situation and yet also a freedom: that woman's freedom is effectively suppressed by the situations which men inflict upon her, yet never thereby definitively destroyed. For Sartre, I argued, Beauvoir's notion of oppression as a situation in which freedom is *forced* to 'fall back into the in-itself' was theoretically impossible. For Sartre, be it that of the slave or the torture victim, freedom is, short of death, indestructible. Thus, strictly speaking, Beauvoir was saying something that it was impossible to say from the point of view of Sartre's ontology. But once we accept Merleau-Ponty's argument, that freedom is not an attribute of a pure subject, but emerges in the dialectic of a body-subject with the material and social world, freedom admits of degree and Beauvoir's position becomes tenable.

The *probability* that a woman will suddenly transcend the weight of the institutions which constitute her oppressive situation need be no greater than the *probability* that somebody will abandon an inferiority complex after twenty years. We do not, after all, have to take the stance of an objectifying Third in order to talk of the generality of woman's situation; for existence *is* general. Just as being a proletarian or being middle class is 'my way of being in the world within [an] institutional framework'(PP 443), so too we could say that to be a woman is to 'carry within me' an institutional framework which I have not consciously chosen for myself, but within which I exist. For both Beauvoir and Merleau-Ponty, oppression involves more than an objectifying look. It is not a relation of pure subjectivities, but of situated existences whose freedoms 'co-exist' for Merleau-Ponty, or are 'interdependent' for Beauvoir. Beauvoir's remark that '[i]t is this interdependence which explains why oppression is possible and why it is hateful'(EA 82), is one which Merleau-Ponty could have echoed. It is also a remark to which his account of the social world as a dialectic of intersubjectivity and conflict gives a deeper resonance. It is because, as Beauvoir had also seen, 'one is not free alone' (SNS 142), that we are vulnerable to an oppression which attacks us, not as Cartesian subjects but as embodied, productive, intersubjective and social existences.

A question which concerns Merleau-Ponty is how the oppressed come to experience a common situation and to assert their freedom through a collective movement of resistance, such as a revolution. Class existence is, we have seen, not structurally determined but a 'way of being' within a particular framework. If this framework has, for a considerable time, facilitated the oppression of certain classes by others, the question is: how do these oppressed classes at a certain point come collectively to assert their freedom against it?

It is no more *probable* that workers who experience their oppression as a 'fate' (as an apparently natural and thus irrevocable condition) will choose to revolt than that a person with an inferiority complex will choose after twenty years to abandon it. Paralleling Beauvoir's notion of the immanence of the oppressed, Merleau-Ponty comments that 'if there is a tacit evaluation [of their situation] it represents *the thrust of a freedom devoid of any project* against unknown obstacles; one cannot in any case talk about a choice' (PP 444, my emphasis). For Sartre, a freedom 'devoid of any project' is, of course, a contradiction in terms. Beauvoir had described such a crippled freedom. But without a critique of Sartre's notion of freedom, such as Merleau-Ponty developed, she was unable adequately to explain how it was possible.

How, then, do the oppressed arrive at a moment of resistance? Like Beauvoir, Merleau-Ponty suggests that what must initially take place is an alteration in their *situation*. From 'the concatenation of less remote and more remote ends', a new situation may begin to form, in which initially isolated workers begin to see that what each had deemed to be an individual fate is shared with others. They then can come to live their condition as 'a common obstacle to the existence of each and every one' (PP 445). It is only then that a revolution, as a collective struggle for freedom, is possible. But even then workers do not necessarily think of themselves as proletarians: The revolutionary project is lived through before it is thought. As Merleau-Ponty puts it:

> If indeed I made myself a worker or a bourgeois by an absolute initiative, and if in general terms nothing ever impelled our freedom, history would display no structure, no event would be seen to take shape in it, and anything might emerge from anything else... A social revolution would be equally possible at any moment, and by the same token one might reasonably expect a despot to undergo conversion to anarchism. (PP 449)

In her discussion of situations of oppression, especially of woman's situation, Beauvoir also had recognized that our world is shaped in enduring ways. She had pointed out that a woman could not assert her freedom through what Merleau-Ponty here calls an 'absolute initiative'. She could only do so gradually, as the modification of woman's situation *in general* took place.

Although Beauvoir had tried initially to preserve a Sartrean notion of freedom, distinguishing an indestructible ontological 'core' freedom from an 'effective' freedom which could be limited by its situation, by the time she wrote *The Second Sex* she could not sustain this distinction. For Merleau-Ponty, however, such a distinction was never acceptable in the first place. Freedom comes into being in that dialectic of generality and individuality which Beauvoir had implied but never explicated. There can be no such thing as a freedom which is indestructible because we are vulnerable, permeable body-subjects, and there is no such thing as pure subjectivity. If I am oppressed, I may experience myself as the isolated victim of an anonymous fate. Yet 'my' situation is not strictly speaking 'mine', but part of a more general situation which transcends my immediate experience. As such, it can return to me (as in an emerging revolutionary situation) transformed into an opening on a new project of which I had not previously dreamed. Freedom is always a two-way relation, and is 'not distinct from my insertion in the world'(PP 360). It is this insight which Sartre, finally, was to take up and explore in the *Critique of Dialectical Reason*.

5

Sartre: praxis in situation

Merleau-Ponty died in the Spring of 1961, some thirteen months after the publication of Sartre's *Critique of Dialectical Reason*. In the memorial essay he wrote, Sartre claimed that it was from Merleau-Ponty he had 'learned History'. Merleau-Ponty, he said, 'showed me that I was making History in the same way that M. Jourdain was speaking prose'.[1]

In 1943, we saw, Sartre's ontology could ground only a dyadic account of 'interpersonal relations'. It could not account for history except as the individual constitution of the meaning of the past. '[T]he meaning of the past is strictly dependent on my present project ... I alone in fact can decide at each moment the bearing of the past', he wrote in *Being and Nothingness* (BN 498). Yet Sartre, like Merleau-Ponty, had learned during the course of the War that 'one is not free alone'. The immediate postwar period saw him emerge as a public and committed man of the Left. But how could one consistently engage oneself in a collective struggle to shape history if a collective history was an impossibility, if each of us remained an autonomous subject, the constitutor of a unique situation?

This is not the place to recount the complex itinerary by which Sartre gradually modified his early philosophy, nor to trace systematically Merleau-Ponty's role in that process.[2] However, by 1957, with the writing of *Problem of Method*,[3] Sartre had arrived at the issues which continued to concern him until his last major project, his massive study of Flaubert.[4] The key problem for Sartre was how to make 'intelligible' that movement in which individual projects and the generality of the social permeate and transform each other. He now sought to demonstrate that human life brings into being a dialectic in which individual and social being constitute and re-constitute each other so that each of us is what he calls a 'universal singular'.[5] In *Problem of Method* and in the *Critique*, my main focus in this chapter, Sartre approached this project through a critical dialogue with Marxism.

Marxism, Sartre now concluded, is 'the untranscendable philosophy for our time' (CDR 822) – a truth learned not from philosophy, but from the experience of the War and its aftermath. It had taken, he observed in *Problem of Method*,

> the whole bloody history of this half century to make us grasp the reality of the class struggle and to situate us in a split society. It was the war which shattered the worn structures of our thought – War, Occupation, Resistance, the years which followed. (PM 20)

Yet Marxism is today inadequate to its tasks. It has 'stopped' or 'sclerosed' in the hands of the Stalinist Soviet regime, and the uncritical Stalinised communist parties of the West.[6] Marxist method has become 'dogmatic', purely 'formal'. It regards its own theoretical framework and concepts as unproblematic and, concerned with universalism at the expense of singularity, 'its sole purpose is to force the events, the persons, or the acts considered into pre-fabricated molds' (PM 37). Sartre regards this dogmatic Marxism as a deviation. For Marx himself, dialectical method had not involved forcing all events into a pre-existing strait-jacket.

However, the deviation of modern Marxism is not merely a theoretical error. It is an accompaniment to Stalinist *practice*:

> Marxist formalism is a project of elimination. The method is identical with Terror in its inflexible refusal to differentiate ... The aim is not to integrate what is different as such, while preserving for it a relative autonomy, but rather to suppress it. Thus the perpetual movement *toward identification* reflects the bureaucrat's practice of unifying everything. (PM 48)

In combatting dogmatic Marxism, then, Sartre sees himself as engaged in a form of political struggle as much as intellectual critique.[7] Indeed, he suggests, his own work is one which is called forth by his own time and its particular crisis. For prior to Stalinism, 'dialectical reason' – the Marxist conception of the conflictual logic inherent in history – had not had any reason to scrutinize its own foundational assumptions.

Thus Sartre's own project is itself both 'universal' – in the sense of an expression of the general crisis of his times – and 'singular', since it is written from his own unique situation within those times. 'The locus of our critical investigation', he writes in the introductory section of the *Critique*, 'is none other than the fundamental identity between an individual life and human history' (CDR 70).

Although Sartre takes Stalinism to be primarily responsible for the emergence of dogmatic Marxism, its roots lie in the earlier history of Marxism. For Marx had left his theory, as it were, suspended in mid-air. He did not rigorously specify the philosophical underpinnings of what were essentially taken for granted, working, concepts. Thus, Sartre suggests, it was by default that Engels's 'dialectics of nature' later came to be regarded as the theoretical underpinning of Marxism. And Engels's claim to formulate the scientific basis of the laws which govern the movement of both nature and society was an invitation to the *a priorism* of later dogmatic Marxism.

Thus Sartre's central questions in the *Critique* – how we can demonstrate 'the fundamental identity between an individual life and human history', and whether, thereby, we can establish that history does have an intelligibility – are raised primarily as a challenge to a Marxism which claims *already* and unproblematically to know the direction of history in advance because it has identified *class struggle* as its dynamic. Sartre does not wish to deny the Marxist notion of the centrality of class struggle in the real process of history but, as he puts it:

> If one grants Marx and Engels the idea of class struggle, that is, of the negation of classes by one another, in other words, if one grants them negation, then they are able to comprehend History. But then we still have to explain negation *in the first place*. (CDR 150–1)

The task Sartre sets himself in the *Critique* is to elaborate the ontological 'foundations' for a non-dogmatic and non-reductionist Marxism. His final goal is to be able to establish the intelligibility of History as *one* universal movement of totalization (as world-historical class struggle), but without eliminating the singularity of individual praxis *en route*. Sartre's attempt to found Marxism as a theory of universal History begins from the pole of singularity, from individual praxis, and sets out to show us how it comes about that individual praxis and subjectivity are always social.

Sartre begins by considering what it is that gives rise to individual human praxis, considered at its most abstract level, and, he argues, praxis at its most abstract must always be an act of negation. He then proceeds to demonstrate that any praxis, as negation, always implicates the praxis of many other agents, thereby giving rise to wider human relations than those of a self-other dyad. This having been established, it becomes possible to reveal the various kinds of social relations − or 'ensembles' − which are possible and even necessary to human being. It is only then that it becomes possible to develop an account of class and class struggle from which individual praxis is no longer eliminated and − finally, but inconclusively − to raise the question of the intelligibility of History as one universal movement of totalization.

As in *Being and Nothingness*, the starting-point of Sartre's analysis in the *Critique* remains the individual, but now as the agent of *praxis* − that is, of activity in which the 'practical material field' is transformed − rather than as an absolute subject, a for-itself. But, some commentators have asked, how different is this notion of the practical, transforming agent from that of the nihilating for-itself? Do we not merely have old wine in new bottles? Does Sartre really succeed in developing a social ontology in which the autonomous subject of *Being and Nothingness* is replaced with a notion of socially situated subjectivity, so that the atomic individualism of his earlier work is overcome?[8]

Overview of the *Critique*: concepts and framework

The *Critique* is a vast and ambitious undertaking. It is also hastily and densely written, and incomplete. Sartre had intended to write two volumes. The first, published in April 1960, was conceived as a preliminary work of 'method'. The aim was to get back to 'the elementary formal structures' of human life (CDR 818) in order to show how individual existences are synthetically linked in a unifying movement which is, in principle, intelligible to its participants. By 'structures' Sartre means the structures of human action itself; structures whose logic emerges at its most basic from our organic existence and the requirements of physical survival. The second volume was to move towards the domain of history proper, using the structures of Volume I to show the intelligibility of history at work in concrete examples. However, Sartre abandoned this second volume incomplete, and refused to allow it to be published during his lifetime. Since Sartre chose neither to complete nor to publish the manuscript, I will focus in what follows primarily on the first volume of the *Critique*, although what Sartre wrote of the second volume has now been posthumously published.[9]

There is a kind of circularity to dialectical reason which makes it difficult to expound. For dialectical reason must be a *reflexive* reason, one which reflects on itself in reflecting on the world: 'thought is both Being and knowledge of Being' (CDR 24). Dialectical reason is thus itself part of the movement of Being which it attempts to grasp. It is, moreover, not a passive reflection of Being, but always an active intervention which alters itself by intervening. It follows that, strictly speaking, we can never define its terms, for they have their meaning only *in situ*. Moreover, since dialectical reason attempts to grasp Being as a movement of synthesis, it is concerned with grasping aspects of Being as inseparable parts of developing wholes. Since this applies as much to itself as to any other aspect of Being, it follows that the key notions of dialectical reason cannot be analysed independently of each other. For these reasons we cannot formally define 'totalization', 'negation', or even 'dialectic'. However, it is still possible to offer a provisional account of the central notions.

It is helpful to begin with the distinction Sartre makes between dialectical reason and what he calls 'analytic reason', or 'positivist reason'. Sartre describes analytical reason as a *dissolving* reason. It breaks its objects into their component parts and explains their relations in *exteriority* – that is, by the action of external, causal forces upon them. Nature, according to Sartre, is the realm of inert matter and there is no way that we could establish that nature is, in itself, dialectical. Analytic reason is thus appropriate to the study of nature, but it is wholly inappropriate to the study of the human realm including, it must be stressed, human relations *with* nature. For human being, as praxis, is dialectical through and through, and only dialectical reason might render it intelligible. Thus, Sartre argues, the use of analytic reason to 'explain' the human realm always serves an ideological function: it serves to mask conflict or exploitation by making the present human condition appear natural and thus unalterable (CDR 802). In *The Savage Mind*, Lévi-Strauss deliberately took up Sartre's very words when he insisted that the reason of the human sciences must indeed be a dissolving reason. He, as much as Sartre, clearly saw how central the issue of analytic reason was to the divide between structuralism and existential Marxism.

For Sartre, what distinguishes human activity is that it is *self*-activity, involving conscious agency. Thus human activity also involves a process of *internal* unification of itself and of its surroundings, whereas there is only unification in exteriority operating in the realm of nature. It is this activity of *internal* self-unification which Sartre calls *totalization*. Although Sartre does not discuss the point at any length, it would appear that some kind of minimal totalization must be present in all organic life – for example, in the consumption of nutrients from on organism's environment and their transformation into new forms of energy. However, Sartre's concern is above all with the *human* 'organism' and it is the particular qualities of the human organism which apparently make it alone the origin of dialectical totalization. For if animals do totalize their environments they do so only cyclically. Their totalization lacks the transformative element of human *praxis*, which is the basis for the possibility of History.

Praxis is an action whose goal is, at the most abstract level, consumption, and which transforms its environment in accordance with its goal. Since it is intentional, goal-oriented action, it implies a notion of the subject of some kind. But, unlike the for-itself of *Being and Nothingness*, this *practical* subject is essentially embodied and socially situated. Praxis involves what Sartre still calls a 'project': a movement of temporalization in which action oriented towards the future totalizes a given field (CDR 60–1). But such a project is no longer synonymous with absolute freedom. It is, rather, now the movement of a conditioned freedom.

Yet this practical subject still remains, of course, also consciousness. Praxis, as Sartre puts it, is action which has an initial 'translucidity' or 'transparency' to itself. If praxis did not have this quality, then clearly dialectical reason, as praxis reflecting on itself, would not be possible and we could have no hope of showing that History has any intelligibility. Indeed, it is only because the praxis of the investigator of dialectical reason shares the quality common to *any* praxis of being intelligible to itself that, in elucidating itself and its situation, it might perhaps be able to show also that there is a broader intelligibility to History.

Totalization, for Sartre, involves taking up and materially transforming a situation through praxis. In elucidating this notion, Sartre introduces an important distinction between the process of *totalization* and the *totalities* which are its products. From the point of view of any particular praxis, *totalities* are encountered as *already* existent, inert entities, which can be taken up and transformed through the new act of totalization. A totality is a 'synthetic unity' in so far as it is 'radically distinct from the sum of its parts', yet also 'present in its entirety, in one form or another in each of these parts' (CDR 45). Sartre's examples of totalities here are as diverse as a symphony and a machine. But in each case the totality is a material object which is 'only the vestige of past action'. Its 'ontological status' is that of 'the in-itself, the inert'. It is only through being re-totalized in a new praxis (the orchestral score being performed; the machine being put to work) that it evades dispersion back into the de-totalized condition of pure matter (a wad of decomposing paper; a heap of rusty iron).

Generally, a totalization re-totalizes several pre-existent totalities. The symphony can be animated by the players only with concert-hall, instruments and scores; the machine by the worker only with the raw materials it uses. Totalization is thus always a 'developing unification'. However, its development is always endangered by the inertia embodied in the prior totalities which it totalizes. For totalization is *not* merely an act of negation and transcendence. It also *preserves* what it transcends, and is *itself* subject to negation by the inertia of the prior praxis which it preserves. Sartre stresses in particular the importance of those inert totalities which he calls 'practical objects'– machines, tools, consumer goods, etc. For these

> create the kind of relation between men which we will refer to later as the practico-inert. These human objects are worthy of attention in the human world, for it is there that they attain their practico-inert status; that is to say, they lie heavy on our destiny because of the contradiction which opposes *praxis* (the labour which made them and the labour which utilises them) and inertia, within them. (CDR 45–6)

In the contradiction which opposes both past and present praxis to the inertia of its products lies the *dialectical* nature of totalization. The dialectic is a totalizing activity and its 'laws' are to do with the contradictory yet mutually implicating relations of 'interiority' (praxis, project, synthesis) and 'exteriority' (inorganic matter, inertia, dispersion). Are these antinomies of interiority and exteriority not simply new terms for the dualities of being for-itself and in-itself, it has been asked. Indeed, we saw above that Sartre describes the ontological status of totalities as that of the in-itself. Is not 'totalization' or 'praxis', then, merely a new term for the for-itself?

This is not, in my view, the case. For praxis is *not* the movement of pure nihilation which Sartre had earlier called being for-itself. Because it *preserves* what it totalizes, praxis can give rise only to a conditioned freedom. In totalizing the exterior world, praxis cannot avoid becoming *itself* an embodiment of the inert quality of that world. Thus Sartre does not describe praxis as a nihilation, but as a *mediation*. Praxis, he says, is 'the synthetic mediation of interiority and exteriority' (CDR 351). The relation of praxis to the inert is not, therefore, symmetrical with the relation of the for-itself to the in-itself. For what we might call 'praxis-in-situation' – as opposed to Sartre's earlier notion of 'freedom-in-situation' – does not transform its situation without being *itself* transformed. Praxis initiates a dialectic in which the mutual determinations of interiority and exteriority, of consciousness and matter, give rise to objects, events and structures which, following Merleau-Ponty, we could describe as a 'third genus of being', since they are neither wholly in-itself nor wholly for-itself.

But Sartre's project requires him to demonstrate more than the intelligibility of *individual* praxis as a mediation of interiority and exteriority. He needs also to be able to establish (a) that multiple individual praxes necessarily interpenetrate and modify each other and (b) that they do so in such a way as to give rise to coherent social structures and movements, rather than to random and directionless encounters. It is in addressing these two issues that Sartre develops his 'theory of practical ensembles', attempting to show how individual praxes do indeed cohere into different kinds of ensembles, ensembles which then mutually interact to give rise to a yet wider totalization from which, perhaps, the intelligibility of History may be shown to emerge. If there are general movements in History – not to mention one universal movement, as Sartre would like to be able to establish – they can emerge only as the end-result of individual praxes, each endlessly totalized and re-totalized. Thus, for Sartre, we do not have to choose between holism and methodological individualism in revealing the intelligibility of History – each is a necessary aspect and neither is adequate by itself:

> the dialectical movement is not some powerful unitary force revealing itself behind History like the will of God. It is first and foremost a *resultant*... The dialectic, if it exists, can only

be the totalisation of concrete totalisations effected by a multiplicity of totalising individualities. (CDR 37)

The structure of the *Critique*, following its methodological Introduction, is to proceed heuristically from simple to complex, from abstract individual praxis to concrete (and complex) social praxis. Sartre divides the work into two major sections, 'From Individual Praxis to the Practico-Inert' (Book One) and 'From Groups to History' (Book Two). The first Book begins with a highly abstracted account of what is involved in the praxis whereby the individual human organism seeks to satisfy its biological need by acting on its environment and transforming it. Sartre then proceeds to show us how this praxis, an initial act of negation by the organism, is in turn negated by the inertia it has interiorized. Praxis alienates itself in producing practico-inert objects which impose their own demands, or 'exigencies', on their makers. In this second moment of the dialectic, praxis is negated by what it has produced, and man becomes 'the product of his product'.

Sartre next considers the kinds of human relations grounded in this initial dialectic. Mediated through materiality, or exteriority, men no longer encounter each other primarily as looks, as consciousnesses, but as organisms competing for scarce resources with which to satisfy their needs. Scarcity is what shapes these initial ensembles as ones in which individuals can be shown to be connected to each other, albeit in relations of mutual antagonism. Sartre calls such ensembles *series*, or *collectives*. Although these ensembles come into being primarily through the mediation of 'worked matter',[10] it is important to point out that they also involve an aspect of consciousness: each member *recognizes* the others as fellow human beings with whom he or she is in competition. There is a mutual, if hostile, recognition of the other as the 'same' as myself, which Sartre describes as 'antagonistic reciprocity'. It is because of the moment of consciousness implied in this recognition that series come into being as *totalizations*, and not as purely the products of exterior conditioning.

At the beginning of Book Two Sartre portrays another, qualitatively different, kind of ensemble: one in which, instead of competing, members complement and reinforce each other in undertaking a common praxis. However, the purest form of this ensemble, which Sartre calls the *groupe-en-fusion*,[11] is possible only in exceptional circumstances when, in the face of a common threat of physical destruction, a mutually complementing praxis is the best possible way for each individual to attempt to survive. In the *groupe-en-fusion* – as in the series and in the isolated, individual praxis from which he began his account – Sartre insists that praxis is immediately intelligible to itself, at least in terms of its own purpose or goal. Sartre calls the understanding involved in such a translucid praxis *comprehension*; and he calls the dialectical totalization carried out by such a praxis a *constituting dialectic*.[12]

By contrast, Sartre goes on to discuss in the remainder of Book Two what he calls a *constituted dialectic*. This is a dialectic in which praxis is no longer open to immediate comprehension by individual agents. Its opacity arises from the fact that it is not a dialectic of individual praxis, but a dialectic of ensembles. Sartre sets out these ensembles, which he calls *organizations* and *institutions*, in a continuum according to the degree to which the core of original common group praxis has become thing-like, or 'reified'. In organizations and institutions, the ensemble itself takes on a degree of autonomy in relation to its members. Although the origin of such an ensemble lies in individual praxis, it is a new whole, not a mere sum of its parts. It is not, therefore, to be made intelligible through an analytic method which attempts simply to reduce it to its component individual praxes.

It follows that the question of the intelligibility of History must, finally, be the question of the intelligibility of a dialectic of ensembles which no individual directly comprehends him- or herself as totalizing. If, as Sartre would like to establish, we are able to discern one reason in History, we must be able to explain how, apparently, there can be 'totalisation without a totaliser'(CDR 817). That is, we must explain how, from the complex multiple interactions of many and diverse ensembles, *one* intelligible, totalizing movement can emerge. This must, furthermore, be explained *in situ*, and not by pretending, God-like, to survey history from a vantage point outside it. If History is not open to a direct comprehension, it must be open to what Sartre calls *intellection* – to a painstaking investigation by the situated investigator.

For Sartre, what is at stake in this endeavour is, of course, the possibility of a *class* analysis of History. Unless we can show how ensembles of diverse kinds are brought into being through individual praxis and act and re-act upon each other, we cannot show that there is such an entity as the working class or the capitalist class. And, unless the existence of classes can be established, we cannot establish the existence of a 'class struggle' out of which, as Marxism claims, the reason of History emerges. Sartre thus concludes the first volume of the *Critique* with a discussion of the possibility of a constituted dialectic *within* a class (the working class), followed by a discussion of the possibility of a totalizing struggle *between* the working class and the bourgeoisie.

If 'totalisation without a totaliser' might be possible, Sartre argues, this could be so only because the praxis of each class is, broadly speaking, *intelligible* to the other. Thus each class must *interiorize* the praxis of the other in developing its own, just as chess players interiorize each other's strategy (CDR 812 ff). Struggle has to be shown to be a conflict of *intelligible praxes* and not, as for dogmatic Marxism, a clash of forces of production:

> if *praxis ceases to be aware* of its end, its means, of the means and ends of its adversary, and of the means of opposing the hostile praxis, it simply becomes blind and therefore ceases to be *praxis*. (CDR 806)

If there is an intelligibility to History this is possible only because the investigator's own totalizing activity and those which are being studied are all praxes in situation.

Sartre does not manage to establish that history is, finally, totalization without a totalizer – only that this is a formal possibility. His failure to complete the second volume of the *Critique* (which was to treat of history proper) leaves his whole project – and the status of Marxism for him – hanging in mid air. But however severe the *Critique*'s shortcomings in relation to its grandiose claims as a theory of *history*, as a theory of *society* it is a work of the first importance. By examining Sartre's notion of situation in the *Critique*, and showing how praxis-in-situation differs from freedom-in-situation, we shall be able to see what Sartre had 'learned' since 1943. He had learned less about history *per se* than about intersubjectivity and sociality. He had learned about the conditioned nature of freedom, and about the impossibility of a subject which is a pure consciousness.

Praxis-in-situation: individual praxis

Critical investigation, we have seen, can take place only within the movement of totalization which it seeks to investigate. It is a *situated* investigation. In investigating itself, it also investigates the movement of totalization within which it is situated. It can cast light on this broader movement only because the investigation is itself a form of praxis and thus comprehends the basic properties of *any* praxis. What we now need to clarify is why it is that for Sartre *all* praxis is praxis-in-situation. In *Being and Nothingness*, in the last instance it was always freedom which brought the whole meaning of its own situation into being. In the *Critique*, Sartre begins instead with an account of the individual human organism, engaged in totalising its material environment in order to satisfy need. Although, at first sight, this appears to be only a new way of describing the nihilation of the in-itself by the for-itself, the ontological implications of Sartre's new terms are in fact profoundly different.

Since dialectical reason must not begin by assuming what it sets out to establish – that is, social being and history – its starting-point must be the isolated individual. Bracketing social experience, at least temporarily, the dialectical investigator must begin from abstract individual being and demonstrate how it implies social being. But what is the starting-point for investigating the abstract individual? Following a method analogous to Cartesian doubt, Sartre argues that what we discover to be indubitable about our own existence is neither consciousness nor, as Merleau-Ponty had argued, sense experience, but 'organic need'.

Man, like any other organism, continually faces the possibility of death, and must continually act to sustain life by eating, keeping warm, etc. Praxis, at its most abstract, originates from the necessity for the human organism *actively* to transform the environment, or 'Nature', in order to sustain itself. Thus investigation must

> set out from the immediate, that is to say from the individual fulfilling himself in his abstract praxis, so as to rediscover, through deeper and deeper conditionings, the totality of his practical bonds with others and, thereby, the structures of the various practical multiplicities and, through their contradictions and struggles, the absolute concrete: historical man. (CDR 52)

The origin of the dialectic is seen to lie in a contradiction within material being, generated by the peculiar region of material being which we call 'man'. Need, in its most abstract form, is the necessity for the organism to consume nutrients, oxygen, etc., in order not to die. It is, says Sartre, 'the first totalising relation between the material being, man, and the material ensemble of which he is a part'. Although a 'material being', man is distinct from the 'material ensemble' in which he participates because he is simultaneously inorganic and organic (CDR 80). Of course animals, and even plants, could also be described in this way. One of the difficulties with Sartre's account is that he identifies 'Nature' or the material world with *inorganic* matter and as *inert*, counter-posing it to 'man' as uniquely organic and active. Thus what distinguishes human praxis from animal behaviour is never made fully explicit. Sartre's refusal to attribute *any* agency to nature – a refusal which Merleau-Ponty certainly would have rejected – raises serious difficulties about the behaviour of at least the higher animals. For Sartre fails to consider that there may be a middle ground between human praxis, on the one hand, and the mechanical processes of inanimate matter, on the other. To account for tool using behaviour by apes, or even for the dog that barks at an intruder or begs for food, would be difficult within his framework.[13]

The starkness of his distinction between nature as inert matter and man as a special kind of active matter becomes even clearer in Sartre's discussion of death. Death, the dissolution of organic being into the inorganic, is kept at bay only by the praxis through which man interiorizes his means of sustenance. Thus, 'need sets up the *initial contradiction* because the [human] organism, in its being, depends directly (oxygen) or indirectly (food), on unorganised being' (CDR 81). Sartre refers to the movement whereby man interiorizes the inorganic variously as *totalization*, as *transcendence* and as *negation* of the inorganic. However, the death of the organism should not be conceived as *its* negation by the inorganic. For negation – thus dialectical totalization – is what *man* brings to other forms of matter, and not vice versa. Against Engels's notion of a dialectic of nature, Sartre insists:

> a material change is neither an affirmation nor a negation... The only possible use for the *order of negation* is to distinguish one direction from another. Resistance and, consequently, negative forces can exist only within a movement which is determined in *accordance with the future*, that is to say, in accordance with a certain form of integration. (CDR 84–5)

If we conceptualize nature exclusively according to a Newtonian notion of the mechanical movement of matter, then Sartre's critique is reasonable. But, we have long left the era of Newtonianism, and it had little to say about animal behaviour. If, for example, a human being is killed by the attack of an animal, this surely could be described as a 'negation' of the victim 'in accordance with a certain form of integration' on the part of the animal. It is because Sartre conceives matter at *only* the most abstract level, thus as inorganic, that he fails to acknowledge the existence of the kind of purposiveness in nature that Merleau-Ponty had recognized when he placed animal and human behaviour in a continuum.[14]

But even if we leave aside the question of animal behaviour, it is still perverse to describe nature as above all *inert*. Floods and hurricanes are certainly *unmotivated*, but they involve intensive transformations of energy that make them real forces. Moreover, they are encountered as such by human beings – they enter our world as such: a point Merleau-Ponty had recognized in acknowledging also the way the natural world can transcend our projects. If Sartre's description of nature as inert matter was an initial abstraction, from which he had then proceeded to concretize his account (as he would do for human praxis), then we could perhaps accept his account as an initial starting-point. But this is not what he does. Only his account of *humanly* transformed matter undergoes deepening as the work progresses, and nature remains an abstraction.[15]

Although Sartre's conception of matter is problematic, he is still justified in claiming that what death reveals most clearly is a double status – as simultaneously organic *and* inorganic – under which human life is lived. This double status is the source of contradiction not only *between* the organism and its environment, but also *within* the organism. What we have here, Sartre suggests, 'is really a matter of two statuses of the same materiality, since everything points to the fact that living bodies and inanimate objects are made of the same molecules' (CDR 81).[16]

The presence of the inorganic within the organism is also, however, what makes *praxis* possible. It distinguishes praxis from the for-itself. For praxis cannot be the pure nihilation of the inorganic by the organic. It cannot be the analogue of the pure nihilating movement of the for-itself. It must, instead, be an act of *mediation* between different forms of the inorganic. In praxis man makes himself a 'tool'. He uses his own inorganic qualities (weight, mass, etc.) to modify inorganic being to satisfy his (organic) need. However, in doing this, he finds himself also subject to the laws of inorganic matter, even as he negates and totalizes the latter through his praxis.[17]

For Merleau-Ponty, man is a 'place of unrest', source of a dialectic within being because of his contradictory existence as an incarnate consciousness, as a body-subject. Similarly now, for Sartre, it is man's status as a contradictory being within Being – both subordinate to the laws of inert material being and transcending that being – which makes him the point of origin of dialectical being. Sartre does not use Merleau-Ponty's notion of a third genus of being to describe this status. Yet something similar is implied by the notion that man is both inorganic and organic, at once matter and the transcendence of matter.

Whatever the difficulties with Sartre's views on matter and nature, it is still clear why praxis-in-situation is radically distinct from freedom-in-situation. For praxis involves our acting as a material force on our material environment. It thus involves our making ourselves inert in order to act, and requires us to interiorize the inertia of the external material world. It is in this double-sided movement of praxis, in which interiorization is also exteriorization, that the practical material field, or 'milieu of exteriority' is totalized as a *situation*. This is to say, praxis creates an internal bond with its objects, and with the contingently given, external, material conditions in and on which it acts. In the project of overcoming need, the organism

> unifies the field of instrumentality around itself, so as to make it into a totality which will provide a foundation for the individual objects which must come to its aid in its tasks. The surrounding world is thus constituted practically as the unity of materials and means. (CDR 87)

This constituting of the surrounding world is, however, now only one aspect of a double-sided relation, whose other aspect – the one Sartre's account lacked in *Being and Nothingness* – involves the *re*-constituting of praxis as *itself* object-like in its products.

Sartre calls this second aspect the 'negation of the negation'. For in negating and totalizing its situation, praxis is itself negated. This second negation is itself twofold. For, as we have seen, praxis not only requires man to make himself an inert 'tool', but also objectifies itself in its products: praxis makes itself into tangible, material things. It is because of the inert quality of matter that this objectification of praxis is possible: the unity which praxis imposes on matter would be wholly ephemeral, dissipating the moment praxis ceased, were it not for the inertia of matter. For it is its inert quality which ensures that matter holds the imprint of praxis after it has ceased – that, for example, molten wax retains the form printed on it by a seal (CDR 161). In this notion of the objectification of praxis in matter, Sartre has also provided an account of the temporal stability of the project that, as Merleau-Ponty had observed, had been lacking in *Being and Nothingness*.

When matter retains the forms imposed on it by praxis, it is not only the material act (the muscular effort involved in the act of sealing, for example) which is retained. Additionally, the human *signification* of the act (e.g. the authority symbolized by the seal) is retained. And Sartre argues that social institutions and values are as much objectifications of prior praxis as are 'practical objects'. Frequently, 'worked matter', or the practico-inert, appears as a power of alienation and coercion against us. But Sartre makes it very clear that it is not the objectification of praxis *per se* which is at the root of this problem. Rather, it is the social relation that Sartre calls *reification* which is the source of the problem. Reification

> is not a metamorphosis of the individual into a thing, as is often supposed, but the necessity imposed by the structures of society on members of a social group, that they should live the fact that they belong to the group and, thereby, to society as a whole, as a molecular status ... Their objectification is modified externally by the inert power of the objectification of others. (CDR 176)

Thus – despite Frederic Jameson's assertion that 'there can be no question but that for Sartre matter is somehow the source of evil' – matter is for Sartre also the positive *precondition* for praxis, and not only the source of its alienation.[18]

Social situations: mediations in exteriority

Having established that individual praxis is, even at its most abstract, dialectical, Sartre's next task is to try to show how a multiplicity of such individual praxes are interconnected. He must show how it is possible in general that there should be human relations:

> History itself does not cause there to be human relations in general. The relations which have established themselves between those

initially separate objects, men, were not the products of problems of the organisation and division of labour. On the contrary, the very possibility of a group or society being constituted – around a set of technical problems and a given collection of instruments – depends on the permanent actuality of the human relation (whatever its content) at every moment of History, even between two separate individuals belonging to societies with different systems and entirely ignorant of one another. (CDR 96)

Starting by assuming men to be initially separate, the next step is to show how in principle any or all of them could be connected. We must be able to establish that there are human relations that do not arise from a direct 'face to face' encounter, such as was implied in the look. Rather, we must seek the grounds of indirect relationship: *mediations*, which will relate one praxis to another even when their agents are ignorant of each other's existence.

If History is to be intelligible, this can only be because we comprehend the multiple and complex mediations through which abstract, individual praxes are totalized in ensembles. As Sartre develops his account, the ensembles described become increasingly complex, but they all involve totalizations and re-totalizations of two distinguishable kinds of mediation: those between individual praxes in *exteriority* and *interiority*. In any ensemble, both forms of mediation will always be present, though with differing degrees of significance. However, for the sake of clarity, I will discuss each in turn.

Mediation in exteriority gives rise to linkages between individual praxes through a commonality of the 'practical material field' in which each praxis is situated. Such mediation, in its most abstract form, gives rise to essentially passive connections, to 'passive synthesis', in which 'inert totalities' are brought into being. In so far as such exterior mediation takes place within what Sartre calls a milieu of 'scarcity', this mediation leads to relations of antagonism and reification. Mediation in interiority is, by contrast, effected through the subjective aspects of praxis. It involves a moment of comprehension, in which praxis grasps itself as both totalizing and as totalized by the praxis of others.

Praxis cannot take place unless the individual organism makes itself inert, exteriorizing itself as a tool and objectifying its praxis in the matter which it transforms. Through a long series of extended examples, Sartre next sets out to show, first, how various social relations – that is, relations between a multiplicity of individual praxes – are established through the mediations of matter and how these mediations transform that praxis; and second, how the human relations mediated through worked matter bring into being *antagonistic* ensembles – those conflictual unities which he calls *collectives* and whose structure he describes as *serial*. Finally, he wants to show how even qualitatively different ensembles – those primarily mediated in interiority and whose praxis is non-antagonistic – will also be repenetrated by the inertia of the practico-inert field which they have together totalized.

Sartre demonstrates the first of these points through the example of the Chinese peasantry. In a situation of endemic land-hunger, the peasants have, over the centuries, deforested China in trying to produce more arable land. For each individual, the intention of the praxis of removing trees was only to extend cultivable land. However, repeated by a multitude of individuals, this has led to consequences no individual intended – soil erosion, periodic floods and thus the destruction of such land. For, unwittingly, they have together totalized *one* material field. There is 'no joint undertaking', but the transformation of each individual undertaking, through its mediation with others which are the same, issues finally in a 'joint result'(CDR 163–4). This, each encounters as a 'counter-finality', as the 'alienation' (the making other) of his or her own praxis.

In this example, Sartre stresses, there is only the most rudimentary totalization of praxes through matter as 'mere Nature'. Men are passively totalized in their relation of isolation.[19] However, the riverine civilization, which develops to combat the flooding through massive public works, involves an active interiorization of the practico-inert. The prior praxis of deforestation is interiorized as the requirement for a new praxis which will negate and transcend it through the construction of new practico-inert objects – dikes, embankments, etc. But this new praxis, while transcending the prior praxis of deforestation, is itself constrained by the fact that it also preserves what it totalizes: there is what Sartre calls an *exigency* arising from the practico-inert, which imposes specific requirements on the new praxis – that the dikes must be continuously repaired, for example. Thus praxis – unlike the freedom of the for-itself – is always constrained by the exigencies of the prior praxis which it interiorizes and totalizes.

In a series of examples Sartre goes on to show not only how prior praxis imposes its exigencies on new praxis, but also how each new praxis engenders its own unanticipated 'counter-finalities'. His examples range from the paradoxical collapse of the Spanish economy in the sixteenth century owing to the influx of new wealth from the Americas, to the invention of the steam engine, and the exigencies which industrial labour imposes on the life of a woman factory worker in modern France.

In this last example Sartre illustrates a power of humanly mediated worked matter so great that it robs praxis of any effective choice. Describing a low-paid woman factory worker who 'decides' to have an abortion to avoid having a child she could not feed, Sartre describes her action as a 'destiny'. Her entire historical condition dictates that she could not choose otherwise:

> she *realises* through herself what she *is* already; she carries out the sentence which has already been passed on her, which deprives her of free motherhood. (CDR 235)

In such a destiny, and in its moment of subjective comprehension which Sartre calls *necessity*, praxis is merely making oneself the material force through which things happen. It remains distinct from a natural material force only in that the agent still comprehends what she or he has enabled to happen:

> the man who looks at his work, who recognises himself in it completely, and who also does not recognise himself at all; the man who can say both: 'This is not what I wanted' and 'I understand that this is what I have done and that I could not do anything else' ... this man grasps, in an immediate dialectical movement, necessity as the *destiny in exteriority of freedom*. (CDR 226-7)

Thus, Sartre now concedes, socially mediated worked matter can limit freedom to the point where no effective 'choice' is possible. 'Necessity' would appear to be the recognition, finally, of what Beauvoir had called 'immanence', of what Merleau-Ponty had described as 'a freedom devoid of any project'(PP 444).

In all of Sartre's examples, what we see in varying degrees is 'the domination of man by worked matter' and the way in which that domination is interiorized as a social bond. This presupposes Sartre's claim that all individual praxis takes place in and is mediated by *scarcity*. 'Scarcity', Sartre tells us, is 'contingent': it does not have the same ontological status as 'need', for it is 'perfectly possible to ... conceive of a dialectical *praxis*, or even of labour, without scarcity'. However, were there to be praxis without scarcity, we would not have men or history as we know them (CDR 124). Although Sartre raises – rather sceptically – the possibility that there could be a future without scarcity,[20] he is emphatic that, with regard to our own past and present, scarcity is all-pervasive. Indeed, it is scarcity which provides an initial, passive mediation of *all* praxis. For at the most abstract level, the possibility that History could be shown to be one universal totalization resides, for Sartre, in the universality of scarcity. In the era of the world market, at least, scarcity passively links all praxes on a global scale, and it suggests the possibility of at least a minimal unification of world History.

However, crucial though the notion of scarcity is for Sartre, its status as contingent yet universal remains rather unclear. Initially, scarcity appears to be an empirical fact: there simply is not sufficient means of subsistence available to satisfy the organic need of every human organism on the face of the Earth. As a 'fact' of human life, universal scarcity is, of course, highly contestable. For even today hunger can be shown to be an outcome of the mal-distribution of resources, not of their absolute lack. However, as Sartre's discussion continues, it becomes clear that scarcity is not merely an empirical fact, but rather the lived *possibility* that there might not be enough, whether or not this is actually the case. Scarcity is thus interiorized in human relations as the threat that the praxis of others will negate my praxis, and as the alteration of the praxis of each through the interiorization of this threat by all. This dynamic, which Sartre would appear to regard as universal, is what brings into being *serial*, or *collective*, ensembles.

In collectives, the mediation of individual praxis through the practico-inert material field is interiorized by each individual in such a way as to bring into being a new spiral of the dialectic: the dialectic of alterity. Sartre again proceeds through a series of examples, in each of which praxis is shown to undergo not only the *alienation* of its project by worked matter, but also a second form of being made other, or *altered*. This second form, which Sartre calls *alterity*, takes place through the direct mediation of other praxes. In this dialectic, the *collective* comes into being as 'the unity of interpenetration of individuals as beings-in-the-world-outside-themselves' (CDR 255–6).

Sartre's simplest example concerns a face-to-face ensemble, a set of people queuing at a bus stop. Each pursues a different praxis, in that each plans to take the bus for his or her own ends. In what sense, then, do they form an ensemble? In the first instance, says Sartre, their individual praxes are *passively* totalized through the practico-inert (through the corner where they wait, the bus stop, the bus which they wait for). They thus share a 'common interest' that the bus should come, and this 'unites them from outside' (CDR 258–9). This is not, however, where totalization ends. For each realizes that there may not be enough seats on the bus for all of them; and in joining the queue each recognizes that the exterior law of number (and not the unique qualities of his specific project) will determine who gets on the bus. Furthermore, as each realizes, it is through the *others* that his own place in the queue is determined: each *is* – and recognizes himself to be – his 'being-outside-himself' as given in the ordering of the queue (CDR 261).

It must be stressed that while this dialectic of alterity requires an interior moment of comprehension on the part of each agent, it is not primarily a subjective phenomenon.[21] A real alteration of individual praxis takes place in exteriority, through what Sartre calls 'the Logic of the series'.[22] Thus, in another example, that of the free market, any individual seller confronting any buyer discovers that the price at which he can sell his commodity is not arrived at through his particular relation with a particular buyer, but by all the absent buyers and sellers in the market collective. Although not physically present, what any other seller would sell at (and buyer buy at) determines what must be agreed in this particular transaction (CDR 277 ff).

Sartre's final example of collective being concerns the early nineteenth-century French proletariat. Against the commonly held Marxist assumption that collective exploitation breeds class solidarity, Sartre maintains that the most fundamental form of class being is serial. In addition to being serialized as competitive sellers of labour-power, workers find their exploitation revealed in the exigencies of the labour process as only 'the passive unity of all', in which each lives the isolation of others as his own. Class being is lived, above all as *destiny*: as their collective *impotence* in the face of the machines, the employers, the labour market, all of which unite them in relations of either passivity or competitive antagonism (CDR 306 ff).

Sartre concludes that if an *internally* unified praxis of class solidarity – what he calls a 'practical sociality' (CDR 340) – is to emerge, it cannot do so through the mediation of the practico-inert field. There has rather to be a fundamentally different kind of ensemble, one which is the radical negation of the practico-inert. This, in its purest form, he calls the *groupe-en-fusion*. It is the free, joint, negation of the practico-inert. But like any dialectical totalization it also perpetuates what it negates, and comes to be permeated by the practico-inert, albeit in new and more social forms: those of the *organization* and the *institution*. Sartre's main example of the *groupe-en-fusion* is the storming of the Bastille (CDR 345 ff). Here, once the group had completed its initial project and taken control of the Bastille and its cannons, the exigencies of the practico-inert re-entered its praxis: the cannons had to be maintained in readiness, a permanent guard mounted, etc. Tasks had to be divided up and properly organized. Thus individuals find that the perpetuation of their common praxis also imposes certain practico-inert exigencies upon them.

Social situations: mediations in interiority

Mediations of the practico-inert are never, of course, purely exterior. They are always totalized, and thus interiorized, by the praxis they mediate. It is through this interiorizing movement that a milieu – a contingently given set of circumstances – is transformed into a *situation*: that a 'lived bond' between praxis and its practical material field is brought into being. Thus praxis-in-situation – unlike freedom-in-situation – encounters necessity as well as freedom and is 'the product of its product'. Moreover, it is always, to a greater or lesser degree, praxis in social situation, since it interiorizes other praxes and is interiorized by them. In exploring these totalizations, Sartre develops two fundamentally new concepts, *reciprocity* and the *Third*.[23]

By reciprocity Sartre means a relation of mutual recognition between two agents of praxis. This recognition may be either antagonistic or, Sartre now allows, co-operative. It 'can be either positive or negative'(CDR 113), the mediation of worked matter determining in any concrete case which it is to be. It follows that, unlike being-for-others, reciprocity is not a relation of two consciousnesses. It is a relation of two embodied agents of *praxis*. Hegel's account of the 'master-slave dialectic', in which 'each consciousness seeks the death of the Other' (which Sartre had largely paralleled in *Being and Nothingness*) erroneously ignores the practical nature of their relation. Against Hegel, Sartre now points out: '[t]he origin of struggle always lies, in fact, in some concrete antagonism whose material condition is *scarcity*, in a particular form'(CDR 113). Even so, reciprocity, like 'being-for-others', remains a *dyadic* relation of mutual recognition.

All reciprocity, positive or negative, involves the following four conditions (CDR 112–13): (1) I recognize both the Other and myself as each a means to our own individual ends; (2) I recognize the Other as a praxis – 'as a developing totalization' – while simultaneously objectifying him within my own totalization; (3) through my movement towards my ends, I recognize his movement towards his ends; and (4) when I objectify the Other within my own totalization, I also discover my own objectification within his totalization. What these four conditions imply is that *any* praxis – however alienated or antagonistic – involves a recognition of a synthetic relationship with other praxes. Just as Merleau-Ponty had talked of a fundamental 'communion' which must exist for conflict even to begin, and of a social world in which men both 'deny and sustain' each others' existence, so Sartre now talks of the reciprocal recognition of praxis by praxis as a fundamental bond between men, even in relations of hostility.

However, by itself the bond of reciprocity is not sufficient to account for the emergence of ensembles, or their totalization within a broader movement of History, for it is a dyadic relation: 'however far the two integrations are carried, they *respect one another, there will always be two* of them, each integrating the entire universe' (CDR 114). Thus it is only through the mediation of Thirds that a multiplicity of such reciprocal dyads may be totalized into ensembles.

Sartre first introduces the idea of totalization through a *Third*, or a 'third party', in describing himself in this role, looking out of a hotel window at a gardener and a road-mender. The two, on either side of a wall, are ignorant of each other's existence. It is thus through Sartre's totalization that their individual praxes are unified – without them knowing it – in a *triadic* relationship. Through Sartre's mediation, 'each of them constitutes the ignorance of the other' (CDR 103 ff). Sartre's account of himself looking at the men from his window is, of course, reminiscent of the look in *Being and Nothingness*. However, looking is now integral to *praxis*. Looking at the men gives Sartre various practical options: to communicate with either of them; to enable them to communicate through him; or 'to play a passive part' and observe them as a 'closed totality' from which he is excluded. But even if he chooses the most passive option, Sartre insists that the observer still remains a situated observer, for his praxis will itself be negated by what it totalizes. Sartre is within the totalised field at the same time as totalizing it, and through his praxis of observation he is himself constituted as 'not a worker', as not experiencing their praxis. Thus we no longer have, as in the Us-object, a dyad overlooked by an objectifying other, but a triad.

Sartre's initial account of totalization through the Third is highly formal. But, as he points out, in concrete events the totalizing function of the Third need not be fixed in the praxis of any one individual. On the contrary, the interiorization of its praxis by an ensemble (be it serial or fused), generally involves a shifting, mediating Third. The relation of third party to the various dyads it totalizes is, as Sartre puts it, 'commutative', with 'each member becoming the third party in turn, like in children's games where everyone takes turns at being the general or the bandit chief' (CDR 119). Each ensemble member can be, in turn, both totalizing Third and engaged in the reciprocal action which each, as Third, totalizes. Each totalizes the ensemble and each is totalized in it.

Returning to Sartre's example of the bus queue, we can now expand on it to see how the moment of interiority in that primarily practico-inert ensemble involves both reciprocal dyads and totalizing Thirds. Let us imagine two more people converging from opposite directions to join the queue. Their relation is one of negative reciprocity. Each has it as his or her project to be the next to join the queue and, in the light of that end, recognizes the other as an equivalent praxis whose project threatens his or her own; each objectifies the other in the totalizing project of arriving first; and each realizes also that the other does the same to him or her.

However, in this example we also have a triadic mediation taking place. For, in relation to the two newcomers each already existing member of the queue acts as an 'alienating Third'. Through each of them the two newcomers are totalized as 'competing for the next place'. Their arrival is also interiorized by each Third as constituting him- or herself as 'not the last', as already having an established place in the queue. Thus, the Thirds are situated within the totalization they effect. They both objectify the dyad of newcomers and are altered through their own totalizing praxis.

It is this same ambiguous position of each member as a Third – both totalizer *and* totalized – which, in special circumstances, can give rise to a *groupe-en-fusion*. What Sartre describes as 'the inversion of alienation' (CDR 378) takes place. Instead of my praxis being undermined by others, it is enriched, strengthened: 'In the *groupe-en-fusion*, the third party is my objectivity interiorised. I do not see it in him as Other, but as *mine*' (CDR 377). When my own praxis returns to me through the 'commutative' circle in which each of us acts as a Third for each other, it does not return to me as altered, but as 'synthetically enriched' (CDR 378) because the praxis of each of us is the 'same'.

For this to occur, there has to be both a particular practico-inert conjuncture and the free choice of the same project with regard to it. The Bastille example suggests that the practico-inert conjuncture must be one in which each individual faces the same threat of annihilation.[24] However, in the face of this threat it is not necessary that a *groupe-en-fusion* comes into being. On the contrary, Sartre stresses that what is involved in the formation of such a group is a free action which transcends the practico-inert. The gathering of threatened residents could as well have been passively totalized in 'serial flight', in a rout in which each tried in vain to flee from the cannon ahead of the others. The free and spontaneous eruption of a fused praxis of resistance produces a qualitatively new, 'second degree' (CDR 309) of sociality.

In his detailed reconstruction of the emergence of the fused group which stormed and took control of the Bastille, Sartre sets out for us the logic of totalization which gives rise to what he calls the *être-un* ('single-being') of such a group.[25] Social theorists frequently conceive groups as organic beings, as having a life independent of their members. Sartre, however, explicitly rejects such a view. If we can talk about the group as a real entity it is not because it is some trans-individual organism, the bearer of a 'collective consciousness' or 'will' of its own (CDR 538–9). Yet neither is the group a mere aggregate of individual praxes. For, in its bonds of interiority, individual praxis comes to be irrevocably altered.

If it is to be intelligible, the *être-un* of the group must be shown to be not what Sartre calls a 'hyper-organism' but a synthetic totalization of individual *praxes*. Thus it would be an error to conceive the *être-un* of the group as a fusion of *persons*. For it is only at the level of a set of specific *praxes* performed in common that a fusion takes place. Indeed, this is why the group threatens to disintegrate as soon as its initial praxis has been completed, and why it can then be held together only by the creation of a bond of internal coercion, a bond which reintroduces alterity within it.[26]

What does it mean to say that a *fusion* of individual praxes takes place within the group? What permits us to talk of its *être-un*? There must be, as Sartre illustrates through the Bastille example, several levels of totalization. Initially, there was only a passive totality, a collective: the Parisians formed the object of the praxis of the troops encircling the city. At first this passive totalization was interiorized by each as alterity. Each, for example, 'was forced to arm himself by others' attempts to find arms... everyone's attempt to get a gun became for the Others the risk of remaining unarmed' (CDR 354). However, as each also recognized that the others were under the same threat of annihilation as himself, a second kind of interiorization was able to develop in which each recognized the other's situation as identical to his own and the other's praxis as also appropriate for himself. Since the situation came to be seen as one, the same for all, action became synchronized (though not yet synthetically totalized) through 'imitation'; all began to shout, march, etc. As a result, multiple relations of reciprocity became possible, a recognition by each of the others, dyad by dyad, as having an equivalent praxis to his own. However, the final fusion of such synchronized, individual praxes into one *common* praxis requires one more totalization – the interior totalization of the *mediating Third*, now called also the 'regulatory Third'.

Discussing the alienated Third, Sartre had argued that only totalization through a multiplicity of Thirds – totalization passing 'commutatively' from one to another – could forge from dyadic relations of antagonistic reciprocity a basic *social* entity: the collective. Each Third was said to be both transcendent in relation to those whom he totalizes, yet himself altered through his own totalizing praxis. Now, in the regulatory Third, all of these elements are again present, but this time in a non-alienated form. For the praxes that simultaneously totalize each other are no longer in competition, but are complementary. Their bond is not now one of otherness and impotence, but of sameness and empowerment.

Sociality, history and the limits to freedom

So far, we have been examining the mediations through which individual praxes (originating in need) totalize each other into various kinds of ensemble. We have mainly been examining what Sartre calls the 'constituting dialectic'. In examining this dialectic Sartre has demonstrated that what he had begun by investigating as individual praxis is always social praxis, for there are both exterior mediations and synthetic bonds through which individual praxes totalize each other, establishing both antagonistic and reciprocal social ensembles.

Thus human praxis can never be a wholly individual action; whether in relations of alienation or those of reciprocal affirmation, human praxes interiorize and alter each other so that no individual could claim to be the unique author of his or her own praxis. Sartre has, finally, given us an ontology in which individual human being and social being are intelligible only as two aspects of one and the same totalization, and a social theory in which methodological individualism and holism are shown to be false alternatives.

This is not, of course, to say that individual consciousness and freedom have now simply disappeared from Sartre's world. Rather, the subject of praxis has become – to use Merleau-Ponty's notion – an 'impure' subject. Not only is the product of his praxis other than he had intended, but his being-outside-himself, for instance his class-being, also penetrates his interior being and conditions future praxis. As 'the product of his product', 'man' is no longer the 'absolute subject' that he was in *Being and Nothingness*.

As Sartre observed in 1966, when asked to comment on the then rising tide of anti-humanism, the subject is 'in a sense...always decentred'. If by 'the subject', he continued, we mean, 'a sort of substantial *I*, or a central category, always more or less given, from which reflection develops, then the subject has been dead for a long time'. However, Sartre hastened to add, the death of this kind of a *thinking* subject is not the death of the subject *tout court*. For as soon as we talk of any kind of transcendence of a given situation or structure, that is, of any kind of praxis, we still require a notion of the subject and of subjectivity. What needs, in Sartre's view, to be explained is how 'the subject or subjectivity constitutes itself from a basis anterior to itself by a continual process of interiorisation and re-exteriorisation'.[27] Foucault, for example, does not give us, in *The Order of Things*,[28] an archaeology, but rather a geology, Sartre complains. For an archaeologist 'studies a period which was conceived and worked upon by men...the result of a praxis whose development the archaeologist retraces'. Whereas what Foucault gives us are a set of immobile strata. Because he denies a place to praxis, Foucault cannot understand *transition*, and 'he replaces cinema with a magic lantern, movement by a succession of immobilities'.

However, Sartre's goal in the *Critique* is not merely to show how the self-constitution of the practical subject takes place in a dialectic of interiorization and exteriorization. Nor is it only to establish the necessarily social nature of individual praxis. Beyond these goals Sartre wants, even more ambitiously, to be able to show that the intelligibility of History as one universal movement emerges in the totalizing conflict of, above all, classes. It is through the exploration of what he calls the *constituted dialectic* – that is, the dialectic of *group* praxes – that Sartre attempts this second and rather less successful undertaking.

Once group praxis has come into being it is no longer reducible to the individual praxes which are totalized in it. For there is an irreversible temporality to the human project. Thus, while never forgetting that it is individual praxis which brings groups into being and sustains them, it is to the dialectical logic of group praxis that Sartre turns in the latter sections of the *Critique*. His aim is to explain how History might be intelligible as one movement of totalization, how, finally, class struggle might be totalized from within, as a movement of 'totalization without a totalizer'.

Just as individual praxis produces practico-inert counter-finalities in which it is alienated, so too does group praxis. In order to avoid the dispersal which always threatens them, groups rapidly create forms of internal inertia. They develop what Sartre calls *structure*. By structure Sartre no longer means those structures of experience, such as temporality or death, which he had discussed in *Being and Nothingness*. Structure now means for Sartre the enduring practico-inert expressions of group praxis. As such, structure represents an *ossification* of group praxis, and it functions as a constraint on future praxis. Moreover, the interactions between structures frequently take on a mechanical appearance, which Sartre calls *process*. In discussing the development of structures and their interactions,[29] Sartre both anticipates the general thrust of later structuralist social theory and also offers a clear delineation of what he sees as the limits to the appropriate role for structural analysis. Thus although structuralism emerged by the 1960s in France as an explicit and militant *rejection* of existential phenomenology, Sartre had already – even before the attack began – indicated both what structuralism might be able to offer and what he took to be its limits.

As we already saw in the Bastille example, once a group has obtained its initial objective it must reinteriorize passivity in order to perpetuate itself. Like the *groupe-en-fusion*, any organization or institution must, in order to perpetuate itself, establish an inert power over its members: a *structure*. 'Power', Sartre observes, 'constitutes itself by producing in everyone the inertia which is the basis of necessity' (CDR 491). Thus, for example, the kinship structures which Lévi-Strauss analysed, or the logic of modern industrial production, in which organization 'must produce within itself the apparatuses of mediation, supervision, and inspection' (CDR 543), *appear* as autonomous determinants of individual life. It is, of course, possible to grasp such structures through the 'dissolving' logic of analytic reason, as Lévi-Strauss had done (CDR 479). It is certainly possible also to give an account of social and historical change as *process*: as a logic of structural interactions. For example, those sociologists who explain the 'pauperisation' of the native population of Algeria under French colonial rule as being the 'necessary result' of the interaction between the structures of a backward agricultural and a modern industrial society are describing a real process. Once colonialism had been installed in Algeria, the 'process of exploitation' did indeed function as a practico-inert system, whose logic could be examined analytically (CDR 721 ff).

However, Sartre insists that such logics constitute only one aspect of historical dialectic. Although much of the second part of the *Critique* is concerned with demonstrating the alienation of group praxis (including working-class praxis) in such structures and their logics, Sartre argues that focusing on the structural aspect alone makes History ultimately unintelligible. For structuralism, like economic reductionism or dogmatic Marxism, is a form of positivism: that is, it assumes as a tacit given an atemporal and non-situated observer – an observer now of macro-structures rather than mere individual facts – who simply states, '[t]his is how things are' (CDR 712). Thus structuralism is unable to grasp the significance of its own observations as themselves the product of a concrete, situated praxis; it cannot locate its own thought as a totalization of a particular social, political and intellectual situation. In short, if it is not to end in what Sartre calls 'empirical irrationality', in which no human intention remains visible, structural analysis can be only one aspect of a dialectical investigation. It must always be reintegrated into an account of dialectical totalization, of praxis. It is this reintegration that structuralism and also post-structuralism preclude by refusing to recognize the moment of practical subjectivity.

It is in exemplifying the notion of praxis as process, or 'praxis-process' in the case of colonial Algeria that Sartre most clearly shows us what he takes to be the appropriate place of the structural moment in dialectical reason. In Algeria, French colonial rule was violently imposed. The perpetuation of this rule, once it was established, involved the development of a set of institutions which installed violence and exploitation as a practico-inert system. For future generations of colonialists, the effects of this appeared as process. For example, wage levels appeared to be settled 'on the basis of specific material conditions which elude the action of the colonialists as much as that of the natives' (CDR 722). Once the system is in place, then, no one appears to be responsible for starvation wages. Yet, Sartre points out, it constantly requires new praxis to perpetuate the system. Similarly, for new generations of colonialists – and for the young French conscript sent out to fight in the 1950s – the violence necessary to maintain the system in the face of the colonized's praxis of resistance also appears as beyond individual control. Violence, like exploitation, has become a process. But it is also a *praxis*. For it is only 'the project of exploitation' (CDR 734) which 'sustains' both the previously established process of exploitation and the violence which is necessary to perpetuate it.

Sartre ends his discussion of Algeria by pointing out that it exemplifies the role of struggle in historical totalization: it is 'struggle' as the 'double reciprocal *praxis*' of colonizer and colonized which gives rise to process as its practico-inert exigency (CDR 734). And it is struggle which either perpetuates or destroys that process through further reciprocal praxis. Struggle can be intelligible only as long as we accord their proper weight both to structure and process, on the one hand, and to praxis, on the other. If, as positivisms of various kinds claim, struggle should be conceived as only the clash of structures (or of productive forces) and not as practical totalization and interiorization, then we would have to admit that 'the human order is strictly comparable to the molecular order'(CDR 734). And were this the case, only an analytic reason, one which posits the 'unintelligibility of History as a definite fact', would be possible.

If struggle is neither pure praxis nor pure process, but always praxis-process, what does this tell us about human freedom? As we already saw in Sartre's treatment of the constituting dialectic, freedom is now *practical* freedom, subject to the exigencies of organic need and the alienating power of the practico-inert. Thus freedom may be so reduced as to involve no more than recognizing that the carrying out of our 'sentence' is a 'necessity'.

What Sartre's account of the constituted dialectic now adds to his notion of practical freedom is a yet fuller exposition of its alienation in social relations. Group praxis objectifies itself in institutions, rigid structures which assert their own counter-finality against their authors; yet these counter-finalities appear even more powerful than those of more simple forms of worked matter. No clear division is possible between those forms of the practico-inert which are mainly material (such as machines) and those which are mainly social (such as relations of production or state power). Yet, as dialectical investigation proceeds from abstract individual praxis towards concrete social praxis, the practico-inert itself is encountered in increasingly social forms and, simultaneously, praxis becomes increasingly opaque to itself. It is above all in the practico-inert structures of power, arising through the praxis of struggle between groups, that freedom most appears to lose itself in thing-like process.

By the end of the *Critique* Sartre had addressed the difficulties which *Being and Nothingness* had posed as a basis for social theory: the absolute freedom of the subject as for-itself, the necessarily dyadic interpersonal relation of the look, the lack of mediations between individuals, all had been addressed in reformulating the notion of the subject as an agent of praxis-in-situation. However, Sartre's ultimate goal in the *Critique* – to show that the whole of human history can be intelligible as one dialectical movement in which class struggle gives rise to 'totalization without a totalizer' – had by no means been attained.

That Sartre abandoned work on Volume II of the *Critique*, where he had promised to show us this totalization at work, is less a cause than a symptom of his failure. It has been suggested that there were above all political reasons for Sartre's abandonment of Volume II: the failure of the Soviet Union to reanimate a world proletarian movement, as Sartre had hoped it would after de-Stalinization, meant that the movement of totalization continued to be effectively blocked. This being so, Sartre's intellectual project was also blocked and had to be abandoned. But this can be only a part of the explanation. Given that Sartre's optimism about a revolutionary revival was never unbounded, he clearly did not see his project as fully tied to a revolutionary future. Thus it is also to internal difficulties within Sartre's project that we must look for an explanation of his failure. Of these, perhaps the most pressing concerns the notion of *one* History, or of *universal* History.[30]

Sartre claimed that he had 'learned history' from Merleau-Ponty. But in the commemorative article where he made this remark, he also pointed to significant divergences between Merleau-Ponty's views and his own. Although they referred to the 1940s, his comments are also relevant to the *Critique*, published only the previous year:

If the Truth is one, I thought, we must, as Gide said, seek it not elsewhere but everywhere... We would be hunters of meaning, we would speak truth about the world and about our own lives. Merleau found me optimistic. Was I so sure that there was meaning everywhere?[31]

For Merleau-Ponty, while being is One and we are 'condemned to meaning', that meaning is profoundly ambiguous and easily transformed into non-meaning. It is, above all, in the social world that the *non-sens* of history emerges along with its *sens*. While Merleau-Ponty accorded considerable weight to oppression and class struggle in trying to account for the violence in human affairs, he also insisted on the irreducible role of contingency, especially in the making of public history. Thus, to Merleau-Ponty Sartre's entire project must have appeared misguided: for Merleau-Ponty it was in principle impossible to establish one universal intelligibility of history.

Sartre later described *Being and Nothingness* as 'a monument of rationality'.[32] Yet the *Critique* even more strongly merits this description. For Sartre is not merely extending Marx's observations about the unifying effect of the world market. He is trying to make the case that *all* individual human praxis, *everywhere*, is in principle intelligible within one universal movement of totalization. It is a claim of staggering enormity.

It sometimes appears as if Sartre is only making an ideal claim – a claim about a hypothetical future point in history when, in a reign of freedom, men will make the 'one Truth' of History in common. Indeed, that is what he says in *Problem of Method*, writing that

> Our historical task, at the heart of this polyvalent world, is to bring closer the moment when History will have *only one meaning*, when it [History] will tend to be dissolved in the concrete men who will make it in common. (PM 90)

But Sartre is also, it is clear, saying something more. When he talks of scarcity as a unification of a universal practical material field, when he speaks of an individual – be it Flaubert, Valéry, Stalin, or himself – as a universal singular whose praxis is a totalization of all past and present praxis, he is making the claim that it ought now (and not only in some ideal future) to be possible to establish that the Truth of History is One. It is a claim which can be sustained, however, only at the expense of introducing a kind of formalism which undermines Sartre's own methodological bases.

The project of establishing the intelligibility of History as, finally, one totalization, can be pursued only at a level so formal as to undermine Sartre's own claims as to the necessarily situated nature of dialectical reason. For if all praxis is to be intelligible as one totalization, this could be so only at the most undifferentiated level, where there is the least regard for concrete situation. Sartre's method in the *Critique* is to begin with the abstract praxis of the individual organism and then to move to ever greater concreteness in revealing the totalizations through which a multiplicity of such individual praxes creates ensembles and practico-inert structures of various kinds. However, there comes a point at which the attempt to grasp the multiple totalizations of totalizations must return us to abstraction: the universal is as abstract as the initial singular. Thus it is only at a level so formal that lived experience and concrete situation have effectively been lost to view, that the universality of History might be established. This becomes apparent if we return briefly to Sartre's treatment of scarcity. Scarcity is what, for Sartre, unifies all praxis within one and the same *universal* practical material field. What, finally, links the internal conflicts of a North African nomadic tribe with the history of the French class structure, or any other social formation we might care to name, is not the world market, colonialism, or capitalism *per se*, but the fact that all are conditioned by one and the same universal, global field of scarcity. But this is a proposition so universal that it tells us virtually nothing. It does not concretely reveal that all praxis is universal, for the significance of scarcity for praxis can be revealed only in concrete instances, and not at the level of universality.

Similarly, the notion of individual praxis as a universal-singular can tell us that a praxis is universal only in the most abstract sense. While Sartre may well succeed in showing us how Flaubert's project totalizes French society in the mid-nineteenth century – its class structure, the revolutions and so on – this is hardly a totalization of universal proportions. Indeed, it is striking that most of Sartre's examples (as opposed to his arguments) are based on, at the widest, national histories. Of course the implication of the notion of the universal singular is that in totalizing the France of his day Flaubert also totalized its place in the 'world system', and thus the praxis of anonymous workers in distant parts of the globe which Flaubert knew nothing about. But here the argument becomes formal to the point of emptiness; we cannot *concretely* demonstrate that any given praxis is a *universal* totalization; it may be said to be so only in principle, or abstractly. At the level of showing us *sociality* coming into being through the dialectic of individual and group praxis, the *Critique* works brilliantly. But as an argument about the universal intelligibility of human history, it falls into abstraction and fails.

Moreover, even at its brilliant best, the *Critique* remains too narrow. A 'monument of rationality', it establishes spiral after spiral of dizzying totalization to demonstrate the dialectical emergence of social being from Sartre's indubitable starting place: praxis overcoming individual organic need. But while one can grant Sartre the indubitability of individual organic need, it does not follow that the praxis which negates such need must be the unique point of origin of all social being. Sartre's monument contains no space in it for love or friendship (unlike Marcel's thought), for generosity (unlike Beauvoir's), or for forms of intersubjectivity grounded in the body (unlike Merleau-Ponty's). Thus while, in comparison with Marcel, Beauvoir, or even arguably Merleau-Ponty, Sartre presents us with the most rigorously developed social ontology, he does so at the cost of excluding significant dimensions of social experience from consideration. This is not to say that we should deny that need is fundamental, nor to diminish the significance of the dialectic which it originates in human life. But need is mediated, indeed humanized, through other kinds of intersubjective experience, such as love, generosity, play and art, none of which is wholly reducible to it. These are dimensions of social existence which Sartre ignores in the *Critique*. He would perhaps have done well to heed Marcel's warnings against the dangers of 'abstraction', and to have remained truer to his own original commitment to phenomenological method.

Even so against anti-humanism and the alleged 'end of the subject', Sartre's work stands as a sombre and cautious reaffirmation of the values of freedom and rationality. For, he insists, however intense the alienation of our actions, we collectively remain their authors. We thus always retain an element of responsibility for the consequences of our actions and, with that responsibility, a possibility of altering our future. Indeed, Sartre's views are arguably over-sombre. The human world is, without doubt, one of scarcity and conflict, such as he reveals. But it is also, as the other thinkers I have examined stressed, one in which relations of generosity and communion take place. What then is needed, beyond the *Critique*, is a further dialectical investigation which would explore the kinds of totalization outside scarcity which Sartre neglects and their complex interplay with totalizations in scarcity. Such an expansion of Sartre's project would go a long way towards giving us adequate means for a 'recovery of the subject'.

Conclusion

Sartre's *Critique* did not make a great impact on the French intellectual scene of the early 1960s. It is striking that, in *Force of Circumstance*, Beauvoir allots only one sentence to its reception.[1] Sartre himself continued to maintain a prominent public position as a man of the Left into the 1970s, but the intellectual winds were shifting. 'Anti-humanism' was becoming dominant, with structuralism the vogue in the 1960s, post-structuralism by the 1970s. It is not that the ideas of the anti-humanists were wholly new. Indeed, some of the essentials of structuralism can be viewed as reformulations, albeit radical reformulations, of the Durkheimian social science which was dominant in France before the First World War.[2] Rather it was a shift in political and intellectual climate, linked to the prolonged postwar expansion and modernization of the French economy, that enabled them to achieve a new dominance, a 'resurrection' of a 'philosophy without a subject'.[3] If the social turn of French existentialism had been made possible by the unique postwar intellectual and political conjuncture, France in the age of established Gaullism was very different; although the resurgence of the idea of a self-regulating and objective system obviously is not explicable merely as the epiphenomenal expression of the stability of the economy at the time, neither are the two wholly discrete occurrences.

Lévi-Strauss's attack on Sartre (in the last chapter of *The Savage Mind*) epitomized the shift that was taking place. It was to be followed by attacks on Sartre and Merleau-Ponty as naïve humanists, exponents of an out-dated 'philosophy of the subject', from numerous quarters. Within Marxism, Althusserian structuralism proclaimed Marxist humanism to be an ideology, distinct from the mature Marxist 'science of history'.[4] While Althusser's initial target was ostensibly East European Marxist humanism, an implicit attack on French existential Marxism was always present in his work, becoming explicit in his *Essays on Self-Criticism*.[5] From another quarter, the work of an older thinker, Lacan, began to occupy the centre of psychoanalytic theory and practice in the 1960s. Lacan effectively dislodged both existential psychoanalysis and classical Freudian theory with a theory of the unconscious modelled on Saussurean linguistics and an insistence on the necessarily fragmentary or 'split' and unstable nature of the self.

In 1961, the year of Merleau-Ponty's death, Michel Foucault published the first edition of *Madness and Civilization*.[6] Foucault was born in 1926 and came of age in the postwar period, when the existentialists were at the height of their influence. Foucault was a student of Jean Hyppolite, who had been responsible for translating and writing a major commentary on Hegel's *Phenomenology*.[7] He also attended Merleau-Ponty's lectures, and his first book, published in 1954, was itself a work of existential psychology.[8] But by 1961 Foucault was, like most of his generation, in militant revolt against his masters. As he much later wrote, his early study of 'forms of experience' had left him dissatisfied, for it relied on a 'philosophical anthropology' that was, he came to believe, ahistorical.[9] However, in setting out to demonstrate what he afterwards still chose to call 'the very historicity of forms of experience',[10] Foucault in fact mounted, from 1961 onwards, a militant attack on the notion of an active *subject* of experience. 'Experience' for Foucault came to be reduced in the 1960s to 'the history of systems of thought',[11] or to the history of 'discursive practices' which, he claimed, *constitute* the subject. In the 1970s his focus shifted and he began to examine the relation of systems of knowledge to practices of power. However, this shift did not cause him to abandon the argument that subjectivity is an 'effect', or a construct, but only to rework it through an account of the effects that power has on (and through) individual bodies.

By the early 1970s, the notion of the subject attributed to the existentialists was under attack from at least two further directions, the deconstructivist strategies of Derrida and the 'philosophies of desire' of Deleuze and Lyotard.[12] Derrida's subversion of the notion of linguistic structure by that of the 'play' of 'difference' soon came to be taken as an account of the world beyond texts – or rather, the world was taken to *be* text, and nothing more. By contrast, for the philosophers of desire the subject was denied in the name of an inchoate and eruptive libido against which consciousness could be only a movement of repressive unification.

CONCLUSION

These diverse thinkers of the 1960s and 1970s span a tremendous variety of fields: from political economy to psychoanalysis, from the study of the treatment of the insane and the criminal to literary theory. Methodologically they range from a neo-functionalist structuralism to an insistence on the radical discontinuity and even randomness of the human, and from realism to a militant nominalism. They are, in many ways, strange and incompatible bedfellows. But their hostility to humanism is the substratum that links their work. All of them confronted the existentialist argument that social agency cannot be theorized without reference to the individual human subject. All of them claimed to find in the arguments of the existentialists no more than a Cartesian notion of the autonomous subject, and dismissed the existentialists on these grounds.

We have already seen, in Sartre's objections to Lévi-Strauss, and in his argument that history cannot be intelligible as either *process* or *praxis*, but only as *praxis-process*, a defence of the notion of situated subjectivity against the objectivist stance of structuralism. The Achilles' heel of structuralism is its privileging of the knower: a detached observer from without or above, the de-situated theorist's claim to observe objective structures in operation casts him or her in the role of the classical knowing subject; it tacitly returns us to a neo-Cartesian epistemology. In addition, by observing in the world only what Sartre calls process, structuralism precludes the possibility of autonomous normative thought or action. While falsely claiming value-neutrality on the part of the observer, it reduces normative arguments, judgements and practices in the world it studies to epiphenomena: values can be no more than the ideological effects or expressions of deeper structural processes.

But what of post-structuralism? Linguistic models, such as Derrida's, are it seems to me broadly open to the same objections as structuralism. They simply replace an account of the purposive, functional, or ordered interaction of structures with an account of the play of signifiers. But those post-structuralisms that focus on desire and the body, while certainly not free of the problem of the relation of the theorist to the theorized or the tendency to preclude the normative, present a challenge of a different sort to a theory of situated subjectivity. For in their examination of how desire is harnessed to social and historical forms, to force and to power, they return to a focus on the individual, even on individual experience. However, their conception of the individual is very different from either the classical or the situated subject. It is in Foucault's work of the 1970s, in which his earlier structuralist concern with epistemic systems is displaced by a focus on the practices of power and the relation of these to the body, that perhaps the most persuasive challenge to the notion of situated subjectivity is to be found.

In *Discipline and Punish* (1975), Foucault makes clear his divergences from structuralism and defines as one of his main concerns the way disciplinary practices, exercised over the individual human body, come to shape 'the modern soul'. The significance of the growth of modern penal systems, with their focus on reform of the criminal, cannot, he argues, be adequately captured by simply describing the new systems of knowledge or the legal and institutional changes with regard to delinquency that have emerged since the eighteenth century. It will not do to focus, like Durkheim, on 'only the general social forms'. On the contrary, addressing not only Durkheim but also more recent structuralist method, Foucault writes,

> If one confined oneself to the evolution of legislation or of penal procedures, one would run the risk of allowing a change in the collective sensibility, an increase in humanization or the development of the human sciences to emerge as *a massive, external, inert and primary fact*. (DP 23, my emphasis)

Foucault's objections here appear strikingly similar to Sartre's critique of Lévi-Strauss. They seem to echo Sartre's insistence that class struggle cannot be reduced to pure exteriority, to a process such as the blind clash of productive forces. Human history, Foucault is also telling us, is more than the sum of its facts. It cannot be adequately grasped from without, as external or inert. But while he is anxious to distance himself from the neo-Durkheimian structuralist study of mere 'social fact', Foucault still wishes to reject the Sartrean notion of interiority. There cannot be, for him, that practical and situated subjectivity which comes into being in the dialectic of praxis and the practico-inert of which the recognition of its own necessity is an inescapable moment.

For Foucault, 'the subject' remains an 'effect'; it is constructed or constituted. While the history of changes in the study and the treatment of, in this instance, 'criminals' cannot be adequately told except as a history of *practice*, such practice needs to be accounted for without even a historicized notion of the subject. 'I don't believe', Foucault says in an interview, 'the problem can be solved by historicising the subject as posited by the phenomenologists, fabricating a subject that evolves through the course of history'.[13] For as he had argued in his earlier work, and still held in the 1970s, the 'constituting' or reflexive subject is itself merely a historical idea, a construct that emerged in the seventeenth century and which now has had its day. We can write a history of the emergence (and decline) of the *idea* of subjectivity, but subjectivity cannot itself be an agency in history.

Foucault's task in *Discipline and Punish* is, then, to develop an account of changing practices, in which agency can be shown to be located neither in objective forces and structures nor in the subject. As against Sartre's attempt to account for change as the dialectic of both praxis and process, Foucault argues for a third notion of agency as neither. Rather, social agency is located in the effects of power, or 'power-knowledge' on the body. 'Knowable man (soul, individuality, consciousness, conduct, whatever it is called)', is, he claims, 'the object-effect' of dominating 'power-knowledge'(DP 305).

Much of the substantive content of *Discipline and Punish* is a description of the development of what Foucault calls 'technologies' of power that operate through a fine-tuned regulation of the body. In the era of monarchy, punishment had been 'a ceremonial of sovereignty', using public punishment, torture and execution to instil in its terrified spectators 'the physical presence of the sovereign and of his power' (DP 130). But in the 'reformatories' developing from the late eighteenth century, the aim was different – the production of 'docility'. Punishment was no longer an assertion of sovereignty, but a set of techniques for the reform of the criminal. It was 'a technique for the coercion of individuals' and 'it operated methods of training the body ... by the traces it leaves, in the form of habits, in behaviour' (DP 131). The reformatory represents the archetypal set of technologies for inculcating docility. But, in modern society more broadly (the feudal extraction of surplus through levy having been displaced by the extraction of surplus at the point of production), labour-power has to be made docile, to be disciplined.[14]

However, this training through the body is not, according to Foucault – and herein lies his originality – to be conceived as the use of force 'on' the body; it is not a repression of a previously existing self, be it a self of desire or a self of consciousness. On the contrary, Foucault argues, power 'invests' the body, which becomes its 'instrument'. Through the thorough and detailed application of technologies, the body is manipulated so that it itself produces the desired effects and, in the process, the 'soul' is produced as 'the present correlative of a certain technology of power over the body' (DP 29). The exercise of power in 'disciplinary society' does not take place either through the use of direct violence, or through manipulations of consciousness, that is, through 'ideology'. In a move which appears to avoid accounting for power as either an operation at the level of consciousness or as direct physical force, Foucault argues that power is *sui generis*, reducible neither to ideology nor to violence.

We have seen, in the work of the existentialists, a repeated attempt to theorize human experience, action, institution and even history, as irreducible, or in Merleau-Ponty's words, as 'a third genus of being'. Both the notions of the body-subject and the practico-inert are, from opposite poles, ways of grasping this irreducibly hybrid nature of human being 'in situation'. But they are ways which Foucault tries to avoid, arguing that the moment of subjectivity, what he refers to as the soul, is called into being by power which has its basis in nothing but its own practice:

> It would be wrong to say that the soul is an illusion, or an ideological effect. On the contrary, it exists; it has a reality; it is produced permanently around, on, the body by the functioning of a power that is exercised on those punished – and, in a more general way, on those one supervises, trains and corrects ... This real, noncorporal soul is not a substance; it is the element in which are articulated the effects of a certain type of power and the reference of a certain type of knowledge ... The soul is the effect and instrument of a political anatomy; the soul is the prison of the body. (DP 30)

Thus for Foucault, subjectivity remains always constituted. Even though, once invested with power, subjectivity is active, and even though what produces it is a *technology* – that is, *human* knowledge and practice, and not a simple material force – subjectivity can never be granted any constituting role. What Foucault seeks to describe and theorize as the technology of power is an agency which is neither free subjectivity nor Durkheimian social fact. However, as Foucault's analysis develops, these rejected antinomies repeatedly resurface within it. In the final analysis, both an objectivist, neo-Durkheimian, notion of the functioning of power and a notion of the autonomous subject are tacitly present in his work, each implied in the attempt to exclude the other.

CONCLUSION

Although Foucault grants that the development of disciplinary society accompanies the shift from the extraction of surplus product through levy to its extraction in the labour process, he is anxious to avoid talking about classes of *agents* as having interests, or as *intentionally* using disciplinary techniques for their own ends. It is the disciplinary techniques themselves which carry social agency, not individuals or social classes. But in trying to exclude human intentionality from his account, what Foucault ends up doing is to personify and grant intentionality to the techniques. For example, he tells us at one point that discipline 'had to solve a number of problems for which the old economy of power was not sufficiently equipped' and that it 'clears up confusion' and 'establishes calculated distributions' (DP 219). In such statements, rationality is transposed into practices *as if* they were persons. On the one hand, it appears to be impossible to exclude from the narrative the language of the classical subject – the language of problem solving, clear thinking, calculation. On the other, by transposing rationality from individual subjects to practices, Foucault still terminates in a functionalism not dissimilar to that of Lévi-Strauss, in which 'primary' facts and external processes have their own purposes.

Moreover, the claim that discipline works directly on the body, so that the soul is produced as its effect, raises the question of how this production of the soul is actually effected. The claim that discipline works at the level of the body is put in question by Foucault's own accounts of disciplinary institutions in which the visibility of the inmates is the primary tool of discipline. Thus he writes:

> The exercise of discipline presupposes a mechanism that coerces by means of observation; an apparatus in which the techniques that make it possible to see induce effects of power and in which, conversely, the means of coercion make those on whom they are applied clearly visible. (DP 170–1)

But how is it that observation can 'induce' effects of power? One does not, for example, train dogs or horses by keeping them under continuous surveillance, but by a far more directly corporeal system of reward or punishment. Bentham's Panopticon, and other plans for reform and discipline based on continuous observation must presuppose a subjectivity which can be harnessed to disciplinary ends – but which also is free to resist them. Something like Sartre's account of the look, of shame as a relation to self in the presence of the other, is implied in the power that is attributed to the panoptic gaze, a power that functions independently of direct material coercion and with what can only be described as the complicity of the subject:

> He who is subjected to a field of visibility, *and who knows it, assumes responsibility for the constraints of power*; he makes them play spontaneously upon himself; he inscribes in himself the power relation in which he simultaneously plays both roles; he becomes the principle of his own subjection. (DP 202–3, my emphasis)

There seems to be no way for Foucault to explain how this non-material power he describes can take effect without the assumption that subjectivity remains constituting. Futhermore, Foucault also acknowledges that panopticism does not, in fact, routinely produce docility. The final effect of the prison generally is to produce delinquency. There are, of course, sociological explanations offered for this. But what is also implied, at the level of the individual, is active non-compliance, resistance. There is then a subterranean recognition in *Discipline and Punish* of an element of *freedom*, even in oppression.

This subterranean recognition begins to surface explicitly in some of Foucault's very last work, as I described in the Introduction. But then, rather than embracing that notion of an 'impure' or situated subjectivity for which his own analyses so loudly cry out, Foucault simply abandons his earlier claim that knowledge and consciousness are always effects. He reverts instead to the classical conception of the autonomous subject. With the claim that 'thought is a freedom in relation to what one does, the motion by which one detaches oneself from it, establishes it as an object, and reflects on it as a problem',[15] he returns to the terrain of Descartes and the disembodied, de-situated, subject.

How are we to explain Foucault's wild gyrations, from the denial of individual constituting consciousness, to the personification of human consciousness in autonomous practices, to a return to the classical autonomous subject? It would seem that his attempt to avoid both subjective idealism and Durkheimian objectivism does not succeed, but merely results in his oscillating from one to the other. The conclusion is surely that we cannot consistently talk about ourselves without admitting that we are embodied and situated *selves*: that is, experiencing, intentional, acting, subjects in situation.

CONCLUSION

'Humanism' is not, for all its ideological overlay, its epochal, class, or cultural specificities, to be dismissed as a pure fiction, or construct. And if 'anti-humanism' has been right to point to those diverse forces which bear down on, which enter and even shape the self, the corollary is not that subjectivity is no more than the complex effect of those forces. Rather, the agenda left us by the self-defeating character of the anti-humanist project, well exemplified in Foucault's trajectory, is to reformulate the notion of the subject as at once constituting and constituted – in short as situated. The French existentialists offer us an invaluable set of tools for such a reformulation.

Notes

Notes to introduction

1 Annie Cohen-Solal, *Sartre: A Life*, trans. Anna Cancogni (New York: Pantheon Books, 1987).
2 For an overview of this return see Peter Dews, *Logics of Disintegration* (London: Verso Books, 1987), pp. xii-xiv; see also Alan Montefiore (ed.), *Philosophy in France Today* (Cambridge: Cambridge University Press, 1983) for a sampling of the diverse themes and modes of recent French philosophy. For an example of the current turn away from anti-humanism see Luc Ferry and Alain Renaut, *La Pensée 68: essai sur l'anti-humanisme contemporain* (Paris: Gallimard, 1985).
3 The most influential exception has been Richard Rorty. Although his book, *Philosophy and the Mirror of Nature* (Princeton: NJ Princeton University Press, 1979), has not effectively shifted the centre of Anglo-American philosophy, it has helped to make post-structuralist continental philosophy an at least marginally respectable topic of conversation.
4 Cited in John Passmore, *One Hundred Years of Philosophy* (Harmondsworth: Penguin, 1966), p. 487.
5 John Rawls, *A Theory of Justice* (Cambridge, Mass: Harvard University Press, 1971). For other examples see Ronald Dworkin, *Taking Rights Seriously* (Cambridge, MA: Harvard University Press, 1977); Robert Nozick, *Anarchy, State and Utopia* (New York: Basic Books, 1974); Michael Walzer, *Spheres of Justice* (New York: Basic Books, 1983).
6 op. cit., p. 11.
7 See, for example, Derrida's discussion of Foucault, 'Cogito and the History of Madness', in *Writing and Difference* [1967], trans. Alan Bass (Chicago: University of Chicago Press, 1978). See also his critique of Lévi-Strauss in Part II of *Of Grammatology* [1967], trans. Gayatri C. Spivak (Baltimore, MD: The Johns Hopkins University Press, 1974). For a critique of Althusser's 'structuralism' along similar lines see Vincent Descombes, *Modern French Philosophy*, trans. L. Scott-Fox and J. M. Harding (Cambridge: Cambridge University Press, 1980), p. 126. For an interesting

brief discussion of the relationship of post-structuralism to structuralism see Perry Anderson, *In the Tracks of Historical Materialism* (London: Verso Editions, 1983), ch. 2.

8 For a lucid overview of this argument see Kate Soper, *Humanism and Anti-Humanism* (London: Hutchinson, 1986).

9 Michel Foucault, 'What is an Author?', in *Language, Counter-Memory and Practice*, edited by Don Bouchard (Ithaca, NY: Cornell University Press, 1977), p. 138.

I am omitting from this rather schematic overview of alternative positions the work of Habermas and his adherents. But from the point of view of the divide I am discussing, Habermas lies on the side of 'the subject', with his emphasis on communication and its ideal conditions. See especially *Communication and the Evolution of Society*, trans. Thomas McCarthy (Boston MA: Beacon Press, 1979).

I would also place utilitarian and rational choice theory on the 'subject' side of the divide. Though both generally operate with a rather thin and under-specified conception of the subject, they must assume that the subject is the autonomous possessor and prioritizer of its own desires and interests. See, however, Jon Elster, *Sour Grapes* (Cambridge: Cambridge University Press, 1983) for an interesting nuancing of this notion of the self.

10 The phrase is Steven Lukes's. See his *Marxism and Morality* (Oxford: Clarendon Press, 1985).

11 Michel Foucault, 'Truth and Power', in *Power/Knowledge*, edited by Colin Gordon (New York: Pantheon Books, 1980), p. 117. The French word, *constituent*, may be translated in English as either 'constituent' or 'constituting'. I prefer to use the latter term for its greater sense of on-going activity.

12 Michel Foucault, 'Polemics, Politics and Problemizations: an Interview', in *The Foucault Reader*, edited by Paul Rabinow (New York: Pantheon Books, 1984), p. 388.

13 ibid. pp. 381–2.

14 Michael Sandel, *Liberalism and the Limits of Justice* (Cambridge: Cambridge University Press, 1982), p. 150.

15 ibid., p. 80.

16 ibid., p. 172.

17 In addition to the 'communitarian' critique of the autonomous subject, an even more trenchant critique has emerged from within feminist theory. See, in particular, Carol Gilligan's argument that different notions of self and connectedness to others are present in the conceptions of justice which women and men hold, *In a Different Voice: Psychological Theory and Women's Development* (Cambridge, Mass: Harvard University Press, 1982), and see also the discussions of the implications of this claim for ethical theory in Eva Feder Kittay and Diana T. Meyers (eds), *Women and Moral Theory* (Totowa, NJ: Rowman and Littlefield, 1987). For arguments from within feminist political philosophy see, for example, Nancy Hartsock's argument that the notion of the autonomous 'self' as constructed in opposition to the 'other' involves a specifically 'masculinist'

world view, in *Money, Sex and Power* (New York: Longman, 1983); see also Kathy Ferguson's critique of the traditional notion of the self as specifically male, 'Male Ordered Politics: Feminism and Political Science', in Terence Ball (ed.), *Critique and Renewal in Political Science* (Albany, NY: State University of New York Press, 1987), pp. 209–229.

18 For a helpful overview of these debates in the 1960s and 1970s see Richard J. Bernstein, *The Restructuring of Social and Political Theory* (Philadelphia, PA: University of Pennsylvania Press, 1978).

19 'The Eighteenth Brumaire', in Karl Marx and Frederick Engels, *Selected Works in One Volume* (New York: International Publishers, 1980), p. 97.

20 Thus, for example, Louis Althusser writes as follows:
[T]he structure of the relations of production determines the places and functions occupied and adopted by the agents of production, who are never more than the occupants of these places, insofar as they are the 'supports' [*Träger*] of these functions. The true 'subjects' (in the sense of constitutive subjects of the process) are therefore not these occupants or functionaries, are not despite all appearances... 'real men' – but the definition and distribution of these places and functions. The true 'subjects' are these definers and distributors: the relations of production... And if by chance anyone proposes to reduce these relations of production to relations between men, i.e. human relations, he is violating Marx's thought.
Reading Capital [1968], trans. Ben Brewster (London: New Left Books, 1970), p. 180.

21 'I am no doubt not the only one who writes in order to have no face', *The Archaeology of Knowledge* [1969], trans. A. M. Sheridan Smith (London: Tavistock Publications, 1972), p. 17. See also, 'What is an Author?', op. cit., p. 138.

22 *Central Problems in Social Theory* (Berkeley, Calif.: University of California Press, 1979), p. 44.

23 'Structuration theory' is most fully developed by Giddens in *The Constitution of Society* (Berkeley, Calif.: University of California Press, 1984).

24 Fred Dallmayr, *Twilight of Subjectivity, Contributions to a Post-Individualist Theory of Politics* (Amherst MA: University of Massachusetts Press, 1981), p. 6.

25 Richard J. Bernstein, *Beyond Objectivism and Relativism* (Philadelphia, PA: University of Pennsylvania Press, 1983). p. 172.

26 ibid. p. 230. Other significant works by Anglophone thinkers which include (or at least imply) a call to 'rethink the subject' rather than to abandon it include Alisdair MacIntyre, *After Virtue* (South Bend, Ind.: Notre Dame University Press, 1981); William L. McBride, *Social Theory at a Crossroads* (Pittsburgh, PA: Duquesne University Press, 1980); Charles Taylor, *Philosophical Papers*, 2 Vols (Cambridge: Cambridge University Press, 1985); Scott Warren, *The Emergence of Dialectical Theory* (Chicago: University of Chicago Press, 1984).

NOTES TO INTRODUCTION

27 For two recent attempts to place one thinker, Sartre, in political and intellectual context, see Anna Boschetti, *The Intellectual Enterprise: Sartre and Les Temps Modernes*, trans. Richard McCleary (Evanston, IL: Northwestern University Press, 1987) and Howard Davies, *Sartre and 'Les Temps Modernes'* (Cambridge: Cambridge University Press, 1987).
28 Jean Wahl, *Tableau de la philosophie française* (Paris: Gallimard, 1962), p. 149.
29 See *Sartre*, a film text by Alexandre Astruc and Michel Contat (Paris: Gallimard, 1977), p. 40. Sartre states that it was Bergson (whom he read in his final year at school) who both fired his enthusiasm for philosophy and oriented him towards a philosophy of the concrete. For Merleau-Ponty's discussion of the importance of Marcel see his 1959 lecture, 'La Philosophie de l'existence', *Dialogue*, vol. 5., no. 3, 1966, pp. 307–22.
30 'The War Has Taken Place', SNS 142. This essay originally appeared in October 1945 in the first issue of *Les Temps Modernes*, the journal founded by Sartre, Beauvoir, Merleau-Ponty and others.

Notes to chapter 1

1 Jean Hering, 'Phenomenology in France', in Marvin Farber (ed.), *Philosophic Thought in France and the United States* (Buffalo, NY: University of Buffalo Publications in Philosophy, 1950), p. 75.
2 'Conversations Between Paul Ricoeur and Gabriel Marcel', TW 222. See also Herbert Spiegelberg's discussion of Marcel's role in the history of French phenomenology, in *The Phenomenological Movement*, vol. 2, (The Hague: Martinus Nijhoff, 1976), pp. 422–44.
3 *Existentialism and Humanism* [1946], trans. Philip Mairet (London: Methuen, 1966), p. 26.
4 Marcel encountered Hegel through his interest in the work of the British neo-Hegelian, Bradley.
5 Apart from Bergson and Bradley, the other thinkers to whom Marcel acknowledged an intellectual debt were the American idealists, particularly Hocking and Royce. He also saw considerable affinities between his own work and that of William James, with whom he corresponded for a period. James himself was, of course, also significantly influenced by Bergson. The relationship between existentialism and pragmatism deserves a fuller exploration than it has yet received. But for an initial treatment see Richard J. Bernstein, *Praxis and Action* (Philadelphia, PA: University of Pennsylvania Press, 1971).
6 See Leszek Kolakowski, *Bergson* (Oxford: Oxford University Press, 1985), pp. 103–5.
7 Bergson's major discussions of consciousness and time are to be found in two of his earlier works: *Time and Free Will* [1889], trans. F. L. Pogson (London: George, Allen & Unwin, 1971) and *Matter and Memory* [1896], trans. Nancy M. Paul and W. Scott Palmer (London: George, Allen & Unwin, 1970). On the distinction between 'closed' and 'open' societies see

8 The talk was later published under the title, 'La Philosophie de l'existence', *Dialogue*, vol. 5, 1966–7, pp. 307–22.
9 Marcel makes this claim in the essay, 'Existence and Human Freedom' [1946], published in *The Philosophy of Existentialism*, trans. Manya Harari (Secaucus, NJ: The Citadel Press, 1980), p. 53.
10 See his account of his childhood and youth in 'Essay in Autobiography' [1947], in *The Philosophy of Existentialism*, op. cit., p. 109 ff.
11 'An Autobiographical Essay', in Paul Schilpp and Lewis Hahn (eds), *The Philosophy of Gabriel Marcel* (La Salle, IL.: Open Court, 1984), p. 17.
12 'Author's Preface to the English edition', MJ xiii.
13 In Schilpp and Hahn, op. cit., p. 581.
14 Bertrand Russell, *The Philosophy of Bergson* (Cambridge: Bowes and Bowes, 1914), p. 24.
15 Indeed, in this militant opposition to systemization Marcel strikingly anticipates one of the main elements in later French 'deconstruction'. Taken as a whole, of course, Marcel's philosophical problematic is radically incompatible with Derrida's. Yet there is still an interesting continuity traceable in French thought, from the existential critique of rationalism which begins with Marcel through to Derrida's critique of 'logocentrism'.
16 As Marcel later admitted, his interpretation of Descartes is a neo-Kantian one; Descartes is open to a more existential reading in which the *cogito* need not be interpreted as an 'epistemological subject' but as 'essentially the affirmation, 'I am'''. See TW 227. However, Marcel was not alone in reading Descartes through Kantian lenses. It was against the Kantianized Descartes of Brunschvicg, Lavelle and others that the postwar existentialists also rebelled.
17 'L'Etre incarné', EPC 29.
18 See Robert Lechner, 'Marcel as Radical Empiricist', in Schilpp and Hahn, op. cit., pp. 457–69.
19 'An Essay in Autobiography', op. cit., p. 128.
20 Martin Heidegger, *Being and Time* [1927] trans. John Macquarrie and Edward Robinson (New York and Evanston IL: Harper & Row, 1962).
21 On the French discovery of Heidegger see Martin Jay, *Marxism and Totality* (Berkeley, Calif.: University of California Press, 1984), p. 334 ff.
22 See also the discussions of the body in MJ, pp.242–50, 310–11, 315–16 and in MB, Vol. I, pp. 92–4 and 99–101.
23 'An Essay in Autobiography', op. cit., p. 127.
24 'On the Ontological Mystery' [1933], in *The Philosophy of Existentialism*, op. cit., pp. 9–46.
25 Love, in so far as distinct from desire or opposed to desire, love treated as the subordination of the self to a superior reality, a reality at the deepest level more truly me than I am myself – love as the breaking of the tension between the self and the other, appears to me to be what we might call the essential ontological datum. (BH 167)

26 See the essays written between 1942 and 1944, published in HV.
27 Merleau-Ponty wrote of the Occupation period,
    One compromised oneself whether one stayed or left; no one's hands are clean ... We have unlearned 'pure morality' and learned a kind of vulgar immoralism which is healthy. The moral man does not want to dirty his hands. It is because he usually has enough time, talent, or money to stand back from enterprises of which he disapproves and to prepare a good conscience for himself. The common people do not have that freedom: the garage mechanic had to repair German cars if he wanted to live. ('The War has Taken Place', SNS 147)
    The essay was published in 1945 in the first issue of *Les Temps Modernes*. Sartre also treated this issue in a play entitled 'Dirty Hands', in *'No Exit' and Three Other Plays*, trans. Lionel Abel (New York: Random House, 1955).
28 The latter paper was initially given in 1933, and was published in BH.
29 'On the Ontological Mystery', in *The Philosophy of Existence*, op. cit., pp. 10 and 12.
30 Many years later Marcel recorded his growing 'anguish' and 'anxiety' about Nazism beginning as early as 1932. 'Naturally', he observed, 'it is impossible for me to state the exact place this concern occupied in my life. But I think I can say that it tended to color what I might call my feeling, rather than my vision, of life. How could I have felt happy in a world so menaced?', ('An Autobiographical Essay', in Schilpp and Hahn, op. cit., p. 34).
31 Also MJ 234–5 and see the essay, 'A Metaphysic of Hope', in HV: 'The truth is that there can strictly speaking be no hope except where the temptation to despair exists' p. 36.
32 Some of these connections between Marxist critiques of alienation and Catholic doctrine were more explicitly developed by Marcel's contemporary – and protagonist – Emmanuel Mounier. See John Hellman, *Emmanuel Mounier and the New Catholic Left, 1930–1950* (Toronto: University of Toronto Press, 1981).
33 'The Critique of the Gotha Programme', in Karl Marx and Frederick Engels, *Selected Works in One Volume* (New York: International Publishers, 1980), p. 324.
34 Karl Marx, *Capital*, Vol. 1, trans. Samuel Moore and Edward Aveling (London: Lawrence and Wishart, 1970), p. 422.
35 Marcel does not indicate any familiarity with the then current German- and English-language literature on 'mass society'. He does, however, appear to have been influenced by the work of the Spanish writer, Ortega y Gasset, who, writing as early as 1930, also linked technocracy with depersonalization and the collapse of Christian values. See *The Revolt of the Masses* (New York: Norton, 1957). Original Spanish edition, 1930. Bergson's distinction between 'open' and 'closed' societies would also seem to be a source for much of Marcel's discussion.
36 For an early, parallel 'left' analysis of the role of deracination and fear in the emergence of Fascism see, Erich Fromm, *The Fear of Freedom* (London: Routledge & Kegan Paul, 1942).

37 In 'An Autobiographical Essay', in Schilpp and Hahn, op. cit., p.63.

Notes to chapter 2

1 'The Itinerary of a Thought', interview given in 1969, reprinted in Jean-Paul Sartre, *Between Existentialism and Marxism*, trans. John Matthews (London: Verso, 1983), p. 33.
2 Thus, if we attempt to grasp the self as a 'real existent', it disappears. It can only be apprehended as 'ideal', since the subject's relation with himself is 'a way of not being his own coincidence, of escaping identity while positing it as a unity' (BN 77).
3 See, for example, Ronald Aronson, *Jean-Paul Sartre, Philosophy in The World* (London: Verso, 1980), p. 72 ff. Also Margaret Whitford, *Merleau-Ponty's Critique of Sartre's Philosophy* (Lexington, KY: French Forum Publishers, 1982), esp. pp. 17-20.
4 'Itinerary of a Thought', op. cit., pp. 41–2.
5 The example Sartre gives is an extreme one: the case where I am free to destroy my life by letting myself fall off a precipice (BN 30 ff).
6 Sartre argues that Freudian psychoanalysis involves such a self-objectification and flight.
7 This is the problem of 'presence to self' (see esp. BN 73–9). Consciousness of self must be always a 'troubled' consciousness since '[t]he being of consciousness does not coincide with itself in a full equivalence' (BN 74). For an interesting comparison of Sartre's treatment of presence to self with Derrida's argument against the possibility of self-identity see Christina Howells, 'Sartre and Derrida: qui perde gagne', *Journal of the British Society for Phenomenology*, vol. 13, no. 1, Jan. 1982, pp. 26–34.
8 Francis Jeanson, writing in 1947, insisted that Sartre was engaged above all in a work of critical clarification, which would make such a 'conversion' possible. Jeanson also argued that the goal of opening a way to the conversion was what linked Sartre's undertaking in *Being and Nothingness* with his commitment to socialism. See *Sartre and the Problem of Morality*, trans. Robert V. Stone (Bloomington, Ind: Indiana University Press, 1980), esp. Part Three, ch. 3, pp. 203-22.

Robert Stone, in his Introduction to the English translation, takes a similar view to Jeanson's. Comparing *Being and Nothingness* to *Capital*, he claims that it 'advanced a *reductio ad absurdum* argument against bourgeois individualism analogous to Marx's demonstrations of the self-defeating character of capitalism in the previous century' (p. xiii). However, it is striking that both Jeanson and Stone look to Sartre's writings *other* than BN to sustain such an interpretation. It is hard to discover any sense of a dynamic of change in BN, such as one encounters in *Capital*. It is, in my view, a distortion to try to read BN as merely about bourgeois individualism, rather than as about human existence in general.
9 *Cahiers pour une morale* (Paris: Gallimard, 1983).

NOTES TO CHAPTER 2

10 This becomes particularly clear in Sartre's critique of Heidegger's notion that there exists a primordial *Mitsein*, or sociality (BN 244–50).
11 Sartre's discussion here is of spoken language but, since he claims that his argument applies to all techniques, it must apply also to written language.
12 People have made of speech a *language which speaks all by itself*. This is an error which should not be made with regard to speech or any other technique... if meanings are fixed in in-itself while we preserve a human transcendence, then the role of man will be reduced to that of a pilot employing the determined forces of winds, waves, and tides in order to direct a ship. (BN 516).

This passage anticipates Sartre's later arguments with structuralism and post-structuralism, to which I return in chapter 5.
13 Talking of the plays he wrote during the War, Sartre later recounted:
The other day, I re-read a prefatory note of mine to a collection of these plays – *les Mouches, Huis Clos* and others – and was truly scandalized. I had written: 'Whatever the circumstances, and wherever the site, a man is always free to choose to be a traitor or not.' When I read this, I said to myself: it's incredible, I actually believed that!
'The Itinerary of a Thought', op.cit., p. 33–4.
14 These are not the operative or external structures studied by structuralism, but rather structures of experience.
15 'These ends in fact are pursued in terms of a particular empirical situation, and it is this pursuit itself which constitutes the surroundings *as a situation*' (BN 567).
16 'The Itinerary of a Thought', op. cit., p. 35.
17 'It is *my place, my body, my past, my position* insofar as it is already determined by indications of Others, finally my *fundamental relation to the Other*' (BN 489).
18 Sartre here recasts Hegel's account, in the *Phenomenology of Mind*, of the emergence of self-consciousness through the 'master-slave dialectic'. For Sartre's explicit critique of Hegel, see BN 235–44.
19 Although Sartre chooses to examine vision as the central means of apprehension between Self and Other, his account would not exclude the experience of the Other through different senses, such as hearing or touch.
20 See Jeanson, op. cit., esp. Part Two, ch. 5 and Part Three, ch. 3.
21 'These considerations do not exclude the possibility of an ethics of deliverance and salvation. But this can be achieved only after a radical conversion which we cannot discuss here' (BN 412, note 14).
22 As Richard Zaner has remarked in discussing Sartre's treatment of the body:
To say that the 'dimensions' of the body are radically, ontologically separate, is to lose the body as the unitary embodiment of consciousness... To say that the being of the pour-soi is not connected to the being of the body of consciousness is to raise the insuperable Cartesian problem of how the one being can ever be united with the other being.

The Problem of Embodiment [The Hague: Nijhoff, 1971], p. 122.
23 See Thomas R. Flynn, *Sartre and Marxist Existentialism* (Chicago: University of Chicago Press, 1984), esp. ch. 2. As Flynn points out, the basic interpersonal relation is for Sartre the 'looking/looked at dyad', and this precludes the possibility of a 'plural look' (p. 19).
24 Those of Sartre's writings of the 1940s which reflect his growing concern with social and political issues include the following: *Existentialism and Humanism* [1946], trans. Philip Mairet (London: Methuen, 1948); *Anti-Semite and Jew* [1946], trans. George Becker (New York: Schocken Books, 1948); 'Materialism and Revolution' [1946], in *Literary and Philosophical Essays*, trans. Annette Michelson (New York: Collier Books, 1962); *What Is Litèrature?* [1947], trans. Bernard Frechtman (New York: Washington Square Press, 1966); *Cahiers pour une morale*, op. cit; *Entretiens sur la Politique*, with D. Rousset and G. Rosenthal (Paris: Gallimard, 1949).
25 Legislating the meaning of words is one of the most crucial tasks of Hobbes's sovereign. See Sheldon Wolin, *Politics and Vision* (Boston, Mass.: Little, Brown and Co., 1960), pp. 257-62. Sartre cannot account adequately for the existence of language in BN. But later, in the *Critique*, it becomes explicable as an element of the 'practico-inert' (see chapter 5 for my discussion of this concept.).
26 Modes of objectivist explanation would include, for Sartre, orthodox Marxism (with its notions of the laws of social motion), behaviourism and, of course, the Durkheimian tradition. Later, as we will see, Sartre also attacked structuralism for its objectivism.

Notes to chapter 3

1 See *The War Diaries of Jean-Paul Sartre*, trans. Quentin Hoare (New York: Pantheon, 1984). Published posthumously, these notebooks were written between September 1939 and March 1940. They contain a mixture of personal introspection, descriptions of army life and extended discussions of the philosophical issues most central to *Being and Nothingness*.
2 *The Prime of Life* [1960], trans. Peter Green (Cleveland, OH: The World Publishing Co., 1962), p. 346.
3 'In philosophical terms, he was creative and I am not... I always recognised his superiority in that area. So where Sartre's philosophy is concerned, it is fair to say that I took my cue from him because I also embraced existentialism myself', Beauvoir, in Alice Schwarzer, *After 'The Second Sex,' Conversations with Simone de Beauvoir*, trans. M. Howarth (New York: Pantheon Books, 1984), p. 109.
4 ibid. See also, Sartre, 'Self-Portrait at Seventy', in *Life/Situations*, trans. Paul Auster and Lydia Davis (New York: Pantheon Books, 1977), pp. 58-9; M. Sicard, interview with Sartre and Beauvoir, entitled 'Interférences', *Obliques*, nos. 18/19, 1979, pp. 325-9.

5   Beauvoir later described these two essays as the works which she had most self-consciously written within Sartre's framework, see Sicard, op. cit., p 328.
6   Not much has yet been written on Beauvoir's role in Sartre's intellectual development, but see Margaret Simons, 'Beauvoir and Sartre: the Philosophical Relationship', *Yale French Studies*, no. 72, 1986, pp. 165–79; see also my article, 'Simone de Beauvoir: Between Sartre and Merleau-Ponty', in Ronald Aronson and Adrien Vandenhoven (eds), *Sartre Alive* (Detroit, Mich.: Wayne State University Press, 1990).
7   *The Prime of Life*, op. cit., p. 433.
8   *The Blood of Others* [1945], trans. Y. Moyse and R. Senhouse (London: Secker and Warburg/Lindsay Drummond, 1948).
9   The book takes its title from the imaginary conversation with which it opens between Pyrrhus (king of Epirus, born ca. 318 BC) and his adviser, Cinéas, concerning whether or not there is any point in setting out to conquer the world.
10 Beauvoir, like Sartre, unfortunately uses 'man' to denote all human beings, irrespective of gender. In *The Second Sex*, she additionally uses 'man' to refer to specifically male human beings, and one has to determine from the context which she means.
11 It is interesting to note that Sartre, some years later, elaborated extensively on the notion of 'generosity' in the *Cahiers*, see esp. p. 514 ff.
12 Thomas Anderson argues, in *The Foundation and Structure of Sartrean Ethics* (Lawrence, Kans.: The Regents Press of Kansas, 1979), p. 94 ff., that Beauvoir fails to make the case that I need the recognition of all men to be free: if my plumber does not recognize my project as a philosopher, his lack of recognition does not matter to me. In response, it has rightly been pointed out that the issue is not one of *actual* recognition for Beauvoir, but of the equality of conditions which would *enable* all others freely to recognize me. See Robert V. Stone, 'Simone de Beauvoir and the Existential Basis of Socialism', *Social Text*, no. 17, Fall 1987, pp. 123–33. Sartre used a similar universalizing argument to Beauvoir's more than two years later, in *Existentialism and Humanism*, op. cit.
13 *The Prime of Life*, op. cit., pp. 434–5.
14 See Descartes's 'Meditations', in *The Philosophical Writings*, trans. John Cottingham and Dugald Murdoch (Cambridge: Cambridge University Press, 1985).
15 G.W.F. Hegel, The phenomenology of Mind [1807], trans. J.B. Baillie (London: George Allen and Unwin, 1966), pp. 228–40.
16 Sartre later uses the term 'ensemble' in the *Critique* to denote the various kinds of social groupings he examines. This passage is, as far as I can establish, the first published use of the term by either thinker.
17 Beauvoir also dwells on this theme in the essay, 'Idéalisme morale et réalisme politique', in *L'Existentialisme et la sagesse des nations* (Paris: Nagel, 1948), pp. 55-101. Merleau-Ponty was exploring the same theme at much the same time, in the essays published in 1947 as *Humanism and Terror*.

18 Karl Marx, Frederick Engels (ed.), *Capital*, Vol. III (New York: International Publishing Co., 1967), p. 820.
19 The work appeared in two volumes which, together, ran to over 900 pages of text. The one-volume English translation by H. M. Parshley is considerably abridged and is also very weak. Parshley, an American professor of biology, was particularly ill-equipped to translate Beauvoir's philosophical terminology. I have frequently re-translated passages, but I have still given page references to the British and US editions of the Parshley translation.
   For a fuller discussion of the problems of the Parshley translation, see Margaret Simons, 'The silencing of Simone de Beauvoir: guess what's missing from *The Second Sex*', *Women's Studies International Forum*, vol. 6, no. 5, 1983, pp. 559-64.
20 Judith Okely, *Simone de Beauvoir* (London: Virago, 1986), p. 122. See also, Michèle le Doeuff, 'Simone de Beauvoir and Existentialism', *Feminist Studies*, vol. 6, no. 2, 1980, pp. 277–89; Mary Evans, *Simone de Beauvoir: A Feminist Mandarin* (London: Tavistock Publications, 1985); Dorothy Kaufmann McCall, 'Simone de Beauvoir, *The Second Sex*, and Jean-Paul Sartre', *Signs*, vol. 5, no. 2, 1979, pp. 209–23.
21 This use of the notion of 'reciprocity' strikingly anticipates Sartre's use of it in the *Critique*.
22 *Force of Circumstance* [1963], trans. Richard Howe (New York: G.G.P. Putnam's Sons, 1964), pp. 185–93.
23 See Michèle le Doeuff, 'Simone de Beauvoir and Existentialism', op. cit.
24 For a very different reading of Beauvoir, one which emphasizes woman's *own* role in the constitution of her situation, see Judith Butler, 'Variations on Sex and Gender: Beauvoir, Wittig, and Foucault', *Praxis International*, vol. 5. no. 4, January 1986, pp. 506-16. My own view, however, is that a careful reading of the text cannot sustain Butler's interpretation.
25 Parshley translates Beauvoir's major section heading, *Formation*, as 'The Formative Years', thus weakening the notion of an active production of the self implied in the French term.
26 For Foucault's critique of 'the repressive hypothesis' see, above all, *The History of Sexuality*, Vol. I [1976], trans. Robert Hurley (London: Penguin Books, 1981).
27 *L'Expérience vécue* – translated rather unfortunately by Parshley as 'Woman's Life Today'.
28 One might well reply to Beauvoir that such qualities are also found in most men. Identifying man and his situation with freedom, Beauvoir has a tendency to idealize the male world and male qualities. For a fuller discussion of this point see Mary Evans, op. cit.
29 In the 1940s Engels's analysis of 'the woman question' still formed the unquestioned basis for the PCF position on women.
30 Karl Marx, 'Economic and Philosophical Manuscripts', in *Karl Marx, Early Writings*, trans. and ed. T.B. Bottomore (New York: McGraw Hill, 1964), p.154.
31 Just how much time this involves is, of course, largely socially specified. Some women choose not to reproduce at all. But they still live the conflict,

32 according to Beauvoir, for (unlike men) they have to decide to deny their 'natural functions'. In any case, such women are the exceptions: woman in general remains and will remain the perpetuator of the species.
32 Several commentators have argued, I think correctly, that Beauvoir underestimates the degree of freedom that can be involved in such activities. See Mary Evans, op. cit.; Susanne Lilar, *Le Malentendu du deuxième sexe* (Paris: Presses Universitaires de France, 1969); Ann Whitmarsh, *Simone de Beauvoir and the Limits of Commitment* (Cambridge: Cambridge University Press, 1981). Beauvoir has also been attacked by the Lacanian feminists in France, such as Irigaray, Cixous and their adherents, who seek to valorize not only feminine 'difference' but also 'motherhood'. For a brief overview, see Dorothy Kaufmann, 'Simone de Beauvoir: Questions of Difference and Generation', *Yale French Studies*, no. 72, special issue on Beauvoir, 1986, pp. 121–31.
33 The phrase is Merleau-Ponty's, cited in a note (TSS 61; 29). Marcel had, of course, used the same phrase, but with a somewhat different meaning.

Notes to chapter 4

1 For an account of this group and its activities see Simone de Beauvoir, *The Prime of Life* [1960], trans. Peter Green (Cleveland, OH: The World Publishing Co., 1962). pp. 382 ff. See also Annie Cohen-Solal, *Sartre: A Life*, trans. Anna Cacogni (New York: Pantheon Books, 1987), Part II, ch. 3.
2 For a history of the journal and of the politics of the group around it see M.-A. Burnier, *Choice of Action*, trans. Bernard Murchland (New York: Random House, 1968). See also Anna Boschetti, *The Intellectual Enterprise; Sartre and Les Temps Modernes*, trans. Richard McCleary (Evanston, IL.: Norwestern University Press, 1987); Howard Davies, *Sartre and 'Les Temps Modernes'* (Cambridge: Cambridge University Press, 1987); Arthur Hirsh, *The French New Left* (Boston, Mass.: South End Press, 1981), esp. ch. 2.
3 In *Adventures of the Dialectic* [1955], trans. Joseph Bien (London: Heinemann, 1974). For Sartre's account of the quarrel, see 'Merleau-Ponty', in *Situations*, trans. Benita Eisler (Greenwich, Conn.: Fawcett Publications Inc., 1965), pp. 188 ff.
4 'La Phénoménologie de la perception', *Les Temps Modernes*, vol. 1, no. 2, Nov. 1945, pp. 366-7.
5 Samuel B. Mallin, *Merleau-Ponty's Philosophy*, (Newhaven, CT: Yale University Press, 1979), p. 32.
6 See 'Merleau-Ponty et le pseudo-Sartrisme', in *Privilèges* (Paris: Gallimard, 1955), pp. 187-250.
7 ibid., pp. 188 ff.
8 In the 1959 lecture, Maurice Merleau-Ponty, 'La Philosophie de l'existence', *Dialogue*, vol. 5, no. 3, 1966, pp, 307–22.
9 I continue to draw here on the *Phenomenology*. However, the same account still holds, broadly speaking, in Merleau-Ponty's last major

work, the posthumously published volume, *The Visible and the Invisible*, trans. Alphonso Lingis (Evanston, IL: Northwestern University Press, 1964).

10 Because 'sensations' (such as 'red') are always given to us as they inhere in objects, I will not distinguish in what follows between Merleau-Ponty's account of 'sensation' and his account of the 'perception of objects'.

11 For Merleau-Ponty's fuller elaboration of his ideas on perspective see, 'Cézanne's Doubt', SNS, pp. 9-25.

12 It has frequently been remarked that *ambiguity* is the hall-mark of Merleau-Ponty's philosophy. Hugh J. Silverman both overviews the secondary literature on this theme and gives his own careful interpretation in 'Merleau-Ponty's Human Ambiguity', *Journal of the British Society for Phenomenology*, vol. 10, no. 1, Jan. 1979, pp. 23–38.

13 The term *sens*, which Merleau-Ponty uses frequently, means 'direction' or 'sense', as well as 'meaning'. Since no one English word carries all of these connotations, I will retain the French throughout this chapter.

14 The passage goes as follows:
[a]ll of the *Phénoménologie de l'esprit* describes man's efforts to reappropriate himself... until subjective certainty finally equals objective truth and in the light of consciousness he becomes fully what he already obscurely was. As long as this last stage of history remains unattained – and should it ever be reached, man, deprived of movement, would be like an animal – man, as opposed to the pebble which is what it is, is defined as a place of unrest (*Unruhe*).

15 'The Primacy of Perception and its Philosophical Consequences' [1947], trans. James Edie, in James Edie (ed.), *The Primacy of Perception* (Evanston, IL: Northwestern University Press, 1964), p. 17 (my emphasis).

16 The centrality of Merleau-Ponty's concern with conflictual relations tends to be overlooked by those who go to him in search of a theory of communicative politics. See, for a recent example, Bernard Dauenhauer, *The Politics of Hope* (London and New York: Routledge & Kegan Paul, 1986).

17 A point recognized by Sartre in his characterization of the Other as being for me 'an explosive instrument'(BN 297). The thrust of Merleau-Ponty's argument here is, I think, aimed at Sartre.

18 There is, as Merleau-Ponty puts it, 'a circuit between the self and others, a Communion of Black Saints. The evil that I do I do to myself, and in struggling against others I struggle equally against myself' (S 212). See also 'Metaphysics and the Novel' and 'Hegel's Existentialism', both in SNS. In the latter Merleau-Ponty refers explicitly to *Pyrrhus et Cinéas* in arguing that existentialism need not be individualistic but can be a *social* philosophy. See SNS 69-70.

19 Hence the possibility of ethnographic study: we could not understand 'foreign' peoples if we did not already share with them the fundamental experiences of sociality. See, for example, Merleau-Ponty's discussion of the Western relation to Chinese thought (S 139).

20 See, *Themes from the Lectures*, trans. John O'Neill (Evanston, IL: Northwestern University Press, 1970), pp. 40–1.

NOTES TO CHAPTER 4

21 For more extended discussions of Merleau-Ponty and structuralism than I offer here see James Daly, 'Merleau-Ponty: a Bridge Between Phenomenology and Structuralism', *Journal of the British Society for Phenomenology*, vol. 2, no. 3, 1971, pp. 53-8; Colin Smith, 'Merleau-Ponty and Structuralism', *Journal of the British Society for Phenomenology*, vol. 2, no. 3, 1971, pp. 46-52; William Gay, 'Merleau-Ponty on Language and Social Science: the Dialectic of Phenomenology and Structuralism', *Man and World*, vol. 12, 1979, pp. 322-38; James Schmidt, *Maurice Merleau-Ponty, Between Phenomenology and Structuralism* (London: Macmillan, 1985); James Edie, 'Merleau-Ponty: the Triumph of Dialectics Over Structuralism', *Man and World*, vol. 17, 1987, pp. 59–72.

22 On Merleau-Ponty's reading of Saussure see especially Edie, op. cit. and Schmidt, op., cit., ch. 4.

23 Merleau-Ponty was to further elaborate his views some years later, in *The Prose of the World*: 'there is an "I speak" which ends doubt about language in the same way that the "I think" terminated universal doubt. Everything I say about language presupposes it, but that does not invalidate what I say; it only shows that language is not an object, that it is capable of repetition, that it is accessible from the inside', (p. 24). Merleau-Ponty abandoned this work, probably written in 1951, incomplete and it was only published posthumously, ed. Claude Lefort, trans. John O'Neill (Evanston, IL: Northwestern University Press, 1974). Merleau-Ponty certainly offers a rather eccentric reading of Saussure. However, the issue here is not the correctness or otherwise of this reading, but the distance between Merleau-Ponty's notion of structure and that of the 1960s structuralists.

24 Particularly *Elementary Structures of Kinship* [1949], trans. James Ball *et al.*, (Boston, Mass.: Beacon Press, 1969). When Merleau-Ponty wrote this account, Lévi-Strauss was yet to identify himself as a militant anti-humanist.

25 *The Savage Mind* [1962], (Chicago: Chicago University Press, 1966), pp. 247-8.

26 On Merleau-Ponty and Hegel see my article, 'Merleau-Ponty, Hegel and the Dialectic', *Journal of the British Society for Phenomenology*, vol. 7, no. 2, 1976, pp. 96-110; also Barry Cooper, *Merleau-Ponty and Marxism* (Toronto: University of Toronto Press, 1979), esp. pp. 14-22.

27 Karl Marx, 'The Eighteenth Brumaire of Louis Bonaparte', in Karl Marx and Frederick Engels, *Selected Works in One Volume* (New York: International Publishers, 1980), p. 97.

28 *Capital*, Vol. 1, trans. Samuel Moore and Edward Aveling (London: Lawrence & Wishart, 1970), p. 178.

29 Merleau-Ponty gave considerable weight to the colonial aspects of the capitalist order in making this judgement. Anti-colonial struggle was already well under way in the French empire by the late 1940s, especially in Indo-China and Algeria, and Merleau-Ponty was in large part responsible for the anti-colonial stand which *Les Temps Modernes* took from December 1946 onwards.

30 Thus it did not take a profound shift of *theoretical* ground for Merleau-Ponty to declare by 1955 (in *Adventures of the Dialectic*) that communism had, in the light of further events and information, lost its claim to be supported at all. Politically, this move meant a nuanced return to liberalism, with support for the person and policies of Mendès-France in the mid 1950s, and a less critical stance towards capitalism. For a fuller discussion of Merleau-Ponty's break with Marxism see Sonia Kruks, *The Political Philosophy of Merleau-Ponty* (Brighton: Harvester Press, and Atlantic Highlands, NJ: Humanities Press, 1981), chs 6 and 7. See also Barry Cooper, op. cit., chs 5-7; Kerry H. Whiteside, *Merleau-Ponty and the Foundation of an Existential Politics*, (Princeton NJ: Princeton University Press, 1988), chs 7–9.

31 These dilemmas are not, of course, unique to Marxism; liberalism also finds itself put in question by the divorce between intention or principle, on the one hand, and consequences, on the other. For Merleau-Ponty's critique of liberalism see Kruks, op. cit., ch. 4.; also Whiteside, op. cit., ch. 6.

32 Some commentators have argued that Merleau-Ponty misreads Sartre's account of freedom here. My own view is that Merleau-Ponty's reading of Sartre is persuasive, but for a different opinion see, for example, Margaret Whitford, *Merleau-Ponty's Critique of Sartre's Philosophy* (Lexington, KY: French Forum Publishers, 1982).

Notes to chapter 5

1 Jean-Paul Sartre, 'Merleau-Ponty', in *Situations*, trans. Benita Eisler (Greenwich Conn.: Fawcett Publications, 1965), p. 176. Originally published in a commemorative issue of *Les Temps Modernes*, shortly after Merleau-Ponty's death, as: 'Merleau-Ponty Vivant', *Les Temps Modernes*, vol. 17, no. 184 1961, pp. 304–76.

2 This theoretical itinerary has been excellently traced by Thomas R. Flynn, *Sartre and Marxist Existentialism* (Chicago: University of Chicago Press, 1984). For a discussion of Merleau-Ponty's place in Sartre's intellectual development see Ronald Aronson, *Sartre's Second Critique* (Chicago: University of Chicago Press, 1987), ch. 1.

3 The essay was originally written in 1957 for publication in an issue of a Polish periodical devoted to French culture. It was then republished in a revised form in *Les Temps Modernes* and, in 1960, as the prefatory essay to CDR.

4 *The Family Idiot*, trans. Carol Cosman (Chicago: University of Chicago Press, Vol. I, 1981 and Vol. II, 1987). French original: *L'Idiot de la famille*, Vols. I and II (Paris: Gallimard, 1971); Vol. III (Paris: Gallimard, 1972).

5 In his study of Flaubert, Sartre attempted to show the intelligibility of such a movement through the method of biography. Flaubert was a 'universal singular' who, through his project, embodied the social and

political milieu he was born into and yet created, through and from it, his own unique works of literature. See also, on the notion of the universal singular, Sartre's discussion of Kierkegaard, 'Kierkegaard: The Singular Universal', in *Between Marxism and Existentialism*, trans. John Matthews (London: Verso, 1983), pp. 141–69.

6   It was the invasion of Hungary, in 1956, which finally caused Sartre to despair of the Soviet Union as a force for human liberation. One wonders whether or not he would have revised his judgement had he lived to see the era of 'perestroika'.

7   Sartre later described CDR as 'a work written against the Communists, while still being Marxist', Jean-Paul Sartre, 'Self-Portrait at Seventy' in *Life/Situations*, trans. Paul Auster and Lydia Davis (New York: Pantheon Books, 1979), p.18.

8   There is a continuum of opinions on this issue. Wilfred Desan, for example, describes even the Sartre of the *Critique*, as the 'last of the Cartesians'. See his *The Marxism of Jean-Paul Sartre* (Garden City, NY: Doubleday Anchor Books, 1965); Ronald Aronson, in *Jean-Paul Sartre, Philosophy in the World* (London: Verso, 1980) and *Sartre's Second Critique*, op. cit., argues that Sartre's Marxism remains flawed by the same persistent individualism as BN. From a more sociological perspective, Gila Hayim argues that the main concepts of CDR are essentially 'social representations' of the main concepts of BN. See her *The Existential Sociology of Jean-Paul Sartre* (Amherst, MA: University of Massachusetts Press, 1980). For arguments suggesting that there is a significant development, but still within a basic unity, in Sartre's thought see, for example, Joseph Catalano, *A Commentary on Sartre's Critique of Dialectical Reason* (Chicago: University of Chicago Press, 1986); Peter Caws, *Sartre* (London: Routledge & Kegan Paul, 1979); Thomas R. Flynn, op. cit. For the view that there is a more radical shift between Sartre's early and late work see Mark Poster, *Sartre's Marxism* (London: Pluto Press, 1979).

9   *Critique de la raison dialectique*, tome II (inachevée), ed. Arlette Elkaïm-Sartre (Paris: Gallimard, 1985).

10 'Worked matter' or the 'practico-inert' (Sartre uses these terms interchangeably) includes for Sartre not only 'practical objects', such as those of economic production and consumption, but also institutions, social structures and even forms of power which have emerged out of the history of human praxis.

11 This has been rendered as 'fused group' in the English edition; not a good translation as it implies a completed and static entity, whereas for Sartre the *groupe-en-fusion* exists only in action and in flux. I will retain the French term in the text.

12 The French is *dialectique constituente*. It is rendered in the English translation as 'constituent dialectic'. Again this lacks the sense of on-going activity which the French implies. I have thus chosen to substitute 'constituting dialectic'.

13 William L. McBride has pointed out that Sartre does in fact indicate a notion of animal praxis in his discussion of household pets in the

'Flaubert'. See his 'Sartre and Marxism', in Paul Schilpp (ed.), *The Philosophy of Jean-Paul Sartre* (La Salle, IL: Open Court, 1981), p. 629, note 33. Had he elaborated a fuller theory of nature in the *Critique*, Sartre would perhaps have allowed a place for animal behaviour between the sphere of inert matter and the sphere of human praxis.

14 Merleau-Ponty, *The Structure of Behaviour* [1942], trans. Alden Fisher (London: Methuen, 1965).

15 As Peter Caws has written,
    The physical sciences deal, we might say, with being before it has become world. The status of this domain cannot be left aside if our goal is an understanding of the universe as a whole ... By taking his stand at too high a level of abstraction, and refusing an analytic of material causes and parts, Sartre risks the collapse of his scheme of explanation in the light of a new reading of the genesis or synthesis of the human (op. cit., p. 96.)
    Although Caws's comment refers to *Being and Nothingness*, the status of natural phenomena and our knowledge of them become even more pressing problems in the *Critique*.

16 The English translation renders the French *statuts* as 'statutes'. However, here and in other passages, I have altered this to 'statuses' or (in the singular) 'status' since 'statute' carries an overly legalistic connotation in English.

17 The man of need is an organic totality perpetually making itself into its own tool in the milieu of exteriority. The organic totality acts on inert bodies through the medium of the inert body *which it is* and which it *makes itself*. It *is inert* in as much as it is already subjected to all the physical forces which reveal it to itself as pure passivity; it *makes itself* inert in its being in so far as it is only externally and through inertia itself that a body can act on another body in the milieu of exteriority (CDR 82).

18 Frederic Jameson, *Marxism and Form* (Princeton, NJ: Princeton University Press, 1971), p. 237. Hazel Barnes points out in 'Sartre as Materialist', in Schilpp (ed.), op. cit., pp. 676-7, that Sartre does carefully distinguish between *objectification* (in which praxis freely inscribes itself in its products) and *reification* (in which, through the intervention of other people, praxis loses its free expression in its products). By contrast Pietro Chiodi argues, in *Sartre and Marxism*, trans. Kate Soper (Brighton: Harvester Press, 1976), esp. ch. 6, that Sartre collapses and confuses these two concepts.

19 'through the mediation of matter, men have realised and perfected a joint undertaking because of their radical separation' (CDR 165).

20 This point is, of course, crucial in discussing the possibility of a non-alienated, socialist future. While Sartre does not absolutely preclude such a possibility, his position does not allow him much optimism either.

21 However, at the subjective level, Sartre says, the experience is lived as an outrage, as an absurd scandal: 'the conflict between interchangeability and existence (as unique, lived praxis) must be lived at some level as a *scandalous absurdity*' (CDR 260).

22 *La Raison de la série*, rendered as 'the Formula of the series' in the English translation.
23 In fact both concepts were already presaged in his earlier writings, 'reciprocity' in the discussion of 'generosity' in the *Cahiers* and the 'Third' in the discussion of the 'us-object' in BN. However, both concepts are elaborated in new and original ways in CDR. For an evaluation of the full significance of the Third see Thomas R. Flynn, 'Mediated Reciprocity and the Genius of the Third', in Schilpp (ed.), op. cit., pp. 345-70.
24 The threat results in this instance from the cannons of the Bastille being trained on the residential *quartier*, whose lay-out is such as to preclude the option of escape. See CDR 351 ff.
25 *L'être-un* is rendered as 'unity' in the English translation, not a felicitous term since unity for Sartre is generally a mechanically imposed unification in exteriority, whereas the *être-un* of the group involves an interior synthesis. I prefer the term 'single-being', but will retain the French in the text.
26 Sartre explores this internal coercive bond through the idea of the 'pledge' or 'oath' which the group imposes on itself to maintain its relations of solidarity. The pledge initiates relations of 'Fraternity-Terror' (CDR 417 ff).
27 The occasion for his remarks was an interview by the journal, *L'Arc*, published in an issue on Sartre. See 'Jean-Paul Sartre répond', *L'Arc*, no. 30, 1966, pp. 87–96. An English translation of this interview appeared as 'Replies to Structuralism: an Interview with Jean-Paul Sartre', trans. Robert D'Amico, *Telos*, vol. 9, Fall 1971, pp. 110-16.
28 Michel Foucault, *The Order of Things* [1966], trans. anon. (London: Tavistock, 1970).
29 Sartre's examples are as diverse as the division of labour within a football team and the logic of violence and counter-violence in Algeria. He develops a typology which ranges from 'organisations', in which the common goal of group praxis still predominates (as in the football team, where each subordinates himself to the common goal of trying to win) through to 'institutions' (especially of state power) where the logic of sustaining the structure at all costs has effectively displaced the aims of the original praxis which brought the group into being.
30 Perry Anderson suggests that it was the political failures of the Soviet Union which caused Sartre to abandon the *Critique*. See *In The Tracks of Historical Materialism*, (London: Verso, 1983). pp. 70–1. Ronald Aronson, in *Sartre's Second Critique*, op. cit., suggests that the main blockage was internal to Sartre's theory, the consequence of what he calls Sartre's 'individualism'. Aronson argues that 'as Sartre construes individual praxis, its intrinsic links with larger totalities can never appear. Without presuming these social links at the outset, as the very basis for the individual's identity, we will never understand how this individual, alone or as a member of a class in conflict, will naturally build larger totalities' (p. 235). My own view, as should be apparent by now, is that Sartre does succeed in showing how individual praxis is *intrinsically* social. The problem (see below) does not lie at

the 'individual' pole of Sartre's work, but at what we might call its 'universalizing' pole.
31 'Merleau-Ponty', *Situations*, op. cit., p. 168.
32 Jean-Paul Sartre, 'Itinerary of a thought', in *Between Existentialism and Marxism*, op. cit., p. 42.

Notes to conclusion

1 'The *Critique of Dialectical Reason* was published; attacked by the Right, by the Communists and by the ethnographers, it gained the approval of the philosophers' *Force of Circumstance*, trans. R. Howe (London: Andre Deutsch and Weidenfeld & Nicolson, 1965), p. 498. Absolutely nothing more is said on the subject.
2 Foucault's critique of structuralism, discussed on p. 184, clearly makes this connection between Durkheimianism and structuralism. See also Pierre Bourdieu and Jean-Claude Passeron, 'Sociology and Philosophy in France Since 1945: Death and Resurrection of a Philosophy Without a Subject', *Social Research*, vol. 34, no. 1, Spring 1967, pp. 162–212. Bourdieu and Passeron were sympathetic to sociology and philosophy without a subject, but also aware of their fundamental lack of originality:
  The ethnologists and sociologists, after all, have only made themselves guilty of 'treating social facts as things', as Durkheim expressly taught almost a century ago... To speak of 'structure' rather than 'social body', of the 'unconscious' rather than the 'collective consciousness', of the 'savage mind' rather than the 'primitive mind'; to formulate the new scientific philosophy, which revives Durkheim's approach, in the language of structural linguistics... all these are so many euphemistic channels for hiding, from others and from oneself, the truth of a scientific intent (p. 166).
3 I borrow the phrase from the title of Bourdieu and Passeron's article, op.cit.
4 See Louis Althusser, 'On the Young Marx' and 'Marxism and Humanism', in *For Marx* [1965], trans. Ben Brewster (London: New Left Books, 1977).
5 In his 'Reply to John Lewis' Althusser describes Sartre as Lewis's 'unavowed' master, and accuses Sartre of being a 'pre-Marxist' in philosophical terms. See *Essays in Self-Criticism*, trans. Grahame Lock (London New Left Books, 1973), pp. 59 and 60. Much of his critique of humanist Marxism is clearly directed at Sartre, even though Lewis is the immediate target.
6 *Madness and Civilisation*, trans. Richard Howard (London: Tavistock Publications, 1967). The English translation is based on Foucault's second, and considerably abridged, edition of 1964. The first edition was *Folie et déraison. Histoire de la folie à l'âge classique* (Paris: Plon, 1961).
7 Jean Hyppolite, *Genesis and Structure of Hegel's Phenomenology of Spirit* [1942], trans. Samuel Cherniak and John Heckman (Evanston, IL: Northwestern University Press, 1974). Hyppolite's Hegel was above all the existential philosopher of 'unhappy consciousness'.

NOTES TO CONCLUSION

8 *Mental Illness and Psychology* [1954], trans. Alan Sheridan, (London: Harper & Row, 1976).
9 'Introduction' to *The Use of Pleasure* (Vol. 2 of *The History of Sexuality*), trans. Robert Hurley, in Paul Rabinow (ed.), *The Foucault Reader* (New York: Pantheon Books, 1984), p. 334. This version of the Introduction comes from the first French edition, and is not in the English translation of the book.
10 Ibid., p. 334.
11 Ibid., p. 336.
12 See, for the second direction, Gilles Deleuze and Félix Guattari, *Anti-Oedipus: Capitalism and Schizophrenia* [1972], trans. Robert Hurley (New York: Viking Press, 1977); François Lyotard, *Economie libidinale* (Paris: Minuit, 1974).
13 'Truth and Power', interview from 1977 published in Colin Gordon (ed.), *Power/Knowledge* (New York: Pantheon Books, 1980), p. 117.
14 'This political investment of the body is bound up, in accordance with complex reciprocal relations, with its economic use; it is largely as a force of production that the body is invested with relations of power and domination' (DP 25–6).
15 Michel Foucault, 'Polemics, Politics and Problemizations: an Interview', in *The Foucault Reader*, edited by Paul Rabinow (New York: Pantheon Books, 1984), p. 388.

Index

abstraction 42–7
Algeria 174–5
Althusser, Louis 2, 3, 181–2, 190n.7, 192n.20, 208nn.4–5
ambiguity
  Beauvoir on 91–2
  of freedom 138–9
  Merleau-Ponty on 121, 202n.12
Anderson, Perry 191n.7, 207n.30
Anderson, Thomas 199n.12
Anglo-American philosophy and theory 1–3, 23
anti-humanism 3–5, 132, 179–80, 181, 189, 190n.2
Anti-Semite and Jew 198n.24
Aronson, Ronald 196n.3, 199n.6, 204n.2, 205n.8, 207n.30
Astruc, Alexandre 193n.29
autonomous subjectivity 5–6, 48, 63

'bad faith' 59–60, 97, 101–2
Barnes, Hazel, 206n.18
Beauvoir, Simone de 201n.1
  and *Being and Nothingness* 83–5
  as derivative thinker 84–5, 99–100, 198n.3
  discussion of ambiguity 91–2, 111
  interdependence of freedoms in Merleau-Ponty and 125–6
  on immanence 143–5
  on oppression 95–8, 99–104
  on reception of *Critique* 181, 208n.1
  on split between Sartre and Merleau-Ponty 114-15
  Sartre's intellectual development and 84–5, 199n.6
  social turn of existentialism and 17
  woman's situation and institutions 104–12

work with *Les Temps Modernes* 113
behaviourism 2, 198n.26
Being and Having 41–2
Being and Nothingness 15, 25
  anti–humanist attack on 9
  Beauvoir's relation to 83–6, 93
  Cartesianism in 15–16
  'in-itself' and 'for-itself' 53–6
  Merleau-Ponty's critique of 114, 141–2
  questioning in 57–8
  social relations in 75–80
  subjectivity and freedom in 90–1
Bergson, Henri
  influence on existentialists 14, 193n.29
  Marcel influenced by 24–6, 193n.7, 194nn.11–12
  Russell and 27, 194n.14
Bernstein, Richard J. 8–9, 192nn.18, 25–6, 193n.5
biology and women 100–2, 108–11
Blood of Others, The 85, 199n.8
body
  body and discipline 186–9
  body-for-me 74–5, 110–11
  body-for-others 74–5
Boschetti, Anna 193n.27, 201n.2
Bourdieu, Pierre 208nn.2–3
Bradley, F.H. 193n.4
Brunschvicg, Léon 25, 26, 115, 194n.16
Burnier, M.-A. 201n.2
Butler, Judith 200n.24

Cahiers pour une morale 60, 86, 196n.9, 198n.24
Capital 96, 133, 199n.18, 203n.28
Cartesianism
  existentialism and 14
  Marcel and 24, 49–50
  Marxism and 16–17, 134–5

Index

Sartre's work as 15–16, 205n.8
Catalano, Joseph 205n.8
Caws, Peter 205n.8, 206n.15
Chiodi, Pietro 206n.18
Cixous, Hélène 201n.32
class
   Beauvoir on 94–5
   facticity and 64–5
   Merleau-Ponty on 132, 144
   Sartre on 64–5, 77–8, 148–9, 155–6, 166–7
closed society 25, 193n.7, 195n.35
cogito 28–33, 54–5
   and solipsism 126–7
   Marxism and 133–5, 136
   pre–reflective 54–5, 62
   sensation and 118–19
Cohen-Solal, Annie 190n.1, 201n.1
colonialism 138, 203n.29, 174–5
communication
   abstraction and 46–7
   conflict and 126–9, 202nn.16, 17, 18
   embodiment and 124–6
   objectification and 38–42
communism
   French party 15–16, 113, 138
   Merleau-Ponty rejects 138, 203n.30
   Sartre on failure of 147–9, 205n.6
   see also Marxism
communitarianism 5–6
conflict
   communication and 126–9
   ethics and 95
   of consciousnesses 71–3, 86–8, 95–6
   oppression and violence 95–7
   social and historical situations of 137–41
consciousness
   being-for-itself 55–6
   body as 74–5
   embodiment and 12, 33, 56–62, 114–17
Contat, Michel 193n.29
contingency, situation and 36–7, 138–40
Cooper, Barry 203n.26, 204n.30
Critique of Dialectical Reason 9, 17, 51, 57, 145, 146
   concepts and framework of 149–56
   counter-finalities in 163–4
   critical reception of 181, 208n.1
   narrowness of 179
   praxis-in-situation in 156–61
   totalization in 151–6, 168–71, 177–80

Dallmayr, Fred 8, 192n.24
Daly, James 202n.21
Dauenhauer, Bernard 202n.16
Davies, Howard 193n.27, 201n.2
Deleuze, Gilles 209n.12
Derrida, Jacques 3, 183, 190n.7, 194n.15
Desan, Wilfred 205n.8
Descartes, René 199n.14
   cogito and Marxism 133–5
   consciousness as knowing 54
   humanism and 3
   impact on French philosophy 14
   Marcel on 29–31, 194n.16
   Merleau-Ponty on 117–18
Descombes, Vincent 190n.7
Dews, Peter 190n.2
dialectic
   constituted 156, 173, 175–6
   constituting 155, 205n.12
   dogmatic Marxism and 147–8
   Merleau-Ponty on 121–4, 202n.14
   of practico-inert and praxis 162–7
   totalization and 151–4
   vs. analytic reason 150–1
Discipline and Punish 184–8
Doeuff, Michèle le 200n.20
Durkheim, Emile 3, 181, 184
Dworkin, Ronald 190n.5
dyadic relations
   and politics 139
   conflict and 76–80
   Marcel and 38–9
   oppression and violence in 96
   reciprocity of 167–8

Ecole Normale Supérieure 15, 113
Edie, James 202n.15, 203n.21
Eighteenth Brumaire, The 133–5, 192n.19, 203n.27
Elster, Jon 191n.9
embodiment
   as facticity of freedom 65, 74–5
   'primacy of perception' and 117–19
   situation and 12–13, 33–8, 116
   women's situation and 108–12
Engels, Frederick 192n.19, 195n.33, 199n.18, 200n.29
Entretiens sur la Politique 198n.24
equality
   abstraction and 44–5
   oppression and 98–9
   in social relations 88–9, 199n.12
   women and 105–7

Index

Ethics of Ambiguity, The 85, 91–9, 102, 107, 139
être–un 170–1, 207n.25
Evans, Mary 200n.20, 201n.32
'Existence and Objectivity' 27
existentialism 1–2, 9–13, 16–18, 23–5
Existentialism and Humanism 198n.24
exteriority, praxis in 161–7

Facticity
  and being-for-others 71
  embodiment and 65, 74–5
  'for-itself' and 64–5, 92
'fact-value dichotomy' 3
Family Idiot, The 146, 204nn.4–5
feminist theory, autonomous subject in, 191n.17
Ferguson, Kathy 192n.17
Ferry, Luc 190n.2
Flynn, Thomas R. 197n.23, 204n.2, 205n.8, 207n.23
'for-itself' 53–6, 114, 118
  facticity of 64–5, 92
  freedom and 56–8
  praxis and 151–3
Force of Circumstance 100, 181, 200n.22, 208n.1
Foucault, Michel 191nn.9&12, 207n.28, 208n.6, 209n.15
  anti-humanism and 4–5, 7
  Beauvoir and 103, 200n.26
  existentialism and 182
  repressive hypothesis 103, 200n.26
  Sartre on 172
  on subjectivity 184–8, 192n.21
freedom
  ambiguity of 138–9
  consciousness and 55, 56–62, 90–1
  history and limits to 171–80
  indestructibility of 63, 65, 85–6
  paradox of 70
  situation and 47–50, 62–70, 83, 141–5
  social relations and 86–9, 171–80, 199n.12
  woman's destiny and 102, 104, 109–10, 200n.32
French Communist Party 16, 113, 138
Freudian analysis 182, 196n.6
Fromm, Erich 195n.36

Gay, William 203n.21
generosity 88–9, 199n.11
Giddens, Anthony 8, 192nn.22–3

Gilligan, Carol 191n.17
group praxis 173–6
groupe-en-fusion 154–5, 166–7, 169–71, 205n.11, 207n.24
Guattari, Félix 209n.12

Habermas, Jürgen 191n.9
Hahn, Lewis 194nn.11, 13, 196n.37
Hartsock, Nancy, 191n.17
Hayim Gila, 205n.8
Hegel, G.W.F.
  Beauvoir on 93
  Hyppolite's interpretation of 182, 208n.7
  Marcel and 24, 193n.4
  'master-slave dialectic' in 68, 92, 127, 129, 167, 197n.18
  Merleau-Ponty and 119, 132, 203n.26
Heidegger, Martin 14, 15, 24, 32–3, 76, 87, 119, 194n.20
  Das Man 119
  Mitsein 76, 87
Hering, Jean 23, 193n.1
Hirsh, Arthur 201n.2
Hobbes, Thomas 76–7, 86, 198n.25
Hocking, William 193n.5
Homo Viator 41
Howells, Christina 196n.7
humanism 3, 181, 188–9
Humanism and Terror 129, 136–7, 139
Hume, David 3
Hungary, invasion of 205n.6
Husserl, Edmund 14, 15, 24, 54
Hyppolite, Jean 182, 208n.7

I
immanence 91, 101–4, 143–5
'in-itself' 53–6, 114, 152
  freedom and 58, 62, 65–6
  women's embodiment and 110–11
institutions
  Merleau-Ponty's discussion of 129–31, 136
  structuralism and 130–2
  women's situation and 104–12
instruments and techniques, social relations and, 78–80
intellection 155–6
'intentional arc' of perception 121
interiority, mediations in 167–71
intersubjectivity 8–9, 13, 17, 38, 48–50, 99, 108, 115, 124–9, 129–37
Irigaray, Luce 201n.32

212

Index

James, William 193n.5
Jameson, Frederic 161, 206n.18
Jaspers, Karl 15, 24
Jay, Martin 194n.21
Jeanson, Francis 196n.8, 197n.20

Kant, Immanuel 1, 29–30, 194n.16
Kaufmann McCall, Dorothy, 200n.20, 201n.32
Kierkegaard, Søren 9–10, 24
Kittay, Eva Feder 191n.17
Kolakowski, Leszek 193n.6
Kruks, Sonia 203n.26, 204nn.30–1

Lacan, Jacques 3, 182
Lacanian feminism 210n.32
language
  gender aspects of 18, 87, 199n.10
  Merleau-Ponty on 131–2, 202nn. 22–3
  Sartre and 62, 77, 197nn.11–12, 198n.25
L'Arc 207n.27
Lavelle, Louis 194n.16
Lechner, Robert 194n.18
Lefort, Claude 203n.23
Les Temps Modernes 113–14, 193n.30, 203n.29
Lévi-Strauss, Claude 2–3
  attack on Sartre 181–3
  Merleau-Ponty on 131–2, 203n.24
  Sartre on 173–4
liberalism 2, 5–6, 47–50, 203n.30, 204n.31
Lilar, Susanne 201n.32
'logic of the series' 166, 206n.22
love 38, 42, 73, 103, 194n.25
Lukes, Steven 191n.10

MacIntyre, Alisdair 192n.26
Madness and Civilization 182, 208n.6
Maine de Biran, Marie-François-Pierre 14
Mallin, Samuel B. 201n.5
Man Against Mass Society 41
Marcel, Gabriel
  Catholic religion and 15, 23, 26, 41, 43
  critique of *cogito* 28–33
  critique of depersonalization 42–5
  critique of Sartre 51–2
  early life and career 25–6
  embodiment in 12–13, 33–8, 65, 115–16

freedom and situation 47–50
  influence on postwar existentialism 13–14, 23–6, 194n.9
  Merleau–Ponty and 115–16, 201n.8
  relation to Marxism 15, 43–5, 195n.32
  social relations in 38–42, 61
marriage, equality and 105–6
Marx, Karl 192n.19, 195n.33, 200n.30, 203nn.27–8
Marxism
  Beauvoir on 95–6, 98–9
  French communism and 15–6
  Marcel's relation to 15, 43–5, 195n.32
  Merleau-Ponty on 113–14, 129, 132–9
  Sartre on 'dogmatic' Marxism 147–9, 205n.6
  structuralism and 2–4, 6–7, 174, 181–2
  theory of consciousness in 134–5
  women and 107, 200n.29
mass society 44–7, 195n.35
'master-slave dialectic' 68, 92, 127, 129, 167, 197n.18
Materialism and Revolution 99, 198n.24
matter, Sarte's discussion of 157–61, 163–4, 206nn.18–19
McBride, William L. 192n.26, 205n.13
Meditations 30–1, 199n.14
Mendès-France, Pierre 203n.30
Merleau-Ponty, Maurice 199n.17, 201nn.8, 33
  communism and 138–41
  conflict in social-historical situations 137–41, 168
  dialectics of 121–4
  early life and career 113
  embodiment 12–13, 117–19
  freedom in situation 16, 141–5
  intersubjective situations 124–37
  Marcel's influence on 24–6, 193n.29
  nature 158–9
  perception 117–19
  reaction to Occupation 195n.27
  Sartre and 113–15, 146, 176–7, 201n.3, 204n.2, 207n.31
  'third genus of being' 117, 119, 135, 160, 186
Metaphysical Journal 26, 29, 32, 34–5, 40, 49
Meyers, Diana T. 191n.17
Mitsein 76, 79–80, 87, 106, 124
Mounier, Emmanuel 195n.32
mystery 34–7

Index

nature
  Hobbesian state of 76–7, 86, 198n.25
  Merleau–Ponty on 159
  Sartre on 157–61, 163
Nausea 25
Nazism
  abstraction and 44–7, 49, 195n.36
  existentialism and 16
  negation of the negation 160–1
  'Note on Machiavelli, A' 128–9
Nozick, Robert 190n.5

objectification 38–42, 45–6, 71–3, 77–8, 87–9, 100, 126–8
Occupation of France
  Marcel's reaction to 39–42, 195n.30
  Merleau-Ponty's reaction to 16, 195n.27
  resistance during 113, 141, 201n.27
Okely, Judith 200n.20
'On the Ontological Mystery' 40
open society 25, 193n.7, 195n.35
oppression 95–9, 106, 108–10, 143–5
Ortega y Gasset 195n.35
'Outline of a Phenomenology of Having' 40–1

Parshley, H.M. 199n.19, 200nn.25, 27
Pascal, Blaise 14
Passeron, Jean-Claude 208nn.2–3
Passmore, John 190n.4
perception
  embodiment and 117–19
  ontology of situation and 120–1
  praxis and 135–6
phallocentrism 18
phenomenology 1, 14, 23–4, 193n.1
Phenomenology of Perception 114, 135–6, 141
post-structuralism 1–5, 103, 181, 183–4, 190n.3
Poster, Mark 205n.8
power 78, 90–1, 173–4, 185–8
practico-inert 154, 160–1, 163–4, 173, 198n.25, 205n.10
praxis
  class struggle and 148–9, 156
  freedom and 57, 160–1, 172
  group 169–71, 173–4
  individual 156–61
  perception and 135–6
  reification of 161
  totalization and 151–6
  triadic relationships and 168–71

universality of 178–9
praxis-process 174–5, 183
Prime of Life, The 198n.2, 201n.1
probability, freedom and 143–4
Problem of Method 146–7, 177
Pyrrhus et Cinéas 85–91, 105, 199n.9, 202n.18

rational choice theory 191n.9
Rawls, John 2–4, 6, 13, 190nn.5–6
reciprocity 100, 128–9 167–8, 200n.21, 206n.23
Renan, Ernest 24
Renaut, Alain 190n.2
res cogitans 14
res extensa 14
Ricoeur, Paul 23, 193n.2
Rorty, Richard 190n.3
Rosenthal, G. 198n.24
Rousset, D. 198n.24
Royce, Josiah 193n.5
Russell, Bertrand 27, 40, 194n.14
Ryle, Gilbert 1

sadism 73–4
Sandel, Michel 5–6, 191nn.14–16
Sartre, Jean-Paul 198nn.4–5
  anti-humanism and 9–10
  consciousness and freedom 56–62
  early influences on 15–16
  editor of *Les Temps Modernes* 113
  exteriority 161–7
  freedom-in-situation 62–70
  'in-itself' and 'for-itself' 53–6
  interiority 167–71
  Lévi-Strauss and 173–4, 181, 183
  Marcel and 25, 51–3, 194n.9
  Merleau-Ponty and 113–14, 146, 160, 177, 201n.3, 204n.2
  my situation and the Other 70–5
  on nature and matter 157–61, 163–4, 206nn.18–19
  on violence 174–5
  plays of 197n.13
  scarcity 164–5, 177–8
  social relations 75–80
  study of Flaubert 146–7, 204nn.4–5
  wartime experiences 52, 196nn.1,4
Sartre (film text) 193n.29
Saussure, Ferdinand de 130–1, 182, 203nn.22–3
scarcity 164–5, 177, 206n.20
scepticism 139–41

214

Schilpp, Paul 194nn.11, 13, 18, 196n.37, 205n.13, 206n.18
Schmidt, James 203nn.21–2
Schwarzer, Alice 198nn.3–4
Second Sex, The 17, 84–5, 99–111, 145, 199n.19
self-cause, pursuit of 60, 196n.8
'Self-Portrait at Seventy' 198n.4
sens 121, 138–40, 177, 202n.13
Sense and Non-Sense 136
'seriousness', condition of 97–8
Sicard, M. 198nn.4–5
Silverman, Hugh J. 202n.12
Simons, Margaret 199n.6, 200n.19
situation
  as common product 67–8, 120
  as condition 69–70
  as constituted field 65–7, 69
  embodiment and 33–8
  freedom and 47–50, 90–1, 141–5
  individual praxis and 156–61
  intersubjectivity of 124–9, 129–37
  ontology of 119–24
  other and 70–5
  perception and 117–19
  social relations and 75–80, 137–41, 161–7, 167–71
  structures of 66, 197n.14
  women in 104–12
Smith, Colin 202n.21
social relations
  in *Being and Nothingness* 75–80, 86–7
  conflict and 76–7, 137–41, 175–6
  equality and 88–9
  instruments and techniques as basis for 76–7
  oppression and violence in 95–9
  perception and 120–1, 123–4
  Sartre on 75–80, 161–71
  situation and 70–5, 93–5, 156–61
  struggle in 175–6
  subjectivity and 6–7, 9–10, 192n.20
  violence in 95–7, 137–9
'Socialisme et Liberté' resistance group 113, 201n.1
solipsism 127–8
Soper, Kate 191n.8
Spiegelberg, Herbert 193n.2
Stalinism 147–8, 176, 205n.6
Stone, Robert V. 196n.8, 199n.12
structuralism 1–3, 103, 130–2, 173–4, 181, 183
'structuration theory' 8, 192n.23

'structures of situation' 66, 197n.14
subject
  anti-humanist attacks on 2–5, 132, 179–80, 189
  as intersubjective 13, 17, 99, 108, 115, 124–5, 128
  autonomous 5–6, 14, 84, 86
  body-subject 12, 33–8, 115, 122, 124, 129, 145
  constituted 2, 102, 182, 184–6
  'encumbered' 7, 112
  impure 13, 117, 132, 172
  Marxism and the 134–5
  practical 151
  social 107, 117, 149
  see also embodiment, 'for-itself', praxis

Taine, Hippolyte 24
Taylor, Charles 192n.26
technology
  abstraction and 45–6
  of power 185–6
Theory of Justice, A 2–3, 190n.5
Third 77, 95, 168–71
'third genus of being' 117, 119–20, 135, 160, 186
totalization 151–3, 154, 156, 168–71, 175–6, 178
Tragic Wisdom and Beyond 41

'us-object' 77–8, 80
utilitarian theory 191n.9

Vandenhoven, Adrien 199n.6
violence 89–90, 95–9, 128–9, 174–5
Visible and the Invisible, The 201n.9

Wahl, Jean 14, 193n.28
Walzer, Michael 190n.5
War Diaries of Jean-Paul Sartre, The 198n.1
Warren, Scott 192n.26
'We-subject' 79–80
Weber, Max 3
What Is Literature? 198n.24
Whiteside, Kerry H. 204nn.30–1
Whitford, Margaret 204n.32
women
  limits of independence for 106–7
  oppression of 99–104
  probability of freedom for 143–5
  situation of 104–12

Zaner, Richard 197n.22

PN 56 .F34 INT